Wahoo Sam Crawford

The King of Sluggers

by

Kent Krause

Wahoo Sam Crawford

Kodar Publishing
ISBN 13: 978-0-578-86915-5

Front cover photo: National Baseball Hall of Fame and Museum

In memory of Ronald G. Krause

Other books by Kent Krause:

The All-American King

Men Among Giants

Behind in the Count

Ninety Feet Away:
The Story of the 2014 Kansas City Royals

Keep the Line Moving:
The Story of the 2015 Kansas City Royals

Contents

"When the final book of baseball history is written; when baseball affairs are reckoned in terms of centuries rather than of seasons or decades, the name of Sam Crawford will appear in the list as one of the greatest players of all time."

F.C. Lane, 1916

Chapter 1

"The Most Exciting World Series Game Ever"

A winter chill greeted the players as they awakened that Thursday morning in October. The sun remained hidden behind the clouds, while the mercury loitered around 30° Fahrenheit. Strong winds whistled through the city, intensifying the frigid impact felt by those who ventured outside. Some forecasters predicted snow would fall before day's end.

By midday, the skies cleared and the temperature climbed into the 40s. The chilly morning upgraded to a crisp autumn afternoon. Though high winds continued to swirl, weather would not prevent baseball from being played in Detroit, Michigan, on October 14, 1909. Bennett Park, the city's major league venue, was set to host Game 6 of the World Series at 2:00 pm.

The visiting Pirates arrived at the ballpark hoping to wrap up their first World Series title. A victory the previous day at Forbes Field in Pittsburgh had given them a series lead of three games to two. Their Tiger opponents looked to stave off elimination and force a deciding Game 7. They would have the support of the home crowd, but the energy therefrom would be a bit lacking. With the chilly conditions discouraging many Detroiters from venturing out, only 10,535 fans would witness the diamond proceedings this day. That total was well below the attendance numbers for the previous two Series games played at Bennett Park: Game 3 (18,277) and Game 4 (17,036).

Despite the modest fan turnout, Game 6 of the 1909 World Series held the attention of the baseball world. This Fall Classic featured a clash of the two most dominant teams in baseball. The National League champion Pirates had posted a 110-42 record to end the string of three straight pennants won by the Chicago Cubs. Detroit had tallied 98 victories in the regular season, the most ever won by an American League team up to that point. The Tigers, moreover, had won three consecutive pennants, firmly establishing themselves as the dominant club in the Junior Circuit.

Adding to the interest in this World Series was the individual matchup featuring each league's top player. Pirate shortstop Honus Wagner had batted .339 during the season to capture his seventh batting title, and his 100 RBI and 39 doubles paced the National League. Tiger outfielder Ty Cobb had captured his third straight batting title with a .377 mark. He also led the AL in home runs, RBI, runs scored, and stolen bases. The head-to-head matchup between these two superstars drew almost as much betting action as the battle between the teams.

Pittsburgh's player-manager Fred Clarke turned to his ace right-hander Vic Willis to bring home the title. Despite posting his fourth consecutive season of 21 or more wins, Willis, a future Hall of Famer, would be making his first start in this Series. Detroit skipper Hughie Jennings gave the ball to his 29-game winner George Mullin. The Tiger ace would be making his third start in the Series, losing Game 1, but tossing a shutout in Game 4. Despite this heavy workload, Mullin assured his manager that he was good to go.

It seemed the Detroit right-hander may have overestimated his readiness when the first four Pirates hit safely. Wagner's two-run double was the big blow, giving Pittsburgh a 3-0 lead in the first inning. Before their team had sent even a single batter to the plate, the hometown Detroit rooters grew restless at the prospect of a third straight World Series defeat.

The Tigers, fittingly enough, clawed their way back into the contest. They plated a run off Willis in the bottom of the first. Two more scored in the fourth, tying the game. Detroit took the lead in the fifth and Cobb's RBI-double in the sixth increased their advantage to 5-3. This score remained unchanged heading to the ninth inning. To get the last three outs needed for victory, Jennings stayed with Mullin, who had tossed seven straight scoreless frames after his rocky start.

Pirate second baseman Dots Miller led off the ninth by slapping an opposite field single to right. Bill Abstein then laced a hit up the middle. Batting next for Pittsburgh was "Chief" Owen Wilson. A few years later, Wilson would hit 36 triples in a single season, a record that still stands. On this occasion, he just sought to advance the two baserunners into scoring position. After Wilson laid down his bunt, Tiger catcher Boss Schmidt quickly tracked down the ball and fired to first. The throw, however, sailed wide, drawing first baseman Tom Jones into the basepath. Wilson barreled into Jones in a violent collision that knocked the ball free. By the time Tiger second baseman Jim Delahanty corralled the ball, Miller had scored and Abstein had advanced to third.

Jones lay unmoving near first base. His hard fall to the ground caused some spectators to fear for his life. A doctor in the stands jumped onto the field to offer his services. Jennings and the Tigers trainer hurried over to Jones. Players from both teams gathered around the fallen player. Though Jones avoided serious injury, he had to be carried from the field by his teammates.

Jennings and his Tigers now faced dire circumstances. The Pirates had cut the lead to 5-4 and had runners on first and third with nobody out. Detroit had also lost the services of Tom Jones, one of the team's strongest fielders. Needing a new first baseman, the Tiger skipper turned to his centerfielder to fill the spot.

At six feet tall and 190 pounds with broad powerful shoulders, this star player on Detroit's roster looked every bit the part of a big-league hitter. F.C. Lane, editor of *Baseball Magazine*, described this man as the ideal choice for the "model of a statue of a slugger." During the season, he had batted .314 with a league-best 35 doubles. His .452 slugging average was second-best in the AL. He had already made his presence felt earlier in Game 6 when, in his first at-bat, he ripped a low liner to right center that barely eluded Pirate outfielder Tommy Leach. This RBI double helped shift the early momentum back to the home team.

This man's name was Samuel Earl Crawford, aka "Wahoo Sam."

When a game was on the line, Detroit fans welcomed the sight of Crawford in the batter's box. But standing at first base was another story. During the past few seasons, he had occasionally donned the big mitt and filled in at first. But Crawford was an outfielder—that was his preferred position. He did not like playing first base, the diamond assignment he considered the hardest and most thankless. He especially did not like playing there without any time to prepare. Just a year earlier he had dropped a ninth-inning popup at first that cost his team a game. He would remember that error for years. Prior to this tense World Series moment, Crawford had not played in the infield for nearly two months. His defensive skills at the first sack surely represented a downgrade from the injured teammate he replaced.

Nervous Tiger fans could feel this game and the season slipping away.

In this desperate situation, Jennings left Mullin on the mound. Though he had pitched more than 300 innings during the regular season, and two complete games in the World Series prior to Game 6, the Tiger manager hoped he had enough left in the tank to get out of this jam. With no outs, the runner at third would probably score to tie the game. But maybe Detroit could then win it in the bottom of the ninth, or in extra innings.

George Gibson stepped into the batter's box on the right side of the plate. Some reporters hailed him as the best catcher in the National League. Though known mostly for his defense and durability, Gibson had posted his best offensive season numbers to date with a .265 batting average and 52 RBI. In this key situation, he looked to make contact to drive in the tying run.

Mullin, on the other hand, wanted a strikeout. Or a popup. Or a tap back to the mound. Something that would keep the runner at third, ninety feet away from plating the tying run. The Tiger pitcher broke off a curve. Gibson swung, bat connecting with ball. It was a grounder to the right side—to the new first baseman.

Crawford had not handled an infield grounder this entire series. And now, on the first at-bat following his switch to first base, the ball was coming to him. With the game on the line. An error here would tie the game and open the door for a huge Pittsburgh inning that would all but end the Tigers' chances.

Undaunted by the high-pressure circumstances, Crawford smoothly scooped up the ball and fired a strike to the plate. At the crack of the bat Abstein had broken down the line from third and raced home. Crawford's throw beat the runner. Tiger catcher Boss Schmidt caught the ball on his knees, his 200-pound frame blocking the plate. Abstein, nicknamed "Big Bill," checked in at six-foot even and 185 pounds. Running at full force, he crashed into Schmidt, his spikes slashing the catcher's thigh.

Despite the jarring collision and the searing pain from a six-inch gash in his leg, Schmidt held onto the ball. The runner was out. A defensive gem from a replacement first baseman and a stalwart catcher had preserved Detroit's 5-4 lead. But the Pirates had runners at first and second with only one out. With Mullin's pitch count mounting, the visitors still had a great opportunity to snatch this game away.

The pitcher was due up for Pittsburgh. After considering his options, Pirate manager Fred Clarke gave the bat to Ed Abbaticchio. Known as "Abby" to the Pittsburgh faithful, the pinch hitter had been the Pirates' regular second baseman the previous two seasons. In 1909 he had been relegated to a utility role, though he still possessed a veteran's hitting eye. He had averaged more than 70 RBI a season in his previous two campaigns as a regular.

Fans at Bennett Park and those following the telegraph reports at newspaper offices in Pittsburgh and cities across the nation hung on every pitch as Mullin and Abbaticchio waged a tense battle. Finally, they reached a full count. The runners took off on the 3-2 delivery. Abby swung, but connected with nothing but air. Schmidt then gunned a throw down to third. The Detroit catcher had struggled to contain the Pirate running game— Pittsburgh had stolen 14 bases thus far during this series.

This time though, Schmidt had a chance. His throw beat the runner, but third baseman George Moriarty had to make a sprawling catch while attempting to apply the tag. As Pirate runner Owen Wilson barreled toward the bag, he crashed into Moriarty—the third violent collision of the inning. Once again, spikes drew blood. And once again, the Detroit fielder held onto the ball. Umpire Bill Klem, in the early years of a Hall of Fame career, signaled that the runner was out.

The hard-fought contest at Bennett Park ended with a dramatic strike 'em out, throw 'em out double play. One Detroit writer called the game's final frame, "perhaps the most spectacular inning of any World's Series ever played." While being a Tiger rooter no doubt contributed to that assessment, the end of Game 6 was certainly loaded with tension. Up to the final pitch the outcome could have gone either way. *Chicago Tribune* sports columnist Ring Lardner hailed the contest as "the most exciting World Series game ever."

Detroit had tied the series. For the first time ever, the World Series would be decided by a winner-take-all Game 7. This climactic game would be played two days later, on Saturday,

October 16. Sam Crawford, a veteran of eleven major league seasons, was just one win away from an elusive World Series title. Though playing in his third consecutive Fall Classic, he knew this was to date his best opportunity to win baseball's top prize. "The Cubs beat us fairly," Crawford said about Detroit's defeats in the 1907 and 1908 Series. "Their club was stronger than ours." But Wahoo Sam felt differently about his team's chances in 1909. After Game 1 in Pittsburgh, he was confident of the Tigers' superiority over the Pirates: "Those fellows are our meat. We have a better club than they have and we will win."

Little more than a decade earlier, Crawford was a teenage town team player traversing the dirt roads of eastern Nebraska in a lumber wagon looking for a game. Now, Wahoo Sam instilled fear in pitchers as the hardest hitting slugger in the game. Yet it was his glove and throwing arm that made a crucial play to help his team climb to within a single step of baseball's highest summit.

The eyes of the baseball world would fix upon Bennett Park for the final game of the 1909 season. Four future Hall of Famers would play in this contest—Crawford, Cobb, Wagner, and Clarke. Two of these players would become world champions. Two would not. None of them would ever play in a World Series game again.

Chapter 2

Wahoo

By the end of the first decade of the twentieth century, baseball had spread to all parts of the United States. In 1909, no fewer than 246 teams played in 35 minor leagues across the country. Major league rosters that year included ballplayers hailing from 41 of the 46 states in the Union. Nicknames for the players of this era often revealed their geographic roots: "the Georgia Peach" Ty Cobb, "Wabash George" Mullin, "Tioga George" Burns, and "the Gallatin Squash" Hub Perdue. Perhaps no player in baseball history has been more closely associated with his hometown than "Wahoo Sam" Crawford.

Crawford's story began in eastern Nebraska. There, in 1870, settlers of mostly Czech, German, and Scandinavian roots founded the town of Wahoo in Saunders County. This small settlement in the rural heartland bore few similarities with the industrial melting pot of Detroit where Sam would achieve his greatest fame. In its early days, Wahoo boasted three general stores, a hotel, and a post office. In the next few years, a hardware store and a furniture store opened for business. A courthouse, bank, and grain elevator soon followed. The stage coach stopped at Wahoo every four hours, beginning each day at 7:00 am.

As for the origin of the town's name, several different stories have emerged. Some believe that it came from a Sioux

Indian Chief named Wahoo. Others say it derived from the howling sound that coyotes made. The most likely explanation is that the town name comes from a Native American word for "burning bush," a shrub that grew along creek banks in the area. The Otoe Indians used this plant for medicine. Wherever they got the name, the first residents of the town spelled it "Wauhoo." It would not be long though before the current spelling became the norm.

Wahoo's location in the heart of a productive farming region 30 miles west of Omaha and 30 miles north of Lincoln boded well for the town's growth. It became the county seat of Saunders County in 1873. Some Nebraska leaders even discussed moving the state capital from Lincoln to Wahoo. Though that proposal did not gain traction, the town continued to expand, attracting rail links, businesses, and people. By 1880, Wahoo's population topped 1,000. Ten years later that total would double. Among the town's residents at that time was the Crawford family.

All four of Wahoo Sam's grandparents were born in the United States. A descendent of Scottish ancestors, his grandfather Stephen Orlando Crawford was born in Vermont around 1822. Stephen's first child was born in Milton, Vermont, on October 30, 1842. This boy (Sam's father) was also named Stephen Orlando Crawford. The elder Stephen and Sam's grandmother Elvira (Newman) Crawford had another son, Elliot, in August 1843. Soon after, Stephen Sr. left his wife and two sons and moved to New York, where he, according to Elvira, lived in adultery with another woman. Elvira officially petitioned for divorce in 1850. The U.S. Census that year recorded that she and her two boys lived in Milton with her parents, John and Polly Newman.

The elder Stephen Crawford did in fact live with another woman in northern New York at this time. Apparently not waiting for an official divorce from Elvira, Stephen Sr. had married again and fathered another child. In 1856 he and his second wife Julia moved west to Minnesota with their son Ampudia, settling in Sauk Rapids, a town on the Mississippi River 70 miles northwest of Minneapolis. Having apprenticed in carpentry, Crawford set up what soon became a thriving business as a furniture manufacturer and dealer. Cabinets, bureaus, tables, and rocking chairs were among the items he offered customers in central Minnesota. It did not take the easterner long to achieve a favorable standing in his new community. After Crawford helped complete construction of a long-unfinished building in town, the local newspaper reported that he "is as enterprising a man as there is in Sauk Rapids."

Early in the 1860s, Stephen Sr. moved his furniture business and his residence across the river to St. Cloud. The latter relocation required 19 oxen to transport the actual house structure to its new location. Though a fire at his St. Cloud furniture factory wreaked $4,000 worth of damages in December 1864, Stephen Sr. stayed in business. His prominence in the community also remained intact, evidenced by the "Great Fourth of July Ball" he hosted the following summer at the Crawford House in Little Falls. Tickets were $4 for this public event that featured live music.

The end of the Civil War no doubt added to the celebratory atmosphere of the Independence Day festivities, but darker times soon lay ahead for Sam's grandfather. Stephen Sr. and Julia both fell gravely ill within the next few months. She died on November 4, 1865, following a lengthy head and stomach affliction that her doctor could not diagnose or treat. Just two days later, Stephen succumbed to typhoid. He was about 43 years old. Ampudia, who had spent two years serving in the Union Army, returned home not long before the passing of his parents.

Both of Stephen Sr.'s sons from his earlier marriage to Elvira also fought in the Civil War. They grew up in Vermont and eastern Canada in the 1850s as tensions over the slavery issue escalated to the breaking point. Sam's father Stephen Crawford Jr., known as "Steve," was 18 years old in April 1861 when Confederate guns fired on Fort Sumter. He resided in Westford, Vermont, a small town near Burlington, at this time. He and his brother Elliot enlisted in the Union Army in the summer of 1862, volunteering for nine-month terms. Both were assigned to the 13th Vermont Infantry Regiment—Steve to Company A and Elliot to Company D. Marching south that autumn, the unit camped at Fairfax Courthouse in northern Virginia in December. Lacking tents for several days, many of the troops fell ill with severe colds and fever. Steve was among the afflicted and had to be hospitalized for several months.

After rejoining his unit, Steve fought at the Battle of Gettysburg in early July 1863. On the third day, the 13th Vermont poured fire into George Pickett's right flank, helping to decimate the final Confederate charge of the battle. Three weeks later, the Crawford brothers mustered out of the 13th Vermont at Brattleboro in their home state. Perhaps because he had missed so much time with his unit during his first enlistment, Steve returned to the Union Army for a second term. On January 1, 1864, he enlisted as a private in the 3rd Battery of the Vermont Light Artillery. This unit saw heavy action the following summer, engaging in frequent artillery duels with Confederate batteries during the siege of Petersburg. Steve remained in uniform for the remainder of the war, mustering out of the Vermont Light Artillery on June 15, 1865.

Soon after the guns of war fell silent, Steve and Elliot joined a wagon train headed across the continent for California. Like many easterners at the time, these young men believed that opportunity abounded in the West. When the wagons reached South Dakota, however, they encountered hostile Indians. This engagement resulted in a detour that sent the Crawford brothers south to Nebraska. Steve settled in the small village of Linwood in Butler County, while Elliot established a homestead in neighboring Colfax County. Their mother Elvira soon joined her boys in Nebraska. She settled in Fremont, about 35 miles northwest of Omaha, with her second husband Robert Bullock, a man 14 years her junior.

Steve opened a general store in Linwood. Business must have been brisk, because the 1870 U.S. Census valued his personal estate at $2,300 and real estate at $700. A net worth of $3,000 at that time was a decent achievement for a 27-year-old new to the frontier—the equivalent of around $60,000 in 2020.

Sometime over the next few months, Steve met Ellen "Nellie" Ann Blanchard, a young woman from Iowa who had recently moved to Nebraska with her family. Nellie's father Thomas Blanchard Jr. (Sam's maternal grandfather), was a prosperous merchant in Iowa before the Civil War. Daguerreotyping, a popular photographic process of the time, was among the services he offered to his customers.

In addition to Nellie, born in 1855, Thomas and his wife Sarah (Thompson) Blanchard had a second daughter, Permelia, three years later. A son, George, followed a couple years after that. The family lived in Washington, a town of around 2,000 about 30 miles south of Iowa City, the state's first capital.

Early in the Civil War, 33-year-old Thomas answered the call to defend the Union. On August 6, 1862, he was commissioned as a captain in the 18th Iowa Infantry Regiment. Early in 1864, the unit moved into Arkansas, where it fought several engagements against Confederate troops. On April 18 at Poison Spring, 6,000 rebels attacked a smaller Union force that included the 18th Iowa. The regiment soon found itself surrounded and isolated. Casualties mounted. Though shot in the right knee and facing heavy fire, Captain Thomas Blanchard held up the colors and rallied his men. The gallant actions of Thomas and the regiment's other officers held the unit together in a desperate predicament. The 18th Iowa charged enemy positions seven times before finally breaking through to Union lines.

Despite his leg wound, Thomas continued to command his men in Company I. He remained with his regiment until the end of the war. On July 20, 1865, he mustered out of the Union Army at Little Rock, Arkansas.

Though Thomas Blanchard Jr. survived the Civil War, his marriage did not. After the conflict ended, he traveled across the war-torn South to Georgia. There, in 1868, he married Mary Harris, a young woman from Tennessee whose family had relocated to the Peach State during the war. A few years later Thomas and Mary moved to Belton, Texas, a town lying midway between Austin and Waco. They would have four children together.

Back in Iowa, Thomas's first wife Sarah (Sam's maternal grandmother) married a Union Army veteran named Milton M. Runyon in 1865. The couple then moved to Boone, a town 35 miles northwest of Des Moines. Their household in 1870 included 15-year-old Nellie and 10-year-old George. Permelia, not listed, may have died in childhood.

In 1871, after only a few years in Boone, Milton and Sarah decided to move west to Saunders County, Nebraska, where they established a homestead. Soon after settling in their new location, their daughter Nellie met Steve Crawford, the successful merchant who lived just across the county line. The couple married on July 22, 1872. The groom was 29 years old; the bride was 17.

Steve and Nellie did not wait long to start a family. Their first child, a son named Tracy "Trace" K. Crawford, arrived on November 26, 1873. The following year the Crawfords moved from Linwood a few miles east to Saunders County, where Steve opened a general store in the small town of Plasi. This village was located about twelve miles west of the newly-founded town of Wahoo.

On March 10, 1878, Steve and Nellie's second child, daughter Zadia, was born. A couple years later, the Crawford family moved across the county to the recently-platted town of Clear Creek. Located a dozen miles east of Wahoo on the Sioux City branch of the Burlington Railroad line, Clear Creek showed promise as a trading point. Nellie's mother Sarah and step-father Milton Runyon had also settled in the town, residing just a few houses away from the Crawfords. A member of the county legislature, Milton ran Clear Creek's first hotel in the train depot building. He also served as a Union Pacific station agent and a telegraph operator. Seven years after its founding, the town changed its name to Yutan. It remained a small village in these early years, with a population of around 130.

At some point in the 1870s, Steve's mother Elvira had moved to Linwood, where her husband Robert Bullock served as Justice of the Peace. Elvira fell ill a few years later and died of pneumonia on January 4, 1880. She was about 70 years old. Three months later, Steve and Nellie's third child was born.

Earl Lee Crawford, aka Sam Crawford, came into the world on April 18, 1880. The exact place where this event occurred is something of a mystery. The long-held common belief is that Wahoo was his birthplace. Sam himself apparently never contradicted this assertion. His family, however, did not reside in Wahoo in the months before or after the culmination of Nellie's pregnancy. A newspaper article indicates that Steve still lived in Plasi (Elk Precinct) as late as October 1879. The U.S. Census reveals that the Crawfords, including infant Earl, resided in Clear Creek (soon renamed Yutan) in June 1880. Sam was born in the eight-month window between these two dates, during which time his family moved from Plasi to Yutan. This suggests that he may have actually been born in one of those two towns.

Decades later, some publications identified the house in Wahoo where Sam grew up as his birthplace. This assertion can be ruled out because real estate records show that Steve had not yet bought that property at the time of Sam's birth. But could Sam still have been born in Wahoo? Certainly. The town is located halfway between where his family moved from and where they moved to—and it was much larger than either of those villages. Nellie may have delivered in Wahoo at the house of a friend, a doctor, or a midwife. A hotel is another possibility.

So, once again, where exactly was Sam born? We can confidently say Saunders County, Nebraska, no farther than twelve miles from Wahoo. The most likely candidates are the towns of Plasi, Yutan (Clear Creek), and Wahoo. In baseball, the tie goes to the runner. Without clear evidence to the contrary, we will move on leaving Sam's birthplace as Wahoo.

The Crawford family lived in Yutan for the first six years of Sam's life. Like the 1880 Federal Census, the 1885 Nebraska Census shows the family living in that town. Steve continued to run a general store during these years. A fourth child, Stephen, was born in Yutan on March 28, 1885 (the Wahoo newspaper confirms his birth location). The family name Stephen Orlando Crawford thus extended to a third consecutive generation, though the boy would become known as "Step."

A fifth Crawford offspring, Willie, was born on September 1, 1886. Around this time, when Sam was six years old, the Crawfords settled in Wahoo. Years earlier, Sam's father had bought a lot on the city's east side at Tenth Street and Orange Street. He paid the county treasurer $800 for this property, on which he built a house. A few years after moving to Wahoo the family again expanded. The sixth Crawford offspring, Neal, was born on September 30, 1889.

Steve and Nellie and their children were one of three Crawford families living in Wahoo at this time. None of them were related. Johnson Crawford, a carpenter, and J.S. Crawford, a well digger and contractor, headed the other two clans. The latter won the contract to build the city hall, which would be completed in 1890 at a cost of $12,000. That structure was among several new buildings that inspired pride among Wahoo citizens, a list that included an $85,000 courthouse, a $50,000 high school, an 800-seat opera house, and two first-class hotels. One of the latter was the Riddle House Hotel, part of an impressive three-story brick building in the center of Wahoo's business district.

Sam's father built a store in Wahoo, continuing the profession he had pursued since settling in Nebraska. As Sam recalled decades later, "My dad ran a general store, just a little country store where they sold everything." Steve's means, however, soon declined. Wahoo at that time was a competitive environment for store proprietors. In March 1887, the *Wasp* newspaper ran ads for six businesses in town described as either general merchandise, general merchant, groceries, or general store. Two hardware stores also advertised that month. All of these businesses served a town of just over 2,000. The following year, a Wahoo general store run by S.M. Gilbert failed and had to close. Gilbert was not one of those proprietors listed above as advertisers in the *Wasp*.

Even more significant than his competition were the national and state developments that hampered Steve Crawford's business prospects. An economic depression known as the Panic of 1893 held the United States in its grip for four years. Making matters worse in Nebraska, drought and hot winds wrecked many of the crops in 1893 and the two years that followed. Real estate values plummeted, businesses and banks closed, homelessness increased, and famine threatened to spread statewide.

Wahoo, like the rest of the state, felt the dire effects of this economic downturn. Sam's family did not avoid this impact. Wahoo resident Jim Campbell later recalled that the Crawfords "were good neighbors, but very poor." In addition to his store, Steve sought income from various other sources to support his large family. He worked at a grain elevator and as a stockman. Steve also tried his hand as a part-time real estate broker and occasionally traveled around Nebraska and to other states looking for land investment opportunities. As the years passed, his gainful pursuits waned and he seemed content to live off his Civil War pension. Pat Levin, one of Sam's classmates, remembers Steve idling away his days at a hardware store, returning home only for dinner and after the place closed.

A recollection from another of Sam's classmates offers further explanation for the financial challenges that the family faced. He described Nellie as a quiet homebody, but said that Steve caused problems in the home due to his frequent profanity and because "he liked his liquor too much." Sam's granddaughter Julie Ann Johnson paints an even bleaker picture of the Crawford household, describing Steve as a violent drunk who beat his son. Sam's siblings presumably experienced the same treatment. The liver problems that emerged near the end of Steve's life further suggest an affinity for the bottle. *The Wahoo Democrat* described him as "most peculiar and eccentric," while his friends called him a "diamond in the rough." Though known for his impressive physical strength, Steve apparently could not defend himself against the challenges of alcoholism.

The Crawford house at 959 North Orange Street was not a large abode for a family of eight, but it did have two stories. Overhead was a tin roof—metal roofing of this type was common in the nineteenth century. Next to the pantry was the door that led upstairs, where the Crawford children slept. They attended North Ward School, just a few blocks away on Elm Street. Sam continued his education through the seventh grade.

When not in school, Sam engaged in the childhood activities common to boys growing up in Wahoo in the 1880s and 1890s. He and his friends frequented the gravel pits east of town, not far from where Native Americans sometimes camped. The place was an ideal swimming hole, and it provided a plentiful supply of rocks for the boys' slingshots.

Sam also spent much time on Linden Street, a main drag in Wahoo during those days. In the late 1880s, during the mayoral term of William H. Dickenson, Wahoo installed Nebraska's first incandescent city lighting system. For Sam, the light on the street corner provided another source of boyhood entertainment. "We used to go down to the corner and watch this light go on," he later recalled. "That was a big deal." He and his curious companions also visited the town powerhouse to see where the electricity was made.

As a boy, Sam garnered something of a mixed reputation. One childhood friend remembered him as "a little on the quiet side." Another described him as a "perfect gentleman," in contrast to his brothers who were not so quiet. One of the Crawford brothers gained notoriety as a quarrelsome troublemaker. Sam's behavior created concerns as well around

Wahoo. Some town residents thought he was lazy. This viewpoint worsened when the lad started smoking.

On one point all accounts about young Sam, including his own, are in complete agreement. That is, he loved baseball and always wanted to play. In that, he was not alone among the Wahoo youth. As Sam recalled decades later, "we spent most of our childhood playing ball."

A game called One Old Cat provided Sam with his introduction to baseball. Playing in the street in front of the Crawford house, one kid started as a batter, one was a pitcher, and one was a catcher. The remaining participants played in the field. After hitting the ball, the batter would run to a base and back home. The fielders could put him out by catching his hit on the fly or by pegging him with the ball as he ran. The batter continued to hit until the fielders got him out. Then he went to the field, the catcher became the batter, the pitcher became the catcher, and one of the fielders came in to pitch.

All the kids wanted to be the batter, but the one who owned the ball would always hit first. Not surprisingly, seven-year-old Sam displayed impressive bat skills playing One Old Cat. As he put it, "I think I was able to get more than my share of the batting." Across the country in the late nineteenth century, countless future pro ballplayers, including Ty Cobb and Harry Hooper, played One Old Cat, or a close variation, during their childhoods.

When Sam and his friends got a little older, their interests shifted to real baseball. They trekked over to the town ballpark by the Union Pacific depot (just five blocks south of Crawford's house) to watch the men play. When Sam was nine, a game between a visiting "regular league" team and the Wahoo town team stirred excitement among the local youth. Sam and his friends all wanted to go, but none of them had much luck raising the 25 cents needed for admission. They instead jumped the fence surrounding the baseball grounds and successfully eluded the town constable. Already favoring the catching and long throwing required of an outfielder, Sam paid close attention to the visiting team's centerfielder. The boy watched in awe as the player "ran faster than I ever thought any man could run, and I never thought that a human being could throw as far as he threw."

After the game, young Sam approached his new idol and asked him for advice on how to play center field. The ballplayer told the youngster, "Hunt out some nice soft spot, wait there and let the ball drop in your hands. That's all." Sam never forgot those words about the importance of positioning. "I have learned to some extent the art of hunting out the spot where to stand," he later said as a big leaguer, "but to find that spot is one of the hardest things that an outfielder has to study."

The Wahoo kids played their own games at a ballfield in the vacant lot just north of the North Ward School. Home plate sat in the northwest corner of the school lot. The school building to the south bore hardware cloth to protect its windows. The houses across Elm Street apparently did not have such protection—at least not the residence of a land surveyor named Ault. "We were always in trouble with Ault," Sam recalled, "as the ball would go through his windows and he would keep the ball until the window was paid for." On such occasions, the youths would scratch around for the money to pay the fee to reclaim their ball. This was not easy to accomplish since nickels and dimes were scarce.

Needing another option when financial resources proved lacking, the Wahoo boys took to making their own baseballs. They gathered all the yarn and string they could find and wrapped the strands around a little rubber ball. One of the boys then asked his mother to sew a cover on the ball to hold it all together. The inventive skills of Sam and his friends were not limited to balls. "For bats we'd find some broken bat and nail it up," he said, "or sometimes even make our own."

The boys of Wahoo's North Ward played many hotly contested games against their counterparts from the other parts of town. These occasions often generated arguments and fights. Sam recalled that many a youth ballgame broke up in a squabble, with each side claiming victory. Ed Meduna, a Wahoo youth from the other side of town, remembered these games, noting that one of the North Ward players stood out above the others. "Everyone knew how good Sam was," Meduna recalled, "and when choosing up sides they all wanted him on their team."

Despite his considerable skills on the diamond, baseball was just a game. Entering his teen years, Sam would soon be a young man. And young men needed to concern themselves with more serious pursuits. Something that could provide income and prepare the lad for a viable career option. With his school days over after the seventh grade, Sam Crawford would soon enter the workforce.

Chapter 3

Town Teams

Sam joining the ranks of the employed would have been a welcome development for his father, especially with the onset of an economic depression. Fortunately, the Crawford boy soon found opportunity in the form of Tom and Ed Killian. The Killian brothers were Wahoo businessmen who ran a large store in town that offered a wide range of wares: clothing, furnishings, linoleums, carpets, curtains, groceries, and Queensware dishes. Older brother Tom, a former Wahoo mayor, took an interest in Sam that had positive implications for the boy's career and his long-term health.

With his son Lloyd the same age as Sam, Tom knew all about the ballplaying lad. The merchandiser made the young man an offer: if Sam forsook his indolent ways and gave up tobacco, he would let him run the shoeshine stand in the downtown barber shop. Aware of the financial benefits of working in such a prime location, Sam accepted the deal. "I never smoked again for 50 years," he later recalled. Another variation of this story has Killian offering Sam a new suit for giving up cigarettes. If true, the extra incentive to ditch the Lucky Strikes would not be the last time the Wahoo businessman expanded the boy's wardrobe

The site of Sam's first place of business was the World Building (later named the Clyde Worrall building) in downtown

Wahoo. In the basement, below the Citizens National Bank, town residents could get a haircut and shave at the Gregory and Jensen barber shop. While customers waited their turn in the chair, a blond lad offered to shine their shoes at the bootblack stand near a towel rack on the east wall. As he ensured the footwear of Wahoo retained its gleam, Sam observed the snippets of hair tumbling down the capes of customers seated across the room. Within the floral wallpaper-covered confines of this shop, his future materialized before him.

Sam had good reason to believe he would eventually wield the clippers himself. This is because a few years earlier, his father had apprenticed his brother Trace to learn the barber's trade. After completing his training, the oldest Crawford son opened his own shop in the nearby town of Prague. A couple years later Trace moved back to Wahoo, where he started a tonsorial business with Clifford Barnes. In addition to cutting hair, Sam's brother served his community by joining the Wahoo Fire Department. In October 1895, at the age of 21, Trace married Myrtle Miller, a young woman originally from Avoca, Iowa. Occurring in Lincoln, the wedding provided happy news for a family that had been hit with tragedy two years earlier. On June 10, 1893, Sam's younger brother Willie had died from scarlet fever at the age of six.

As with Trace, the patriarch Steve Crawford decided that Sam too should be a barber. The youth began his tonsorial training with Norm Gregory and Chris Jensen, in the same shop where he shined shoes and where his brother had apprenticed. With the depression limiting the prospects of young men in the area, barbering seemed to offer a solid career path. Sam accepted this reality but derived little excitement from his training. As he later recounted for Lawrence Ritter:

> I was learning the trade the hard way there in Wahoo. And I do mean the hard way. Cleaning cuspidors, and washing windows, and mopping the floor. Then sometimes they'd let me lather somebody and get them ready for the real barber. And sometimes a tramp would

come through and want a haircut, and I could practice on him. That's the way we learned in those days.

Sam soon realized that barbering would not be an easy way to make a living. He watched his razor-wielding mentors stand on their feet all day. On Saturdays when the farmers all came in, the haircutting started at 7:00 am and continued until ten at night. For 35 cents, Gregory and Jensen's customers could get a haircut, shave, and shampoo. Sam gradually learned the skills of the profession, gaining more opportunities to practice the tonsorial craft.

While his enthusiasm for his nascent barbering career may have been somewhat lacking, Sam remained excited about baseball. Newspaper stories about diamond stars like Cap Anson, Wee Willie Keeler, and Cy Young further fueled this devotion. Sam talked about the game nonstop with customers at the shop. His loquacious love for baseball gained him a reputation as the "talkingest" barber in Wahoo. Fortunately, Gregory and Jensen proved to be kind bosses. When business was slow, they allowed Sam to head off to the ballfield. On such occasions, one can imagine the teenager tearing off his apron and bounding up the stairs from the basement shop to race over to the diamond with his friends.

Aside from their successful merchandising enterprise, the Killian brothers were also baseball promoters. In the mid-1890s, they organized a town team in Wahoo. Tom managed, while Ed and a third brother, Amiel, played. The players on this squad wore real uniforms, similar to those worn by the big leaguers. Sam and his friends dreamed of playing for the Killian nine and donning those uniforms. Tom, for his part, was well aware of the burgeoning baseball talents of the kid running his bootblack stand. "There was a young lad in our town who was a mighty good player for his age," Killian later recalled. "Although he was still just a boy he hit the ball so hard he was the star of the nine." In the spring of 1896, when Sam was just 16 years old and still shining shoes, Tom offered him the opportunity to play for the Killian Brothers team. Decades later, Sam still remembered the moment when Tom gave him his first uniform, calling it one the greatest thrills of his life. "I was so proud of it I slept in it," Crawford said.

Despite Sam's young age, he had the right look for a ballplayer. "He was a big, raw-boned fellow, kind of lanky," an opposing sandlot player noted about him. With large hands to firmly grip the bat, Crawford displayed hitting skills that left no question about the wisdom of Tom Killian's choice. Sam remembers actually knocking the cover off the ball on occasion. Granted, this feat of baseball cliché was mostly possible because of the shoddy stitching on the balls they used, but still, that Crawford kid swung a ferocious bat. On the defensive side, Sam could fly across the outfield, and he brandished a strong throwing arm. The prodigy was a natural southpaw who threw and batted from the left side.

Sam played center field when the Killian Brothers began their 1896 season on May 29 against the Omaha Originals. Opening Day stirred excitement among the baseball-starved locals. As *The Wahoo Democrat* reported: "People who have been marking off the days on their vest-pocket calendars that have had no ball games checked on them so far this season can now put away their pencils and scratch around in their pockets for the fifteen cents they have been itching to spend." Though they did not realize it at the time, the paying customers at Wahoo's ballfield that Thursday afternoon in late May were witnessing a historic diamond moment—the semipro debut of Sam Crawford.

In addition to chasing flies, Sam emerged as one of the team's three regular starting pitchers, along with Carl Goucher and Ed Killian. Backed by the slugging and hurling prowess of their youthful ringer, the Killian Brothers won 11 of the 12 games they played that summer. One of the season's high points came on the Fourth of July when Wahoo defeated the University of Nebraska 12 to 5. Sam, batting cleanup, scored twice and stole a base. After starter Ed Killian hurt his arm, Sam also pitched the final three innings, striking out six. In its recap of the game, the *Wasp* hailed Crawford as the best all-round player on the Killian team. A couple weeks later, after he pitched a complete game victory over Fremont, the newspaper again sang his praises: "Sam is to be complimented on his steady pitching and the coolness with which he played."

Sam batted .273 in his first season in a baseball uniform. On the mound, he posted an impressive 1.068 WHIP (walks plus hits per innings pitched), while striking out 53 batters in 44 innings. In August Sam reluctantly packed up his beloved Killian uniform for the year. As the leaves started to turn, he took his athletic talents from the diamond to the gridiron. A returning veteran for Wahoo's high school football team, Sam had played quarterback the previous year. His brother Trace, a five-foot seven fireplug of muscle, had played left halfback. Prep sports eligibility requirements were a bit lax at the time given that neither Sam nor his 21-year-old sibling were enrolled as students in 1895.

In September 1896, the young men on Wahoo's football team started training for another season. An experienced gridiron man named G.A. Hice coached and played left end for the team. Sam now played center. Burly and strong, he proved an effective blocker for his ball carriers, right halfback Amiel Killian and left halfback F.M. Milenz (Trace's replacement). The team started playing in early October and weeks later concluded a perfect six-win season with a 12-6 triumph over Lincoln High.

Though the University of Nebraska football team ("the Bugeaters") had started to generate considerable fan interest by this time, the game was not yet first in the hearts of most state residents. Hard to imagine today, but a competition in the political arena overshadowed gridiron activities in the state in the fall of 1896. That year Nebraska had an opportunity to send one of its own to the White House.

In 1887, Illinois native William Jennings Bryan moved with his wife to Lincoln, Nebraska, where he practiced law. An outstanding public speaker, Bryan soon entered politics, twice winning election to the U.S. House of Representatives. In 1894, he fell short in his bid for the Senate. Despite this setback, Bryan remained a rising young star in the Democratic Party. A staunch supporter of the free and unlimited coinage of silver, Bryan delivered a rousing oratory known as the "Cross of Gold" speech at his party's 1896 national convention. Stirred to a frenzy, the powerful Silverites rallied behind Bryan, nominating him for the presidency. At 36 years old, he was, and still is, the youngest presidential nominee of a major party.

While Sam Crawford was baffling opposing hitters for the Killian nine, the unexpected Democratic nominee launched a massive campaign tour in July. Over the next hundred days, Bryan traveled 18,000 miles by rail crisscrossing 27 states. He delivered more than 500 speeches, focusing on the hotly contested midwestern states. In so doing, he set the model for the modern cross-country presidential campaigns of today.

By Election Day in November 1896, Sam had returned to his barbering duties in Wahoo. He likely heard plenty of political commentary on the national struggle between Bryan and Republican nominee, William McKinley. The Boy Orator of the Platte, as Bryan was called, carried Nebraska, the South, and most of the West. But his message promoting small farmers, small towns, and small government failed to gain traction in the industrial Northeast and in the nation's large cities. McKinley captured 51% of the popular vote and prevailed in the Electoral College 271 to 176.

Years later, Crawford spoke of lathering and shaving Bryan. If factual, this event likely occurred a couple years later, when Sam's tonsorial skills had advanced beyond the apprentice stage. One wonders if Crawford and the Boy Orator spoke of baseball or politics. And did the other people in the shop that day realize that the young barber would soon rival his customer as the nation's most famous Nebraskan?

As he continued to hone his barbering skills in Wahoo over the winter months, Sam looked forward to another baseball season in 1897. Sadly, tragedy again struck the Crawford family in

February when Sam's older brother Trace fell ill with a severe case of appendicitis. He underwent an operation on the 17th, but his condition did not improve. Nine days later, he died at his home in Wahoo. Pastor J.W. Swan of the Methodist Episcopal Church conducted the funeral service. Several members of the Wahoo Fire Department served as pallbearers. Fireman S.H. Sornborger delivered a heartfelt gravesite tribute for his fallen comrade. "No member of this department was more esteemed," Sornborger said, "none could be more missed." Trace is buried near his brother Willie in Sunrise Cemetery east of Wahoo.

On April 16, 1897, the town newspaper reported that the Killian Brothers team had reorganized and hoped to start playing games in another week. Ed Killian was the secretary, pitcher, and left fielder. Sam Crawford was slated to pitch and play left field, alternating with Ed. Amiel Killian would play center field. About to turn 17, Sam still viewed himself as a future full-time barber who played baseball for fun as much as he could. Little did he know what the upcoming season would hold.

Thrilled to again don his Killian Brothers uniform, Sam displayed his skills on the mound and with the bat. His team, however, hit some rough waters early on. On May 5, a squad from Council Bluffs, Iowa, defeated the home team at the Wahoo ballfield. Hitting the ball early, the Clerks, as the local team was now called, led 6-1 after five innings. But the visitors scored six runs in the eighth and eventually prevailed 10-7. Errors from the Wahoo infield and Crawford's loss of pitching control helped fuel the Iowans' late rally.

A few days later, Sam lent his talents to Wahoo's other town team. Known as the Colts, this squad traveled south for a game in Lincoln. There, the University of Nebraska team demolished the visitors 16 to 0. The college boys played stellar defense and ran wild on the bases. Sam accounted for the lone Wahoo highlight when, with two men on in the ninth, he drove a liner deep to the fence. But an amazing running catch doused the Colts' chance to avoid the shutout.

Back with his original team, Crawford and his Killian teammates played well in the following weeks. A personal highlight for Sam came on June 15 when he drilled a three-run homer against the Lincoln Originals. He again demonstrated his skills when the Nebraska Indians came to town. Lawyer and baseball promoter Guy Green recruited the players for this touring squad from the Genoa Industrial and Agricultural School, the Santee Normal School, and two reservations. They played their first two games in Wahoo, dropping both contests against the Killians in late June. After starting out the year with three losses in four games, Green very much wanted a victory to get his team on track. So for the next game he rented the services of Crawford, one of the pitchers who beat the Indians in Wahoo. Though not his finest performance on the mound, Sam delivered three hits to help the Native American team prevail over the Lincoln Originals, 18-12. Crawford's appearance set a precedent for Green, who would occasionally hire talented white players to provide a short-term boost for the Indians' roster.

Two weeks later, with Crawford pitching, the Clerks fell 14-3 to the Hayden Brothers, a department store team from Omaha. A few Wahoo residents vocalized their disapproval of the team's performance. Some even accused Tom Killian of using baseball as a merely money-making venture, even though he invested what little gate remained after expenses back into the team. Frustrated with the unfair criticisms, Killian disbanded the Clerks. A week later another team called the Wahoo Clerks formed. Looking to be more competitive, the new squad included top players from several different businesses in the city. There were a few familiar faces in the lineup: Ed Killian, captain and second base; Amiel Killian, left field; and Sam Crawford, pitcher.

Sam's time with this new outfit of mercantilist all-stars did not last long though. Just a few days after the reorganization, he found another baseball opportunity. The manager of Wahoo's other town team, Tom "Snakes" Crawford (no relation), had made plans for an extended road trip that summer. Enticed by the idea, Sam left the Clerks to become a Colt.

On July 20, Sam homered in a Colts victory over the visiting Lincoln Originals. The two teams played again the following day, with Sam on the mound for the home team. Though he doubled and struck out eleven, five walks and several costly errors allowed the Originals to prevail in "an uninteresting contest." The visitors won again the next day to claim two of three from the Colts.

After concluding the three-game series with Lincoln, Tom Crawford took his team of mostly of 16- to 18-year-olds on the road. They traveled the dirt lanes of eastern Nebraska in a lumber wagon that one of the boys, John Isaacson, convinced his father to let them use. Two horses pulled the covered vehicle (the kind used to haul grain to the elevator) that carried the eleven players on the team.

The Colts headed north from Wahoo to play teams in Fremont, Hooper, Scribner, Dodge, and West Point. When the wagon rolled into a town, one of the players whipped out a cornet to sound their arrival. When the people came out to investigate, Snakes announced that his Wahoo team was ready to play a baseball game against the local nine. "Every little town out there on the prairie had its own ball team and ball grounds," Sam later told Lawrence Ritter, "and we challenged them all. We didn't have any uniforms or anything, just baseball shoes maybe, but we had a manager."

The Wahoo tour was not a money-making venture, nor was it glamorous. It was baseball in a basic 1890s country form. Receiving no salary, the players passed a hat at the games to take up a collection that may or may not have covered their expenses. Their diet consisted mostly of round steak, which they bought at twelve pounds for a dollar. One of the players cooked the meat on a stove and served it with bread and gravy. If the wagon happened upon an orchard, then apples made it onto the menu as well.

Lodging arrangements were similarly spartan for the travelling Wahoo team. Players slept in a tent or in the wagon or on the ground out in the open. On some occasions they might lodge at a fairground or in a barn, if available. According to one of Sam's former classmates, his teammates frequented the taverns in the towns where they played. But Sam eschewed such evening amusements.

Each town provided its own umpire, adding to the on-field challenges facing Snakes and his boys. Sam, who pitched and played outfield, recalled that victories did not come easily. At an early stop in Fremont, 25 miles northeast of Wahoo, the hosts dismantled the visitors 24-4. Twelve Wahoo errors contributed to the avalanche of Fremont runs. A week later, West Point buried the traveling team 18-9, though Sam garnered attention by hitting the only home run in the game. In a rematch the following day, Wahoo tallied only two hits while getting shut out 6-0.

After nearly three weeks living on bread and beefsteak, Snakes and his players headed back home. In terms of on-field results, the Colts tour fell well short of the undefeated precedent set by the 1869 Cincinnati Red Stockings. Traveling with the Wahoo lumber wagon team, nonetheless, had a profound impact on Sam. "We were ballplayers on a trip and loved it," he said. Not only did the tour cement his love for baseball, it also set him on the path for a career in the game.

While in West Point, the young Wahoo slugger impressed the home team's manager. The skipper sent Sam a letter with an offer he could not refuse. West Point would pay him $30 a month to play outfield and pitch. Though Snakes planned to resume the wagon tour by heading to some towns to the west, Sam now had an opportunity to get paid to play baseball. He bid farewell to his traveling teammates and moved 45 miles north to West Point, a town of about 1,800.

Sam debuted for his new team on August 10. In a 5-0 West Point victory in Neligh, Crawford attracted press attention for his fielding prowess. The 17-year-old had joined a talented team riding a hot streak. On August 30, Sam pitched and contributed a home run and a triple to a victory over the Omaha Brewing Association. That triumph gave West Point 21 wins in its last 22 contests.

In early September, West Point played a best-of-five series against Norfolk to determine the state championship. After the teams split the first two contests at West Point, the series shifted to the Wayne County fairgrounds in the town of Wayne. After West Point took the third game, Norfolk knocked Sam from the mound in a 15-0 blowout to even the series. On September 11, the teams headed to Norfolk for the deciding contest. Hometown fans celebrated their team's Game 4 shutout victory with a band and a complimentary dinner at the Oxnard Hotel, to which their opponents were also invited. They may not have been so hospitable had they known that West Point would claim the state title with a 6-2 victory in a hard-fought fifth game. Upon the team's return home, jubilant West Point fans held a banquet to honor their conquering heroes.

The state championship series did not mark the end of the season for West Point. They played more games against Norfolk and other Nebraska teams throughout September and into the following month. West Point concluded its 1897 season on October 8 with a 41-3 shellacking of Fremont. In a game filled with offensive highlights, Sam made news by slugging the longest home run ever hit at the West Point ballfield.

It had been an eventful summer for Sam Crawford. The teenager had donned his cherished Killian Brothers uniform, traveled the small towns of eastern Nebraska on a wagon tour, and received money to play the game he loved. And that fall he won his first baseball championship.

Sam resumed his barbering duties for Gregory and Jensen in the winter of 1897-98. His exploits of the previous summer, however, further eroded his lukewarm interest in a tonsorial career. He had a taste of life as a professional ballplayer, and he wanted more. Instead of standing behind a swivel chair wearing a white coat and wielding clippers, Sam instead dreamed of standing in a batter's box wearing a baseball uniform and wielding a hefty stick.

Baseball aspirations at this time rarely brought encouragement or approval from a young man's parents. Though the game was gaining popularity by the end of the nineteenth century, playing it was not generally considered a respectable occupation. Many people looked upon ballplayers as crude and lazy, or worse. Aspiring baseball stars often faced parental disapproval of their career ambitions in the game. Pitcher Rube Marquard's father expressed a common viewpoint when, upon learning of his son's desire to make a livelihood of playing baseball, said, "Ballplayers are no good, and they never will be any good."

What Steve and Nellie Crawford thought about their teenage son's dreams of playing baseball is unknown. Perhaps they thought it was a fancy that would pass. Perhaps they urged him to focus on his "serious" career option of barbering. Or perhaps they, recognizing his unusual talent, supported his diamond aspirations. Whatever the case, it seems they did not pose a roadblock to their son's continuance down the basepath.

By the spring of 1898, Sam had made a name for himself well beyond Wahoo to a widening semipro baseball circle. His pitching and hitting talents had helped West Point win a state championship. His mammoth blasts had become a frequent topic of conversation among townsfolk and farmers across eastern Nebraska. One fan described how Sam drove a ball "over the David City right fielder's head a mile into a great field of waving corn in the suburbs, through which it cut with the noise of a cyclone."

Crawford's strappingly husky physique also attracted fans, especially the young women in the towns where he played. Ruth Burnhardt, who was a teenager in the 1890s, later recalled: "Whenever Wahoo Sam Crawford played in West Point, I remember all the high school girls were wild to go see him play." An appearance by Sam at the ballfield even warranted skipping school, Burnhardt added.

Sam was also popular with the younger baseball fans in Wahoo and other Nebraska towns. Jim Campbell grew up across the alley from the Crawford house on North Orange Street. He remembered that Sam always had time to play catch. Often joining them was Sam's younger brother Step, who dreamed of following in his older sibling's ballplaying footsteps.

Turning 18 at the start of the baseball season, Sam looked to build on his progress from the previous campaign. Among the inquiries about his baseball services he received that spring was a letter from Wymore manager, L.P. Covington. Sam replied that he would join his team if Covington would land him a barbering job that paid $9 a week. After the manager secured said job at the requested wages, Crawford headed 85 miles south to Wymore, a town of 2,600 residents near the Kansas border. As he did the summer before, Sam joined a talented group of ballplayers. Wymore boasted the best team in southeastern Nebraska at the time.

Early in the 1898 season, Guy Green brought his barnstorming Nebraska Indians to Wymore for a pair of games. The home team prevailed in both contests, 11-10 and 8-2. With the Native American players' clowning antics and exciting style of play, Green's barnstorming team created a Wild West carnival-type atmosphere in the small towns where they played. Following their two defeats in Wymore, the Indians went on a tear, winning game after game as they traveled through Iowa, Missouri, and Illinois. Green's team finished their 1898 tour with an impressive 81-22 record. Over the next 16 years, the Nebraska Indians established themselves as one of the most formidable exhibition baseball teams in the nation. They won more than 1,200 games between 1897 and 1914—and Sam Crawford was the winning pitcher in one of their first victories.

Wymore continued its winning ways after Green's barnstormers left town. A string of triumphs elevated the team as contenders for a state championship. Sam's pitching arm and bat played a key role in several of these victories. In mid-July Wymore cooled off, dropping a pair of games in Omaha. Upon returning home, the team rebounded to sweep a two-game series from a Frankfort, Kansas, team. Crawford pitched the second game, a 16-1 win.

The Frankfort gem would be Sam's last hurrah in Wymore. A few days after that game, he and three of his teammates jumped ship to play for Superior, a town of 1,500 residents 80 miles west of Wymore in southern Nebraska. It did not take Crawford long to reward his new employer with a string of dominant mound performances. He struck out nineteen in a 14-2 victory against Hastings. He then struck out eleven in a shutout win over Grand Island. While beating Hanover he nearly pitched another shutout, but a late error allowed three meaningless unearned runs to score. Wymore, meanwhile, had rebuilt a formidable team by recruiting players from Kansas and Texas. This new assemblage disrupted Superior's victorious stretch on August 15, with Sam taking the loss. He got revenge five days later by tossing a complete-game home victory over Wymore.

The season concluded with an impressive late-summer run, both for Sam and the Superior town team. Baseball, however, was still not a profession that paid his bills. To make ends meet, Sam continued to cut hair during his time in both Wymore and Superior. The barber's pole, with its red, white, and blue stripes, still loomed ahead as a prominent beacon on his career path. The next year would mark the end of a century. It would also prove decisive in setting the future course of Sam's life.

Chapter 4

The Road to the Big Show

By the winter of 1898-99, Sam Crawford had well-established his baseball reputation among the town teams and semi-professional circuits of Nebraska. Though he had earned pay for his diamond work, his wages had thus far been modest—barely more than a dollar a game. Two big questions remained regarding Sam's dream of a career in baseball: 1) Could he succeed against higher-level competition? 2) And could he support himself playing what many at that time still considered a game for children? The two questions were related—an affirmative answer to the first would likely bring the same answer for the second. After a successful year in 1898 at the town team level, Sam headed into the following spring seeking an opportunity to prove himself against faster competition. Otherwise, the pressure to get a "real job" might draw him back to barbering full-time.

Sam did not have to wait long for opportunity to knock. One of his teammates in West Point two years earlier was a pitcher named John McIlvaine. The next year, McIlvaine played for Chatham in the Canadian League. After that league's 1898 season ended, he returned to Nebraska, where he saw Sam again. Impressed by his former teammate's talents, McIlvaine wrote to the Chatham manager recommending Sam for the next season. The Canadian team obliged, sending travel money for them both to head north in April 1899. About to turn 19, Sam would be moving not only out of state for the first time, but to another country. He was ready. "So when I got this chance to play professional ball," he said, "I didn't think twice about it."

The Canadian League of Professional Base Ball Clubs included six teams in 1899: Hamilton, St. Thomas, London, Chatham, Guelph, and Stratford. All of these cities are located in southern Ontario. The distance between the team farthest west (Chatham) and the team farthest east (Hamilton) was only about 140 miles.

Chatham is located on the Thames River, 45 miles east of Detroit, Michigan. Prior to the Civil War, the town had served as a destination for fugitive slaves from the American South seeking freedom via the Underground Railroad. Though situated in an agricultural area with a large trade in grain and lumber, Chatham by the end of the 19th century was developing a manufacturing sector specializing in the production of boilers, engines, iron goods and woolen goods. In 1899 the town had a population of just over 9,000.

The Chatham Reds required its players to report for practice on April 22. Travelling by train from Nebraska, Sam Crawford and Johnny McIlvaine would have likely gone through Detroit, before heading east into Canada. Little did Sam know on this journey that he was passing through a city that would later play a defining role in his professional life.

Though perhaps not as exciting as when he first received his Killian Brothers uniform three years earlier, Sam certainly felt great pride donning the red and blue uniform of the Chatham Reds. Listed on the team roster as a left fielder, Sam was now a minor leaguer. Chatham paid him $65 a month, plus board. Good wages in the 19-year-old's opinion.

The Canadian League started its 1899 season on Wednesday, May 10. Chatham opened on the road against Hamilton, dropping a 3-2 decision. Crawford tripled in the ninth inning, his only hit in four at-bats in his first game as a pro. The Reds won the next day, but then dropped their next two to start the season at 1-3. Chatham's subsequent home stand offered hope for a promising campaign. The Reds swept a doubleheader against Stratford on the 20th to vault into second place. Despite a stretch of poor weather, attendance was strong league-wide. This auspicious beginning for Sam's new employer would not last though.

A losing streak in early June dropped Chatham to fifth place in the six-team league. London, meanwhile, surged ahead with a 14-1 record, threatening to run away with the league title. Such developments typically have an adverse effect on attendance in other cities, and the Canadian circuit was no exception. The last-place Stratford Poets disbanded on June 8th, not even a month into the season. The league transferred the team to Woodstock, Ontario, and revised the schedule.

Chatham had climbed to fourth place by mid-June but continued to struggle with a 12-17 record. Pitching problems sent manager T.M. Tennent on a search to strengthen his mound corps. Sam's buddy Johnny McIlvaine did not make this task any easier when he asked for a release from his contract to accept an offer with another team.

Chatham made a brief surge in late June, but proved unable to sustain the momentum. By the first of July, the Reds remained mired in fourth place. St. Thomas, meanwhile, had been struggling with financial problems. The club played its last game on July 3 and then dropped out of the league. The next day, Canadian League officials voted to drop Chatham and finish the season with just four clubs. Having swept a double-header from Guelph on the 3rd, the Reds concluded their 1899 campaign with a 19-23 record.

Despite playing for a mediocre team that disbanded mid-season, Crawford had established himself as the top hitter in the circuit. He batted a league-best .370 with twelve triples in his eight weeks with Chatham. Because the Canadian League was an official member of Organized Baseball under the National Agreement, its star players attracted notice among the professional clubs back in the states. Joe Schrall, an outfielder for the Hamilton team, helped Crawford's cause by penning a letter to sportswriter Ren Mulford Jr. about Sam's exploits north of the border. Mulford was the Cincinnati correspondent for *Sporting Life,* a national publication that covered baseball. He tabbed the Chatham outfielder as an up-and-coming prospect. Word quickly spread about Crawford. Just a few days after the Chatham club disbanded, Columbus (Ohio) of the Western League, a top minor league circuit, added Sam to its roster. *Sporting Life* reported the transaction: "The Columbus Club ... has signed outfielder Sam Crawford, the Nebraska boy who made such a hit with Chatham."

The four-team Canadian League limped along for another month, before ending its season a month early on August 12. "Lack of interest and poor patronage" were cited as the reasons for its struggles and early demise. Though few would consider the 1899 season a success for Canadian baseball, the league provided an invaluable boost to the career of one of its players. The Chatham Reds gave Sam Crawford the opportunity to show that he could dominate low-level minor league pitching. In just 42 games, he climbed another rung on the professional baseball ladder. And it was still early July—Sam had more than half a season left in 1899 to demonstrate what he could do on the diamond.

Sam would not have far to travel to reach his new hometown in the states. Lying 170 miles south of Chatham, the Ohio state capital of Columbus boasted 125,000 residents at the turn of the century. It would be the largest city Sam had lived in up to that point in his young life. Except, he never lived there. He never even played a home game in Columbus.

Sam joined the Columbus Senators on the road, debuting for them in Milwaukee on July 8. He played center field and batted sixth as his team opened a three-game series in the Cream City. Sam singled in four at-bats, while recording one putout in the field with no errors. But Columbus starter Rube Waddell surrendered twelve hits in a shaky outing, and the visitors fell 7 to 6.

Sam again recorded one hit the next day, and the Senators dropped another slugfest 10-9. Columbus owner/manager Tom Loftus moved his new Nebraska slugger over to left field and up to third in his lineup for the series finale in Milwaukee. Sam contributed a single and three putouts as Columbus prevailed by a score of 3-2.

At the time Sam joined the team, the Senators hovered just over .500 and sat in fourth place in the eight-team Western League. But Columbus remained in striking distance of the lead, just three-and-a-half games behind the two teams tied at the top—Indianapolis and Minneapolis. Much like with Sam's Canadian club, however, poor attendance plagued the Senators. Loftus by this point was searching for a new home for his team.

The Senators next traveled to Minneapolis, where Sam collected his first triple in the Western circuit on July 13. His bat remained hot after his club crossed the Mississippi River to play a pair of games against St. Paul. On July 18, the team travelled back to Minneapolis again. But Sam would no longer be playing for the Columbus Senators. Neither would his teammates. They were not cut, nor were they sent to another club. It was their *city* that got traded.

The Western League and the Interstate League had worked out a deal to exchange locations. Columbus of the Western League would transfer to Grand Rapids, Michigan. The Grand Rapids team in the Interstate League would then move to Columbus. This unusual move likely confused more than a few fans in the respective cities, who opened the newspaper to wonder why all the players on their hometown team had different names. Sam Crawford played a total of eight games for Columbus, none of them in front of the home fans in the city he represented.

The team formerly known as the Columbus Senators took the field in Minneapolis on July 18 now representing Grand Rapids. This abrupt change must not have bothered Sam, who hit his first home run in the Western League. He and his teammates combined for twelve hits in a 10-7 victory over their Minnesota hosts.

Located in western Michigan 30 miles from the shoreline of Lake Michigan, Grand Rapids had a population of 87,000 in 1899. The city's new baseball team, now called the Prodigals, played their first home game on July 20. They were greeted by "a large and appreciative crowd." Inspired by the support and change of scenery, the home team unleashed a 15-hit barrage to bury Minneapolis 15-3. Sam contributed two triples, and Waddell struck out nine in a complete-game victory.

Grand Rapids rode an early wave of hometown enthusiasm to move into third place in the standings. Eventually, both the team's performance and fan support plateaued. Home attendance averaged around 1,100, which was not bad for a city that had recently lost interest in its cellar-dwelling Interstate League club. Attendance numbers were better than the team had received in Columbus, but Loftus had expected better crowds. The Prodigals hovered around the .500 mark and fell further behind the eventual league champion, Indianapolis.

Though his team did not inspire accolades, Sam Crawford continued to attract notice as a rising star. Undaunted by the highest level of competition he had thus far faced, the young Nebraskan continued to thrive. *Sporting Life* took note of his diamond prowess. "Young Crawford ... has all the ear-marks of a rising ball player," the paper's editor wrote in early August. "He has the build, the eye and, in fact, is lacking in nothing to make him just what all his friends predicted of him, one of the most brilliant fielders in the country."

With his batting average well above .300, Sam soon attracted the attention of big league scouts. Grand Rapids started receiving offers less than a month after his Western League debut. On August 12, *Sporting Life* wrote that Cincinnati had purchased Crawford. While this report was premature, it does indicate that major league teams were serious about Sam. Praise for the Wahoo native continued to appear in that same publication: "Crawford, the outfielder, pitcher and general player … has made a decided sensation by his brilliant fielding and remarkably heavy batting. He is a big fellow, and hits like a second [Napoleon] Lajoie."

At this point, there was only one more rung for Sam to climb before reaching the highest level of baseball competition at the time—the National League. And the decision makers in that circuit were giving him a long look. By mid-August five NL magnates had expressed interest in the Nebraska slugger, prompting the press to report on a "Crawford boom" in the Western League. Sportswriters lavished Sam with praise as he continued racking up extra-base hits from the number three spot in the Grand Rapids lineup.

One of Sam's best games during this stretch came on August 24 in St. Paul. He went four for five with a double and scored two runs in his team's 9-4 victory. In the field he recorded three putouts and threw out a baserunner. This stellar play backed the mound work of the Prodigals' other rising star, Rube Waddell. Sam recognized even then that his unconventional teammate was destined for success. He later recounted some of Rube's antics in Grand Rapids, such as skipping games between starts to go fishing, showing up at the ballpark just minutes before he was to take the mound, and pouring ice water over his arm so his blazing fastballs did not burn up his catcher's glove.

Sam continued to hit through the waning days of August. A Cincinnati scout wired his bosses about the burly power-hitter tearing up the Western League. That was enough for Reds president John T. Brush. He soon completed negotiations with Grand Rapids to buy the contract of Sam Crawford. For Brush, the transaction was part of a late season spending spree that saw him acquire three outfielders, a shortstop, a catcher, and a pitcher from the minors. And his agents were negotiating to buy even more players from the Western League. *Sporting Life* speculated that Brush was loading up on young talent in case a rival major league emerged the following year and tried to raid

National League rosters. In such a scenario, Brush did not want to get caught short-handed.

For Sam, Brush's motivations were of less significance than the larger issue—after just four months in the minors, Crawford was a member of a major league baseball team. Wahoo Sam had reached the highest rung on baseball's ladder while still a teenager.

Sam's big league debut would not happen right away, however. The Western League season still had two more weeks left, and he would remain a Prodigal for most of that fortnight. Crawford played his last game in the Western League on September 9. He singled in four at-bats as Grand Rapids lost at home to St. Paul. The Prodigals swept a doubleheader the following day to finish their season in fourth place with a 62-61 record.

Sam had already left town before the Prodigals opened the first game of their final twin bill. Covering 300 miles, his train arrived in Cincinnati that morning. The kid from Wahoo would be reporting to his third different club in five months. It had been a whirlwind of a season that saw him travel across Ontario and several states. He did not mind his time on the road. "All that was pretty exciting for a nineteen-year-old kid," he later said. "I'd never been anywhere before that."

And now Sam Crawford was in the Big Show.

When Sam arrived in the Queen City on the morning of September 10th, the Reds trailed league-leading Brooklyn by 15 games with a month left to play. Cincinnati officials had no illusions that their promising young slugger would lead them to a pennant in 1899. Crawford's late-season promotion was, in actuality, an extended tryout. It was by no means a given that Sam was in the big leagues to stay. In 60 Western League games, he had batted .334, but he needed to prove himself at baseball's highest level if he wanted to drink more than a cup of coffee in Cincinnati.

Reds manager Buck Ewing wasted no time trying out the "great long-distance hitter of the Western" his team had acquired. Just hours after Sam stepped off the train that Sunday morning, he found himself in uniform about to make his big-league debut at League Park in Cincinnati. The Reds were scheduled to host two different teams that day in an unconventional doubleheader. Sam batted cleanup in the first game, delivering two hits in a 10-2 victory over Cleveland. In the second game, against Louisville, he added three more hits, including a triple off Bert Cunningham. If Sam were nervous about facing big league pitching for the first time, it did not show. He went five for eight on the day with no errors playing left field. As *Sporting Life* reported, "Crawford made his debut and scored a big success."

After sweeping the twin bill on Sunday, the Reds set out on a two-week road trip. Their first stop was Washington, D.C. Sam would be visiting yet another new city this year, his first time in the nation's capital. He continued hitting, going one for three in the series opener against the Senators, and followed with three more hits in a doubleheader the next day.

Forty miles away in Baltimore, his former teammate Rube Waddell made his 1899 National League debut for Louisville. Two days earlier, Waddell had been scheduled to pitch for Grand Island in the Western League season finale, but the eccentric lefty departed without notifying his manager. He had boarded the same train that Sam took, bound for Cincinnati. There, Waddell convinced Louisville manager Fred Clarke to give him a shot. Another Prodigal had made it to the Big Show.

For the doubleheader in D.C., Reds manager Ewing, a former catcher and future Hall of Famer, moved Sam into the number two spot in the lineup. That is where he stayed for the fourth and fifth games in Washington. He hit a triple in each of those contests. Nobody knew it at the time, including young Sam, but he was starting to build what would become one of baseball's unbreakable career records.

After the five-game set in D.C., the Reds travelled to Baltimore. For the first time, Sam would share the same field as John McGraw, the 26-year-old Orioles third baseman known for his brash style of play and stellar bat skills (he hit .391 that season). Player-manager McGraw did not put himself in the lineup for any of the three games against Cincinnati. His wife had died from appendicitis two weeks earlier, and he was still reeling from the emotional effects of that shocking loss.

Sam recorded a hit in all three games in Baltimore. The 19-year-old had hit safely in each of the ten major league games he had played thus far. The hitting streak ended with his next game, a series opener in Philadelphia. Though Sam went zero for two, he still contributed with a walk and a sacrifice. He also recorded five putouts in center field, his regular position for the season. The next day, September 21, he hit his first major league home run—the blast coming off Frank Donahue at Philadelphia's National League Park (later known as the Baker Bowl). Sam added a triple in the series finale against the Phillies. The press took note of the young slugger's early success in the league. Reporting on a Reds series, *Sporting Life* said, "Cincinnati … presented two corking good young outfielders in the speedy Barrett and the hard-hitting Crawford."

The Barrett referred to in the quote was Jimmy Barrett, another outfield prospect that Cincinnati had purchased from the Western League at the end of August. Debuting for the Reds just a few days after Sam, the 24-year-old made an immediate impression. Manager Ewing tabbed him as his leadoff hitter and everyday right fielder. Batting in front of Crawford, who still occupied the two-spot, Barrett's bat remained hot. The team finally returned to Cincinnati on the 24th to play a doubleheader against Chicago. Barrett reached base eight times and scored three runs in the two games. Crawford contributed three hits and scored three runs in the twin bill split against the Orphans (not yet called the Cubs). The games were well attended, with 9,000 jammed into League Park. According to the press, "'The locals' new men were the chief attractions."

Cincinnati in 1899 had a strong core of veterans that included future Hall of Famers Jake Beckley at first and Bid McPhee at second, along with the strong fielding shortstop Tommy Corcoran. Sam recalled that his new teammates were not too friendly to him after he joined the team. Big league veterans at the time often gave a cold shoulder to rookies, whom they viewed as competitors for their jobs. Nonetheless, the dynamic outfield duo of Crawford and Barrett elicited great fan excitement in the Queen City during the final weeks of the season. These newcomers, along with rookie southpaw and 20-game winner Noodles Hahn, gave Reds fans reason to be optimistic about the future. Further stoking these hopeful flames were the rumors that President Brush might lure John McGraw to manage his rising stars in 1900.

As the season entered its final two weeks, Sam fell into a slump. Heading into the last weekend of the season, his average had dipped to .279. Fortunately, Cincinnati had three games left against the cellar-dwelling Cleveland Spiders. Sam feasted on the woeful arachnid pitching that weekend, pounding out eight hits in 16 at-bats. When the dust settled after the season-ending doubleheader on Sunday, October 15, Sam had raised his batting average to .307. Eight triples and a homer during his month with Cincinnati pushed his slugging average to a lofty .472.

Though Cleveland's sorry mound corps played a major role in Sam's .300-plus average with the Reds, one cannot say the young slugger did not hold his own against the strong pitchers in the league. He drilled a triple off Baltimore's Joe McGinnity, a 28-game winner that year and one of the league's most dominant hurlers. And he went two for four against his buddy, southpaw sensation Rube Waddell.

All told, 1899 had been an amazing season for the kid from Wahoo. He played for three teams, and batted over .300 for all of them. His glove work in the outfield also proved more than capable. Crawford furthermore earned praise for having one of the best arms among NL outfielders.

Reporters covering the Reds took a liking to Sam right away. Upon learning of his hometown, scribes immediately started calling the newcomer "Wahoo Sam." They also latched onto his haircutting past, referring to him as the "slugging tonsorial artist." *Sporting Life* informed its readers that Crawford was just the second barber to play Major League Baseball. Bumpus Jones, a pitcher who threw a handful of games for the Reds a few years earlier, was reportedly the first. The *Cincinnati Post* reported that Sam had offered to demonstrate his barbering skills on the team's business manager, Frank Bancroft. The latter declined this opportunity to serve as a "practice grounds" for Crawford, advising him to save his razor for the farmers who come into Wahoo over the coming winter.

The Nebraska press, not surprisingly, followed Sam's progress that fall with great pride. The *Omaha Bee* told readers that the Wahoo native had become "the talk of the eastern press and is lionized by the Cincinnati fans." The article continued by stating, "Nearly every day he makes a home run and is already recognized as the best batter on the team." Neither of those claims were true—Sam hit just one home run for Cincinnati in 1899 and veteran Jake Beckley was still regarded as the team's best hitter. The article was spot on though when it continued, "His [Crawford's] Nebraska admirers are particularly proud of the record he is making since getting into fast company."

It was also no exaggeration that Sam stirred enthusiasm among Reds fans, who liked to yell "Wahoo! Wahoo!" when he came to bat. Their team finished the season in sixth place (out of 12), but with a decent 86-67 record. It was not a done deal that Crawford and Barrett would be back on the team in 1900, but the return of both seemed likely. As *Sporting Life* speculated:

> While both men still have much to learn, they are not so green that they should be kept longer in minor leagues. Both have improved considerably since they joined the Cincinnati team, and with proper instruction in the spring practice they will come very near being the finished article next season.

Following the season, several Cincinnati players went on a barnstorming tour of Ohio and then, after a break, several cities in the South. Not among this group of travelling Reds, Sam returned to Nebraska for the winter. While he was one of the 26 players the club had reserved for next season, he did not have a contract for 1900. That was not cause for worry though, since Brush had decided to wait before signing any of his players for the next campaign. Few doubted that Crawford would be on the team when Cincinnati finalized its roster next spring.

Just a few months earlier, Sam rode on a train from Nebraska to Canada. He had at that time never played even a single game of minor league baseball. In October he rode on a train from Ohio back to Nebraska, returning home as one of the most promising young players in Major League Baseball.

Chapter 5

Cincinnati

"People ask me what I do in winter when there's no baseball," Rogers Hornsby once said. "I'll tell you what I do. I stare out the window and wait for spring." Though "The Rajah" did not utter those words until after Crawford's playing days had ended, they likely offer an apt description of how Wahoo Sam felt between October 1899 and March 1900. For the first winter in his young life, Crawford could look forward with near certainty to an upcoming season in which baseball would be his profession. And not just that, he would be playing at the game's highest level. While he certainly derived some enjoyment hearing the congratulations of friends and locals who climbed into his barber's chair that winter, one can imagine Sam returning home after work to swing his bat at imaginary pitches, and mark the days off his calendar in a countdown to Reds training camp.

Hundreds of miles to the east, big-city baseball owners were making momentous decisions that offseason. With the 12-team National League bloated with unprofitable and uncompetitive clubs, the magnates agreed to decrease their number to eight. Cincinnati was in no danger of elimination, but this move reduced the total number of major league roster spots by one third. The competition for unestablished young players like Crawford to stay in the Big Show became much tougher.

Western League president Ban Johnson, meanwhile, harbored ambitions to challenge the NL's status as the only major league. He changed the name of his league to the American League for the 1900 season, but his circuit was still a minor league at the time. For Crawford to remain a big leaguer, he would need to make it in Cincinnati.

The 10th largest city in the nation, Cincinnati was home to 325,000 people at the turn of the century. The burg included a diverse population with large German and Irish communities. In the nineteenth century, the city emerged as a center of meatpacking ("Porkopolis"), iron production, and beer brewing. The Ohio River and fifteen railroads made the city an important transportation and shipping hub. With a population density of 37,000 people per square mile, Cincinnati presented a sharp contrast to the small-town environment of Wahoo. While Sam had played ball in many sizeable cities the previous year, this would be the first time he lived in a large urban setting for an extended period of time.

For Sam, moving to the Queen City in the spring of 1900 was an exciting prospect. He would be making more money than ever before—$150 a month. That totaled $900 over a six-month season, which he considered a lot of money. Good wages indeed, compared to the average annual income of other professions at the time: farm laborers ($460), butchers ($520), clerks ($610), barbers ($620), and foremen ($625). And best of all for Crawford, the youngest player on his team, he would be earning his money doing what he loved. Such was his excitement at playing for Cincinnati, that during the spring he announced his intention to become a year-round resident of the city, where he would run a barber shop during the off-season.

In March, Crawford traveled to New Orleans to report for his first major league spring training. New skipper Bob Allen, a former Phillies shortstop, would be leading the Reds in 1900. The retirement of longtime second baseman Bid McPhee created a hole to fill in the infield. For the outfield, however, five fly chasers would be battling for playing time. Veteran Elmer Smith batted .298 the previous season, while Kip Selbach hit .296 with 38 stolen bases. Another Reds outfielder, Algie McBride, hit .347 in 64 games. The youthful speedster Jimmy Barrett seemed a lock as a starter after batting .370 over the final month of 1899. Though Crawford had similarly shown promise after his late season call-up, it would not be easy to crack Cincy's starting lineup.

Sam showed up to practice in Louisiana ready to prove himself. Reporters noted that he ran to first base faster than he did the previous fall. His and Barrett's impressive speed made Selbach expendable, increasing speculation that the Reds would sell the latter. This prediction was soon realized when Cincinnati dealt Selbach to the Giants. Sam continued to impress in spring training, officially securing a roster spot on the club. That was the good news. The bad news was that he would not be one of the three starting outfielders. Though management believed in Crawford's talent, they felt that he would more easily adapt to a bench role than the older players, Smith (age 32) and McBride (age 30).

Following a banquet at the Imperial hotel in New Orleans, the Reds returned to Ohio on April 7. After an easy victory over Rochester in an exhibition contest, the team appeared ready for regular-season action. Despite relegating him to the bench, Allen praised his young outfielder from Wahoo. "Crawford is undoubtedly a great ball player," the manager said. "He is not only a natural hitter, but he is a great fielder, and one of the best throwers I ever laid my eyes on." How much playing time this assessment would translate into remained unknown.

Cincinnati opened its 1900 season at home on April 19 before a packed house of 12,000 at League Park. As expected, Crawford did not start. He pinch hit in the ninth, but failed to get on base. The home team fell to Chicago 13-10. The next game Crawford came off the bench to score a key run in a Cincinnati victory. A day later he delivered a pinch hit single in a four-run ninth-inning rally that propelled the Reds to a 7-6 win over Chicago.

Just over a week into the season, Algie McBride went down with a charley horse in Pittsburgh. Crawford replaced him in center field and contributed a single and a double to Cincinnati's 19-5 victory. He added two more hits the next day in a win that moved the Reds into a tie for first place.

Crawford looked determined to keep his recently-acquired spot in the starting lineup. Cincinnati's early surge, meanwhile, was one of the biggest surprises thus far in the baseball season. After winning at St. Louis on May 6, the Reds were just a half-game out of first with a 9-5 record. They lost the next contest against the Cardinals when a late rally fell short. Cincinnati would not win again for nearly two weeks, a tailspin that dropped them into sixth place. Just before the losing streak, *Sporting Life* commented that the Reds were not going to follow their typical pattern of futility this season. But once again the team seemed to be following their modus operandi: "to start off with a rush, stand well up to the fore for a while, and then go sliding down in a battered heap."

Despite his team's woes, Sam continued to rake. A month into the season, his batting average sparkled at .328. Reporters noted his defensive skills too, with one writer predicting that Crawford "will take second place to no player in the business when it comes to making a quick, hard and accurate return of the ball." Umpire Hank O'Day concurred, calling Sam the most promising young outfielder to reach the National League in years. News about the Nebraska star spread to American League cities as well. Future managing legend Connie Mack wanted to bring him over to Milwaukee, but Reds management wisely turned down the Brewers $1,000 offer.

The rookie Crawford lived in a boarding house at 245 5th Street with five of his teammates: Algie McBride, Jimmy Barrett, Noodles Hahn, Harry Steinfeldt, and Ted Breitenstein. Veteran first baseman Jake Beckley and his wife rented the house next door. These dwellings were in downtown Cincinnati, a few blocks north of the Ohio River. At nearby Fountain Square, Hawley's cigar store displayed a big white baseball on wires above the street whenever the Reds played a home game. League Park, where Sam and his teammates plied their trade, stood about a mile northwest of his boarding house.

Crawford soon followed the time-honored ballplayer tradition of embracing a superstition. Appropriately enough, the slugging barber believed his hitting was tied to the length of his hair. That is, the shorter his hair, the better he hit—a reverse Samson effect. This theory received "confirmation" when Sam ended a brief slump in mid-May after getting a haircut that was "as close cropped as a convict." Crawford also brought his sartorial sense of style to the Queen City, attracting attention for wearing a flashy vest "that would call out the fire department at Wahoo." Like many of his teammates, Sam sported a diamond ring.

As the losses piled up, Cincinnati's attendance dwindled. One writer commented that this was just retribution for Brush's role in contracting the league down to eight teams. In the second half of May, injuries sidelined Crawford and Barrett for more than a week. These absences came at a bad time. On May 27 the team concluded a two-week homestand in which they had won only three out of 14 games. On a positive note, Cincinnati's two young star outfielders would both return to the lineup for an upcoming series in Boston.

But then came a blow that all but demolished the team's hopes for getting its season back on track. On the morning of May 28th, Decoration Day, a fire destroyed the grandstand at League Park. In addition to claiming most of the seats, the blaze consumed the clubhouse, which contained the team's uniforms, bats, and balls. As Sam later recalled, "We didn't have a shoestring left of our equipment." The fire also claimed the personal effects the players had stored at the clubhouse, including several suits, and none of these possessions were insured.

The team scrambled to acquire bats, gloves, and shoes before traveling to Boston that night. Manager Bob Allen was the only team member with a surviving uniform for the first game against the Beaneaters. The players were in ill-spirits as their train reached Massachusetts. Not surprisingly, the Reds lost all four games in Boston. With no home stadium, the team would have to remain on the road for an entire month before temporary stands could be completed at League Park. Cincinnati's previously scheduled home games in that span were transferred to other cities.

Making matters worse, Brush expected his players to pay for their new uniforms. This from a wealthy owner who paid the lowest salaries in the National League (the Reds were the only club with a payroll under $40,000); who was insured against losses caused by the fire; and who had already required his team to pay for their uniforms (a hefty $30 expense per player) at the start of the season. The players understandably expressed their objections to the team owner's request.

It was not a good year for John T. Brush's approval ratings among Cincinnati baseball fans and sportswriters. A self-made millionaire who rose from childhood poverty to make his fortune as a department store owner and clothing magnate, Brush first entered the baseball arena in 1887 when he bought the Indianapolis Hoosiers. He soon advanced a player classification plan designed to keep salaries in check. Approved by the other National League owners, Brush's idea sparked a player uprising that led to the formation of the Players League in 1890. Though it attracted most of the top stars of the day, the new union-run circuit survived only one season competing against the vast financial resources of the NL magnates. A few years later, Brush further agitated players by proposing lifetime suspensions for the use of profanity on the field. A second revolt was avoided when a court, recognizing the ubiquity of swearing in baseball, rejected Brush's idea by ruling that ballplayers were entitled to utter stronger language than that used by ordinary citizens.

As the 1900 season continued, the Cincinnati press launched a campaign criticizing Brush for charging high ticket prices to watch an inferior product on the field. *The Cincinnati Times-Star* complained that fans at League Park had to pay 75 cents for a decent seat, with the other option being a hard bench with no back and no grandstand shelter from the sun. "Philadelphia, with the finest grandstand in the country," the paper opined, "offers its patrons better seats for 50 cents than the Cincinnati Club gives for 75 cents."

Continuing their crusade all summer, the press claimed to be defending the working people of Cincinnati "who make $10 or $15 a week and less" from the alien owner (Brush lived in Indianapolis) charging them "exorbitant and unreasonable" ticket prices to see the game they loved. The anti-Brush campaign yielded results. Attendance by mid-August dwindled to 500 for some games at League Park. Cincinnati's Board of Legislation joined the attack by passing an ordinance requiring the club to cover the ballpark's bleachers or pay a fine of $1,000. Brush's popularity in the Queen City had waned to the point that one reporter even speculated that the grandstand fire had been intentionally set by "some enemy of the management of the club."

Brush tried to defend himself against what he considered unjust attacks. He argued that the club charged the same prices for the same seats as it did ten years earlier, when "the public was satisfied." The owner furthermore claimed that the Reds had lost $11,000 the previous season, a shortfall that he and co-owner C.G. Lloyd had to bear themselves. Brush added that he had hired an architect to submit estimates for a new fireproof stand for his ballpark. Cincinnati papers were skeptical of the owner's loss claims, alleging that he could manipulate his bookkeeping system to show whatever result he wanted. *The Cincinnati Enquirer* continued to issue a daily call for Brush to sell the team to local buyers.

Despite this toxic atmosphere, the Reds surprisingly improved in June. Though they played all but three of their June games on the road, the team posted a 14-9 mark for the month. Perhaps adversity hardened their resolve, or maybe distance from the daily criticisms leveled at Brush improved their on-field focus. Winning six of seven in mid-July remarkably elevated Cincinnati to within one game of .500. During that stretch, Frank "Noodles" Hahn provided the team's top highlight of the season by throwing a no-hitter at League Park against Philadelphia. Crawford drilled a home run and recorded three putouts in left field to support his teammate's gem. The Reds unfortunately could not maintain this momentum, winning only two out of eleven games in the second half of July. Though the team showed signs of life again in August, the wheels came off completely in September when they flopped to a 9-19 record for the month. Cincinnati finished the season at 62-77, just one-and-a-half games ahead of the last-place Giants.

Up to this point in his brief career, Sam usually thrived whether his team was winning or not. The summer of 1900 would be a different story. After May, the young slugger fell into a slump, struggling at the plate and in the field. The darling of the press up to that point, the Nebraska native now found himself the target of pointed criticism.

June started well enough for Crawford when Cincinnati sent Elmer Smith to the Giants. The move was a vote of confidence, showing that management viewed Wahoo Sam as an everyday outfielder. As the summer wore on, however, the hits flew off his bat with less frequency. Brush suggested that Crawford needed more seasoning. He said that he may have acquired the young outfielder too soon, explaining that he had to sign him when he did to keep Sam from falling to a rival team.

Reporters covering the Reds did not gloss over Crawford's struggles at the plate. "He lost his natural stride during the slump," Ren Mulford Jr. said, "and began stepping back and 'feeling' for the ball." The *Sporting Life* correspondent also noted that Sam was over-anxious with a two-strike count and easy to fool in such situations. By mid-August, Crawford's average had tumbled to .272, a decline of more than 50 points in three months.

Sam incurred even more criticism for his mental errors on the basepaths and in the outfield. In late July, he drew the ire of Brush when New York catcher Jack Warner picked him off third in a key situation. Mulford faulted Crawford for holding onto the ball too long before firing it into the infield. When the problem persisted, the writer's barbs grew sharper. He said the outfielder's think tank was sometimes clogged with chicken. In August, Mulford's frustrations resulted in a mini-rant against Crawford.

> He has fallen down on the easiest of plays. Three of the nine games lost in the East would have been Red victories had Crawford not held the ball in the field. The hardest lesson he has to learn is that it is not possible to catch anything or do anything while the ball is being held for a touchdown out in the high grass. Crawford is only a boy, but three months in fast company ought to be sufficient time to indelibly impress that fact upon his brain pan in letters hot enough to burn.

Despite his struggles, many baseball people still saw a bright baseball future for Wahoo Sam. After the Reds swept Philadelphia at League Park in mid-August, Phillies captain Ed Delahanty predicted that "Sam Crawford is destined to become one of the greatest stars in the League." A 13-year veteran and one of the top hitters in the game (lifetime .345 BA), "Big Ed" knew what he was talking about. His words were likely a much-appreciated vote of confidence for the beleaguered rookie from Nebraska.

As the calendar turned to September, Crawford seemingly still had a month left in the season to get back on track. The Reds traveled to New York for a Labor Day doubleheader at the Polo Grounds. Sam contributed a single and a stolen base in Cincinnati's victory in the first game. He added another hit in the second game, but strained a tendon in his leg sliding into third. He remained in severe pain as his condition failed to improve in the following days. The injury proved serious enough to keep him out of the lineup for the rest of the season.

Though Sam's 1900 season was over, he continued to represent the Reds as a delegate to the Players' Protective Association. This new union had formed earlier that summer with Pirates catcher Chief Zimmer as president and Brooklyn infielder Hughie Jennings as secretary. While declaring it had no radical intentions, the organization compiled a list of demands that included: no trades without a player's consent, limitations on the reserve clause, fewer suspensions, and club payment of player medical bills and uniforms.

Crawford concluded his injury-plagued rookie season with a disappointing .260 batting average. He nonetheless displayed impressive power. Despite playing in only 101 games, he led his team with seven home runs. His 15 triples trailed league leader Honus Wagner (who played in 34 more games) by only seven. Sam's extra-base hits propelled his slugging average to a healthy .429 mark.

In his season review column, Mulford praised Crawford for what he had accomplished at such a young age. "It seems almost incredible that the lad who less than two years ago had never seen anything but prairie grass in Nebraska should be playing ball in the fastest organization in the land," the correspondent wrote. "He has natural talents that will be developed in the school of experience."

Abandoning his plan to open a barber shop in Cincinnati after the season, Crawford returned to Wahoo in October. The colder months between the 1900 and 1901 seasons would be an eventful time for baseball and for Sam. For the young slugger, questions persisted about his future in the game. Though not overmatched by major league competition, his struggles raised concerns about his suitability as an everyday player. Many baseball scribes and Reds fans viewed Sam as a fourth outfielder bench option.

Mulford was among those writers who had Sam pegged as a substitute outfielder for the 1901 season behind Barrett (.316 BA with 44 stolen bases as a rookie) and newly-acquired Dick Harley and Topsy Hartsel. The latter two hit well in the few games they played for Cincinnati after joining the team late in the season. Even after the league assigned Hartsel to the Chicago

Orphans to resolve a claim dispute, Mulford still viewed Crawford as a backup.

Weighing against Sam was his low batting average, the most important offensive metric in the eyes of most baseball people at the time. In November, *Sporting Life* kindly pointed out that Crawford's average was higher than only two other regular outfielders in the league. Mulford commented that Crawford had lost confidence in himself and disappointed those fans who expected him to be another Sam Thompson (a feared slugger of the 1880s and 1890s).

The criticisms reached the town of Wahoo, where Sam had resumed cutting hair in the off-season. Defending himself, the tonsorial slugger explained that his slump was a result of efforts to change his natural batting style (gripping the bat low on the handle and swinging away) to the choked-up contact-oriented technique that most hitters of the day practiced. The explanation holds weight. The history of baseball (and other sports) is replete with examples of knowing mentors trying to "correct" the unorthodox or unique style of a young player. These efforts, as with Sam in 1900, often make things worse. Observers noted that as the season progressed Crawford was pulling away from pitches rather than stepping into the ball as he did in his earlier, more productive, days.

Though he did not mention his manager by name, Sam's words stood as an indictment against Bob Allen. It was not the only criticism leveled against the Reds skipper that fall. *The Cincinnati Enquirer* had been calling out Allen for much of the season. With yet another disappointing campaign in the Queen City, someone had to be the scapegoat. Allen was gone after just one year—the only season he ever managed in the major leagues. To replace him, the club hired recently retired Reds second baseman Bid McPhee, a Cincinnati legend.

The clouds of war, meanwhile, gathered over Organized Baseball. After a successful 1900 season for his American League, Ban Johnson withdrew from the National Agreement, planted new teams in large eastern cities, and declared his circuit a major league. To back this claim, Johnson would of course need major league-caliber players. A large and imperious-looking man with a large and imperious personality, the AL president told his team owners to start raiding National League rosters.

This was not the first time an upstart circuit had tried to lure away the top talent from the established major league clubs. In these circumstances, team owners warn their players that if they jump contract and join the "outlaws," they will be blacklisted and never allowed to play major league ball again. This usually effective threat carried little weight in 1901. Thanks in large part to a strong gate in 1900 and the financing of Cleveland coal magnate Charles A. Somers, the American League had built up a sizeable war chest. AL owners had little trouble outbidding the National League teams that had capped player salaries at $2,400. Player grievances, moreover, had been building against the NL owners, as evidenced by the formation of the Players' Protective Association in 1900.

And so began the Great Baseball War. Players jumped to Ban Johnson's circuit in waves, with top stars like Cy Young, Napoleon Lajoie, and John McGraw joining this migration. Over half of the 182 players on American League rosters in 1901 were former National Leaguers. Wars are typically a bad thing, but this conflict would ultimately end up benefiting baseball, and Sam Crawford.

In the first weeks of 1901, however, a rumor emerged that Sam would not return to baseball. That winter he invested in a grain and feed store and joined the Wahoo Chamber of Commerce. *Sporting Life* reported that rather than shaving the whiskers from farmers, Crawford "has laid down the razor and lather cup to sell corn and feed for 'em." Not viewing this as a full-time career change for Sam, Mulford still believed his most likely occupation come April was backup outfielder for Cincinnati.

Crawford's prospects for returning to the Reds starting lineup greatly improved as winter began yielding to spring. First, outfielder Jimmy Barrett jumped ship and signed with Detroit in the upstart American League. The baseball war had thus dealt Cincinnati a sharp blow by removing one of its top stars. Overnight, Crawford had become a more prized commodity for the Reds' front office.

Sam then took matters into his own hands to further enhance his value for the upcoming season. In mid-March he signed a contract to play for the Philadelphia Athletics of the American League. Philadelphia manager and co-owner Connie Mack coveted Wahoo Sam's talents, having tried to purchase the outfielder the previous season. The press noted that Crawford and Napoleon Lajoie, recently pilfered from the NL's Phillies, would form a hard-hitting duo in the A's lineup.

Though only 20 years old, Crawford had already learned a thing or two about labor-management issues in Organized Baseball. As a member of the Players' Protective Association, he knew all about the struggles that players faced in dealing with the owners and the much-loathed reserve clause. Like many of his colleagues, he recognized the opportunity for leverage that the ongoing war afforded the men out on the field. With his Philadelphia deal in pocket, Crawford successfully negotiated a larger salary with Brush to stay with Cincinnati.

Though welcome news in the Queen City, *Sporting Life* frowned upon Sam's tactics, calling him a "double dealer." The Philadelphia-based publication predicted that the American League would blacklist Crawford. It furthermore included his name among those players covered by the following indictment:

> Under the circumstances it would be imagined that the majority of players would be grateful to the American League and that such of them as belonged to or would join that organization would be loyal to it under all circumstances. Such is not the universal rule, however, as several players, to their shame be it said, have played double with the American League.

Cincinnati was scheduled to open its 1901 season at the still-charred League Park on Thursday, April 18. Rain, however, postponed this contest to Saturday. For Crawford, it was his first start on a major league Opening Day. Freezing temperatures scratched the planned street parade and speech from Mayor Julius Fleischmann, while limiting the crowd to just 3,000. Playing right field and batting cleanup, Sam did not let the weather stop him from logging two hits and a stolen base. The Reds, however, fell 4-2 to the Pirates.

An ongoing deluge in the Midwest pushed the next game back four days. The backwaters of the Ohio River crept into left field and center field of League Park, requiring the construction of a small dike to make play possible. Hits into the outfield lakes became ground rule doubles. No doubt pleased to be stationed in right that day, Crawford looked on as Reds left fielder Dick Harley got drenched repeatedly chasing flies hit in his direction. Sam doubled and scored three runs as Cincinnati outslugged the Chicago Orphans 10-9.

Making his previous-season struggles seem like a distant memory, Crawford started his sophomore campaign on fire. On the 26th at Chicago's home opener, he tripled and stole a base to help the Reds pull out a 12-inning victory. That same day at the Polo Grounds, Giants rookie Christy Mathewson pitched a three-hitter to record his first big league victory. The Reds had traded Matty to New York the previous December. In so doing, Cincinnati parted ways with one of the greatest pitchers in major league history. In return for giving up a future 373-game winner, the Reds received Amos Rusie, a once-great pitcher who had nothing left in the tank by this point. Rusie went 0-1 in just three games for Cincinnati, retiring from baseball by mid-season.

Blissfully unaware of their team's front office blunder, Crawford and his teammates continued their early season tear. On April 27, Wahoo Sam drilled four hits, including a home run and a triple, to propel Cincinnati to another win in Chicago. The young slugger opened the season with a 15-game hitting streak. His defensive skills in right field also improved. Noting Sam's quick throws and decisiveness, Mulford called him a revelation who had conquered his old weaknesses. "The Nebraskan, without exaggeration, it may be said, is 50 per cent better now than he was in June last season."

The Reds remained hot as well. A month into the season, they sat atop the National League standings with a 15-8 record. It was a high time to play for Cincinnati. Crawford added to the fun by developing an off-field hobby as a "camera fiend." He thus took after his maternal grandfather Thomas Blanchard, who specialized in daguerreotypes before the Civil War. Though perhaps unaware of that bit of family history, Sam took to the camera with enthusiasm. He acted as an "official photographer" when he and several teammates spent an off day in St. Louis on a trolly tour of the city and surrounding country. The participating players deemed the excursion the best such outing they had experienced.

The team's good fortunes would not last. Once again as the weather got warmer, the Reds cooled off. They lost four in a row at the end of May. After a brief rebound in early June, Cincinnati dropped 14 out of 15 decisions. Another losing streak would follow in July. The team never again righted the ship in 1901, skidding through a 1-11 stretch in September. A season that started with so much promise ended in the National League cellar.

For Crawford himself, this campaign was fortunately not a repeat of 1900. He remained a bright spot all season long for his struggling team. In a late May contest at the Polo Grounds, he registered two hits against rookie sensation Mathewson. A few days later, he tripled and snared a drive from the bat of Wee Willie Keeler to help preserve a Reds victory over Brooklyn. Later in June, Sam drove in two runs with a tenth-inning triple against Philadelphia to help his beleaguered team end a 10-game losing streak. The press meanwhile resumed treating Crawford as a rising star and even a role model for young baseball fans. In June, *Sporting Life* noted that Sam eschewed tobacco and alcohol. If this report made it back to Wahoo, Tom Killian would have been much pleased to learn that his former mentee still followed his advice.

As the summer weeks passed, Crawford attracted more notice for his power. In a home game in mid-July, he launched what reporters described as the longest hit ever made at League Park. In St. Louis, Sam blasted a "terrific drive" over the centerfielder, allowing Wahoo to circle the bases. A few days later when the same two teams met in Cincinnati, Crawford recorded another inside-the-park homer after driving a ball off the scoreboard in right field. This power display gave Reds fans something to root for and follow in the papers the rest of the season. The team had dropped well below .500, but Sam had a real chance of winning the league's home run title.

On August 21, Crawford lofted a short drive that a diving Chicago outfielder failed to spear. Sam lowered his head and motored around the bases to tally his 13th home run of the year. That round-tripper in effect ended the power race. Brooklyn's Jimmy Sheckard and St. Louis's Jesse Burkett were the other contenders for the NL home run title that year. They finished with 11 and 10 homers, respectively. Crawford finished with 16, the top NL mark for the entire decade. Twelve of Sam's 16 home runs were inside the park, a single-season record that stands to this day.

Why did Crawford, the league's top power hitter, hit only four balls over the fence? The famously "dead" ball of that era provides much of the answer. The baseballs used then were less resilient, and they got softer after repeated hits. Unlike today, the same ball was used for several innings, until, as Sam noted, "it looked like a clod of dirt."

The pitchers also worked their magic on the horsehide spheres. Crawford recounted that "a pitcher could do anything he wanted to with the ball; and most players chewed tobacco and spit on the ball to darken it up so the batter would have a harder time trying to hit it." Launching those soused, soft leather orbs over the distant outfield walls of the spacious turn-of-the century parks was no easy task. But the burly Nebraskan still hit plenty of drives over outfielders' heads to leg out bushels of triples and inside-the-park home runs.

Crawford finished the 1901 campaign with a .330 batting average, 104 RBI, and a superb .524 slugging average. These numbers are even more impressive considering that the foul strike rule (counting a batter's first two foul balls as strikes) was in effect for the first time. By posting such gaudy numbers, Crawford provided a resounding answer to the questions that had dogged him at the end of the previous season. Wahoo Sam was an elite ballplayer, and he was in the major leagues to stay.

The previous winter Sam returned to Wahoo and opened a feed and grain store. During this offseason, he had even more important business in mind. On Wednesday, October 30, 1901, he married Ada Lattin. Both the bride and the groom were 21 years old. Reverend Joseph J. Lampe officiated the ceremony at the home of the bride's parents on California Street in the Omaha suburb of Dundee (later annexed by Omaha). *The Wahoo Democrat* reported that the event was "a quiet, but exceedingly pretty little wedding, a sort of a home affair, with only the members of the two families and some young friends of the bride present." After the ceremony, the couple boarded a train for a honeymoon trip to Chicago and the eastern cities.

Sam's new in-laws were John and Martha Lattin. John was a stock dealer who had owned a farm near Wahoo before moving to Dundee in 1895. His daughter Ada had attended school in Wahoo prior to her family's move. It was thus in the classroom back in the early 1890s where she likely first met her future husband. Their fathers, moreover, were business associates, if not friends, dating back to those years. In the spring of 1893 Steve Crawford and John Lattin traveled together to Wichita, Kansas, to consider a land investment opportunity. Later that year, they headed to Oklahoma with several other local men to try to secure a claim in the Cherokee Strip Land Run. Steve and John were also active members of the populist People's Independent Party in the early 1890s. Steve had earlier supported the Republican Party, serving as a Saunders County committee representative for Elk Precinct in the 1870s.

Though he spent half of the previous two years in Cincinnati, Sam still listed his residence as Wahoo. Following his nuptials, he moved from 959 N. Orange Street in his hometown to a house in Omaha, where he and Ada would live during the off-season months. Earlier that fall his sister Zadia had also left the nest. On September 12, 1901, she married Arthur Monteen of Wahoo. Both were 23 at the time. With those two fall weddings, 16-year-old Step and 11-year-old Neal were the only two Crawford children still living at home with their parents. The previous summer, Step had followed in his brother's footsteps by playing baseball for Wahoo's town team.

The Great Baseball War continued to rage through the winter months. Ban Johnson's "outlaw" American League boasted a successful first year as a major league circuit. AL attendance for 1901 reached nearly 1.7 million, very close to the 1.9 million drawn by National League teams. The new circuit, moreover, continued to raid NL rosters. Senior Circuit efforts to use the courts to uphold the reserve clause won some temporary battles but ultimately proved unsuccessful at stopping the departure of its talent. Meanwhile, the Players' Protective Association (of which Crawford was still a member) loomed as a lingering threat to National League stability. Many questions hovered over baseball as the 1902 season approached.

The status of Sam Crawford, on the other hand, was more solid than ever as he approached his third full season of big league ball. As the reigning home run king, he arrived at spring training locked in as the Reds everyday right fielder. His salary had climbed to $3,500, second highest on the team behind Hahn's $4,100. Now a married man with a lofty income, Sam did not return to his boarding house in downtown Cincinnati. He and his new bride would make their home in Walnut Hills, a hilltop neighborhood northeast of downtown. The Crawfords shared their Queen City abode with Jake Beckley and his wife, and bachelor Harry Steinfeldt.

Adding to the excitement of the start of the 1902 season was the remodeled League Park. Now called the Palace of the Fans, the Reds' rebuilt ballpark featured a majestic grandstand inspired by the neoclassical White City buildings of the 1893 World's Fair. Topped by a pediment that proclaimed "CINCINNATI," the structure resembled a Roman temple built from concrete and wrought iron. A roof supported by square columns covered the seats down both baselines.

The Reds opened the season at their majestic new ballpark on Thursday, April 17. A lively crowd of 10,000 watched the home team fall to Chicago 6-1. The Windy City visitors took the next two games as well. Finally on Sunday, the Reds recorded their first victory at the Palace of the Fans to avoid a four-game sweep. Crawford scored Cincinnati's first run in the victory after doubling in the fourth inning. Wahoo Sam's bat picked up where it had left off the previous season. Unfortunately, so did his team. The Reds stumbled out of the gate with a dismal 3-7 record in April.

Bid McPhee returned as skipper for the 1902 season. In addition to Crawford, Beckley, and Steinfeldt, Cincinnati's returning players included shortstop Tommy Corcoran, catcher Bill Bergen, outfielder John Dobbs, and pitchers Noodles Hahn and Bill Phillips. Among the newcomers to the team was veteran centerfielder William Hoy. Since he was deaf and mute due to meningitis, players at the time (including William himself) referred to him as "Dummy." Overcoming his disability, Hoy batted .288 and played stellar defense over a 14-year career in the majors. Crawford always spoke highly of his teammate. Because Hoy could call for a fly ball with a squawk, Sam had no problems knowing when to try to make a play in right center.

The Reds' fortunes failed to improve in May as losses continued to pile up. Despite the team's abysmal play, Queen City fans still showed up at their fancy ballpark. On May 11, a packed house of 10,000 watched Pittsburgh trounce the home team 10-0. Two days later, the Reds got back on track (for one game, anyway) by demolishing the Phillies 24-2. Crawford contributed three hits and a stolen base to his team's barrage. On Friday, May 16, the Reds celebrated the formal opening of the Palace of the Fans. The visiting Giants, however, soured the occasion by scoring five runs in the ninth to claim a 5-3 victory.

A loss at St. Louis on May 31 dropped Cincinnati into last place. Crawford nonetheless remained a potent slugging threat in the Reds lineup. Mulford wrote that he had improved at place hitting and bunting as well, though he noted that Wahoo left room for improvement at baserunning. Crawford's defensive skills showed no decline—in Boston he gunned down a runner at the plate in the ninth inning to preserve a one-run victory.

On June 12, Crawford rapped three hits and stole two bases in a victory at Philadelphia. The next day he added three more hits, including a triple, at the Polo Grounds. Sam's artillery helped propel the Reds to a four-game winning streak—even beating Mathewson in one of those contests. But the Reds lost seven of their next nine. Seeking to spark his offense, McPhee shuffled Crawford in the lineup between the second, third, and fourth spots. Wahoo Sam continued to deliver, going four for four with a triple in a home game on June 22. The Nebraska slugger still showed his inexperience from time to time though. On one occasion after he grounded a single through the infield, Cardinal right fielder Patsy Donovan pretended the ball got past him. Crawford took the bait and broke for second, allowing Donovan to gun him down.

In a reversal of form from previous seasons, Cincinnati started playing better as the summer days grew hotter. The Reds posted a respectable 15-12 mark in July to climb into fifth place in the standings. Crawford's bat played a key role in his team's resurgence. A St. Louis scribe provided an especially descriptive account of one of Sam's big hits:

> Sam Crawford's visage gave no hint of his demoniacal intentions. "Wahoo" took a couple of strikes before he got in his solar plexus punch. It was a beauty. Neither Barclay nor Smoot could close in on it, and, while both were pursuing the bounding leather to the Pacific Coast sign on

the overflow bleacher fence, Samuel was tearing around the greensward with his cap in his hand and his hairless head shining like a billiard ball on green cloth. He made the round trip with seconds to spare.

As Crawford continued causing "atmospheric disturbances," as the press called his long drives, momentous changes were afoot in the Queen City that summer. John T. Brush sold the Reds to a Cincinnati syndicate that included Mayor Julius Fleischmann and political boss George Cox. August "Garry" Herrmann, Cox's top lieutenant, would take over as team president. By no means through with baseball, Brush would soon buy the New York Giants. The changes in Cincinnati did not stop with new ownership. Earlier in July, the axe had fallen upon manager Bid McPhee. Team business manager Frank Bancroft served as interim skipper for three weeks before Brush brought in Baltimore (AL) outfielder Joe Kelley as player-manager.

Kelley's arrival in Cincinnati followed a series of events in a complex plot stemming from a feud between Ban Johnson and Baltimore player-manager John McGraw. Having lured the star third-baseman to the American League the previous season, Johnson soon grew tired of McGraw's umpire baiting and confrontational style of play, suspending him at the end of June 1902. To retaliate, McGraw set in motion a scheme involving Brush, Kelley, and Kelley's father-in-law John Mahon, the president of the Orioles. Pooling their financial resources and shares in the Baltimore team, these conspirators arranged for the sale of controlling interest in the Orioles to Brush and New York Giants owner Andrew Freedman.

Two National League owners, Freedman and Brush, thus gained control of an American League franchise. The two magnates immediately gutted the Oriole roster by transferring its best players to their respective NL teams. McGraw and Joe McGinnity were among the players who went to the Giants. The Reds acquired Kelley and Cy Seymour, both highly-skilled batsmen. A furious Ban Johnson invoked a league rule to reclaim control of the Orioles, but it was too late—the team's star players were already gone. The National League had won this round.

From Crawford's point of view the most immediate impact of these moves was that he would be playing with two new teammates (Seymour replaced Hoy in center), and he would report to a new manager in the dugout. None of these changes adversely affected his performance on the field. Now batting third ahead of Seymour in the lineup, he continued his torrid hitting. On July 27, he logged a four-hit game in Chicago.

As for the managerial changes, Crawford got along fine with Bancroft, whom he had known since joining the team. When Ada traveled to St. Louis while the Reds were there, the interim skipper gave Sam a day off to spend with his wife. The arrival of Kelley at the end of July also did not present any problems for Sam. The new manager may have even provided a boost for Crawford. As *Sporting Life* reported, "Kelley is paying much attention to the big fellow's development, and the results have been most satisfactory." The entire Reds team in fact started playing better after Kelley took the reins. Cincinnati went 17-12 in August, its best month of the season.

Even with their improved play, the Reds had no chance to catch Pittsburgh for the league championship. The final weeks of the 1902 season would nonetheless carry much drama for Sam Crawford. These events would continue into the offseason and profoundly alter the course of his career and the future of Major League Baseball.

Chapter 6

The Great Baseball War

The Reds and the Orioles were not the only major league teams to experience ownership changes in 1902. The previous winter a syndicate had bought the Detroit club in the American League. An insurance company executive turned railroad builder named Samuel F. Angus was a leading member of this ownership group. The following summer, Angus bought out his partners and gained sole control of the Tigers. The new owner immediately sought to improve his team. Although 1902 was a lost cause for Detroit, mired near the bottom of the AL standings by midseason, Angus ordered manager Frank Dwyer to hit the road to sign new talent for 1903. The magnate especially coveted established National League stars like Wee Willie Keeler, Fred Tenney, and a young Cincinnati slugger who hailed from Wahoo, Nebraska.

Dwyer, a former Reds pitcher, wasted little time carrying out his boss's orders. Rumors surfaced that a mysterious scout from Detroit had approached Sam Crawford and Jake Beckley in Chicago in late July. When the Reds travelled to New York in mid-August, Dwyer took matters into his own hands. Sneaking into the Sturtevant House hotel after midnight, the skipper roused Crawford out of bed to pitch him Detroit's offer. Upon learning of these doings that occurred "after the hour when witches prowl," Reds business manager Frank Bancroft was incensed. He accused the American League president and the Detroit manager of betraying Cincinnati's new owners:

> Think of Ban Johnson in the West, telling what a great friend he is of the Fleischmanns and Garry Hermann, while he sends an agent here to grab their players. I'm surprised at Frank Dwyer. The Cincinnati club kept him one year after he had outlived his usefulness and then had him put on the umpire staff and yet he goes around knifing the National League in the dark.

Reporters speculated on the amount of Detroit's reported offer to Crawford. One source placed it as high as $5,000 for 1903, while another writer reported $4,500. Either way, it appeared that Angus offered Sam a hefty raise over his current salary with Cincinnati. But did Crawford actually sign with the Tigers? Sam himself would neither confirm nor deny what he had done.

The Crawford gossip increased when Dwyer and Detroit pitcher Win Mercer showed up in the Queen City during the Reds next home stand. Rumored to be the Tigers' next manager, Mercer was helping with Dwyer's recruitment efforts. The Detroit duo reportedly sought to reel in Jake Beckley and Cy Seymour too. From the stands of the Palace of the Fans, the raiders scouted their targets.

Having lost star outfielder Jimmy Barrett to Detroit a year earlier, Cincinnati ownership took action to fight off the invaders. Celebrating the dawn of a new era of Reds baseball, the owners held a banquet for their players after they returned home from a long road trip. Two street parades and a fireworks show added to the festivities celebrating the local nine. Joe Kelley played a leading role in the team's counterattack. Meeting with Mercer, the Reds skipper made him an offer to switch sides and come over to Cincinnati. The attempt to flip the raider led one reporter to comment, "Queer thing, this scouting business." Kelley also counseled Crawford, warning him of the instability of the American League. If Sam jumped ship and the

AL folded, he would face the prospect of a lifetime ban from the National League.

The ongoing controversy took a toll on the 22-year-old from Nebraska. Crawford grew increasingly annoyed at the newspaper articles stating that he was already bound for Detroit. Finally, he told Ren Mulford Jr., "I'm liable to sign with Cincinnati just to show up a few of these pinheads who know more about my business than I do myself." Despite his frustration, Crawford continued to rake at the plate. From August 19th through the 22nd, he went 12 for 21 with three triples during a torrid streak of five straight multi-hit games.

While Reds ownership remained hopeful they would keep Crawford, they made contingency plans in case the rumors of his departure were true. In August they signed "Turkey Mike" Donlin, a flamboyant young outfielder who had batted .341 for Baltimore the previous season. No stranger to the bottle, Donlin had just become available after completing a six-month prison sentence for assaulting two chorus girls and public urination. Aside from skill at hitting a baseball, Donlin shared few similarities with the man he might be replacing.

As August drew to a close, Reds president Garry Herrmann wanted resolution on the Crawford matter one way or the other. Issuing an ultimatum, he said that if his right fielder did not sign a contract to remain with Cincinnati, he would be released before the team headed out on its East Coast road trip on September 1. Sam did not back down, declaring "I will not sign a Cincinnati contract at this time, even if I do go east with the team."

With the deadline approaching, Crawford and Herrmann met on August 27. One can imagine the burly young slugger entering the regal office of the team president, a gregarious man known for his German accent, checkered suits, pinky rings, and love of sausages. The conference ended with no deal. They met again the following day in a final attempt to end the impasse. The team president doubled down on his ultimatum by declaring that any player who had signed with another club would be released without further pay. Within the tense atmosphere of Herrmann's office, the two men made progress at reaching a mutually-acceptable number that would keep Crawford in the Queen City. Two days later on Saturday, August 30, the Reds played the final game of their homestand. Sam went two for four with two stolen bases in his team's 13-2 triumph over St. Louis. That morning before the game, he had signed a contract to remain with Cincinnati in 1903 for $5,000, plus a signing bonus.

While this long-awaited agreement brought a huge sigh of relief from Reds Nation, it also confirmed that Crawford had indeed signed an earlier contract with Detroit. Angus later described how that deal went down. After Dwyer's midnight raid in New York failed, the Tigers owner told his skipper to bring Crawford to meet him at the Waldorf-Astoria Hotel. There, Angus handed Sam a check for $1,000. According to Angus, the player replied, "Well, that's the largest check I ever saw with Sam Crawford's name to it, so I guess I'll take it." Months later holding an even bigger check from the Reds, Sam returned the advance that the Tigers had given him. But what of Herrmann's earlier threat to release any player who signed with another club? Not to worry. With the ink of Crawford's name drying on a Reds contract, all had been forgiven by the front office.

Early September was a happy time for Cincinnati fans. Sam was securely back in the fold. Veterans Beckley, Steinfeldt, Corcoran, Hahn, and Phillips were also coming back. They would be joined by newcomers Kelley, Donlin, and fan-favorite Cy Seymour. Local owners had replaced the unpopular Brush, and, after a strong second half, the team finished at 70-70 to climb into fourth place. Queen City rooters indeed had many reasons to feel good about their baseball prospects for next spring.

Crawford himself was also pleased. Mulford wrote that "Sam Crawford is the happiest fellow in the Red party" after not yielding to his early impulse to jump ship. With a hefty raise coming, Sam concluded his stellar 1902 campaign with a .333 batting average and a league-leading 22 triples. Playing in all

140 of his team's games, he topped the NL in total bases, while finishing second in slugging average and third in RBI and hits. The Reds outfielder had firmly established himself as one of the top stars in the league.

But the good feelings in Cincinnati would prove to be short-lived that off-season. For Detroit, this story was not over. Hungry Tigers still prowled about, determined to claim a prize from the Reds roster they believed was rightfully theirs.

Cleveland challenged Cincinnati to a postseason series to determine the baseball champions of Ohio. Led by Napoleon Lajoie, the Bluebirds (not yet called the Indians) finished in fifth place in the American League with a 69-67 record. Joe Kelley reported that the Reds were not interested in playing such a series. Crawford still found an opportunity to play postseason baseball. He, along with Beckley, joined the All-Nationals, a team of NL all-stars scheduled to tour the midwestern and western states over the next two months. Ada would accompany him on this trip, that would eventually reach the Pacific coast.

With the World Series not yet inaugurated in 1902, the NL champion Pirates played a postseason series against a team of American League all-stars that included Lajoie, Cy Young, and Addie Joss. Pittsburgh prevailed in the four-game set, winning two and losing one—the third game ended in a tie. After the final game of the series on October 11, the All-American team started a joint tour with the All-Nationals. Over the next several weeks, the two teams would play each other in more than a dozen cities, including Des Moines, Denver, and Phoenix. The tour provided thousands of fans in states west of the Mississippi an opportunity to witness big league ballplayers in action.

One of the highlights for Crawford came when the touring all-star teams played in Omaha on October 18 and 19. An enthusiastic crowd of 5,000 packed the city's Vinton Street Park for both games. The stands of course included a large contingent from Wahoo, who had filled entire train cars for the short trip east. The crowd roared for Crawford whenever he stepped to the plate or made a catch in left field. Prior to the game, friends and neighbors from Wahoo tossed flower bouquets onto the field and called for him to hit a home run. "I'll knock that home run out if I can," Sam replied. "I'll try mighty hard to do it, and I think I'll get there, too."

Energized by the adulation, Crawford delivered a stellar performance in the first contest with three hits, a stolen base, and two runs scored, including the game winner in the bottom of the ninth. In the field he caught all four chances that came his way and produced a highlight reel (if such things existed at the time) throw to double off a runner at first. As for that home run his fans wanted—in the fifth inning Crawford hit a drive into right field that rolled under the fence, allowing him to circle the bases.

The next day's game provided more of the same. Before Crawford's first at-bat, fans presented him with a large horseshoe-shaped bouquet with "Wahoo" tattooed at the top. Grinning, Sam accepted the flowers and bowed to his admirers. Another big game followed for the local boy, who rapped two doubles and a single in a 7-5 victory for the All-Nationals. While they likely did not have as good a time as Crawford, the other players on the two teams appreciated the large gate from the Vinton Street Park games. Before arriving in Nebraska, several of them had expressed their hope of drawing large crowds in Omaha. These hopes were realized during a successful weekend of baseball.

The all-star teams next headed south to Missouri, where they played in St. Joseph and Kansas City, before their tour headed west to Kansas and Colorado. Several hundred miles to the east, meanwhile, the Crawford controversy heated up again in Detroit and Cincinnati. Even though Sam had signed with Herrmann, Frank Dwyer told reporters he expected the outfielder to "give the Reds the mitten and jump to Detroit in the spring." Going a step further, Angus argued that since Crawford had signed a contract with him first, he "morally and legally" belonged to the Tigers.

Cincinnati sportswriters, on the other hand, still maintained that Crawford would remain in Ohio in 1903. Mulford confidently wrote "I don't think 'Wahoo Sam' is losing his mind," so anyone who thinks he is heading for Detroit is mistaken. The writer added that Crawford "has pledged himself most emphatically to stick to the Reds." Sam provided statements supporting Mulford's assertion. The Nebraskan explained that he had signed with Detroit before Brush had sold the Cincinnati club. After the Queen City syndicate bought the team, Crawford believed that signing with the new Reds owners was now in his best interests. At the end of the 1902 season, moreover, he had directed the grounds crew to make certain changes to the right field topography at the Palace of the Fans. Such instructions would have been unnecessary if he intended to patrol the outfield in another city next summer.

As the all-star tour continued though the autumn weeks, the conflicting reports about Crawford's future increased. The press in Detroit and Cincinnati both seemed confident that their team had secured Sam. *Sporting Life*, a more neutral party in this seesaw battle, indicated that the Tigers had the edge. In late October, the publication reported that Crawford would complete a great trio of outfielders for Detroit in 1903. Another article in the same issue said that players in both leagues expected Sam to join Detroit, and that he "has no intention of remaining with the Reds."

Ban Johnson had to walk a tightrope when weighing in on the controversy. Under normal wartime circumstances, the American League president would want one of his teams to land a star player from the National League. But Johnson, a former Cincinnati sportswriter, was friends with Herrmann. Realizing the value of maintaining this alliance, the AL president said, "no American League club would have attempted a raid on Cincinnati players if my wishes could have prevailed." Angus had thus gone rogue, targeting Crawford in violation of a league directive. Not missing the chance to take a shot at an NL enemy though, Johnson added, "If John T. Brush had remained in control [of the Reds] we would have riddled the team."

Johnson's position on Crawford was not his only source of tension with Angus that offseason. Johnson's proposal to move the Tigers to Pittsburgh created greater controversy among Detroiters at the time. *Sporting Life* criticized the American League for its treatment of Angus, alleging that Johnson and other AL owners wanted to block Detroit from improving its roster. The newspaper said these efforts were hindering the Tigers chances of securing Crawford. Despite his disapproval of Angus and Dwyer's raid, Johnson, ever the politician, said he expected Crawford to join the Tigers for 1903.

The all-star teams, meanwhile, continued their journey through the West. After playing in Albuquerque, New Mexico, on November 1, the tour proceeded to El Paso, Texas, and then to Arizona. When the teams reached Los Angeles on November 9th, the Crawford controversy remained as muddled as ever. Angus expressed his confidence to reporters that Sam would be playing right field for Detroit next season. Chicago sportswriter W.A. Phelon, on the other hand, predicted that Crawford would remain with Cincinnati, Wee Willie Keeler would stay with Brooklyn, and Christy Mathewson would jump to the St. Louis Browns in the American League. In retrospect, one hopes that Phelon did not place any wagers at the track that day.

The Cincinnati-Detroit back-and-forth continued as the All-Nationals and All-Americans played a series of games in Los Angeles. The tour then headed north to San Francisco, Oakland, and Sacramento. In early December, Crawford issued a statement from California to settle the matter of his future employment once and for all. He declared that he would remain with Cincinnati. The man himself had finally made a definitive proclamation to put the matter to bed. Reds fans could once again breathe a sigh of relief that their star right fielder would be back.

For Detroiters, of course, nothing was over. After Christmas, Angus gave notice that he would continue to fight for

Crawford. He dispatched Win Mercer to lead the charge. The newly-hired Tigers manager told the press in early January that reeling in Wahoo Sam remained a "strong possibility." So the controversy, now in its sixth month, lingered on. Unbeknownst to all involved, an actual final resolution was only days away.

The ongoing Crawford issue was just one battle in the larger Great Baseball War that continued to rage through 1902. Though both sides suffered casualties, the American League had gained ground that year. Ban Johnson's circuit attracted 2.2 million fans for the season, outdrawing the National league by a margin of 500,000. The AL president then cut a deal with Tammany Hall leaders in New York, clearing the way to place a new franchise in the city. This successful invasion of the Big Apple was a major victory for Johnson. He also threatened to plant the Tigers in Pittsburgh, directly challenging the profitability of the Pirates.

By December 1902, the National League owners were tired of fighting this costly war. They had lost dozens of players to AL raiders and had to increase salaries to keep more of their men from jumping. Their gate receipts, moreover, steadily declined. NL officials sent a peace delegation to Johnson to open talks to end the war.

The two sides met in Cincinnati on January 9, 1903. After two days of negotiation, the nation's top baseball magnates hammered out a peace agreement establishing the two-league structure for MLB that continues to this day. Under the new National Agreement drawn up at the conference, both the National League and American League were recognized as major leagues. Teams across both leagues would respect each other's reserve clauses, bringing an end to raiding. The new AL team could stay in New York, but Johnson had to agree to stay out of Pittsburgh (the Tigers would thus remain in Detroit). To govern Organized Baseball, the magnates created a three-man National Commission. Functioning as baseball's judicial branch, this body would consist of the AL president (Ban Johnson), the

NL president (Harry Pulliam), and a chairman (Reds president and Johnson ally, Garry Herrmann).

The peace conference also decided on those 16 players who had signed two contracts and were thus claimed by teams in both leagues. After much discussion, the owners compiled a list legally awarding the players to one of the clubs with which they had signed. Mathewson, Vic Willis, and Tommy Leach were among the players staying with the National League. Lajoie, Keeler, and Wild Bill Donovan were among the players awarded to the American League.

With neither Cincinnati nor Detroit's ownership willing to loosen their grip on the slugging outfielder from Wahoo, the issue of Sam Crawford remained a sticking point until late in the negotiations. A majority of the magnates ruled that Crawford should go to Detroit. Herrmann objected, not willing to lose the star outfielder he had signed the previous August. As other contentious issues between the leagues were settled and the two sides neared a final agreement, the Crawford issue stood as one of the final barriers to ending the war. The Reds president finally relented. In the interests of bringing peace to baseball, Herrmann reluctantly allowed Crawford to go to Detroit.

And so after months of controversy and wavering, the decision on where Wahoo Sam would play in 1903 did not lie with Sam after all. All of the lobbying, promises, and threats intended to sway his decision did not matter. Like at Versailles after World War I, a peace conference had redrawn baseball's borders and the territory of Sam was now part of a new nation. Detroiters, Angus and Dwyer included, could celebrate that they had claimed the prize for which they had long fought. This pleasing news was tempered, however, by the tragedy that befell one of the other men who had worked to bring Crawford to the Tigers.

Win Mercer should have been among those people happiest about the Crawford decision. As Detroit's manager-elect, he could look forward to penciling one of the league's top sluggers into his lineup every day. Mercer was a member of the American

League's travelling all-star team, and likely found several occasions on the western tour to try to win Sam over. Had the peace conference not settled the matter, Detroit's player-manager indicated that he was planning to follow Crawford to Nebraska to continue his effort to woo him into the Tigers' camp.

The all-star tour ended in San Francisco in early January. Members of the All-Nationals and All-Americans remained in town for a few days of vacation before heading back east. On January 12, just two days after baseball's peace agreement, Mercer checked into the Occidental Hotel in San Francisco under a fake name. After midnight that evening, he ran a tube of illuminating gas into his mouth and asphyxiated himself.

News of Mercer's death shocked the baseball world. He seemingly had much to live for. At 28-years-old, he had just concluded his best pitching season in five years. His appointment as Tigers manager would provide a further salary bump. With his piercing dark eyes and outgoing personality, Mercer was a fan favorite. Owners often tabbed him to pitch on Ladies Days at the ballpark because the handsome hurler always drew a large crowd of female admirers. Some sportswriters speculated that troubles with women were the reason for his suicide. Others attributed it to gambling debts incurred at the horse track. Mercer allegedly left a final note in which he stated, "A word to friends: beware of women and a game of chance." Historians have still not come to an agreement on the exact reasons for this tragic event.

News of baseball's peace settlement reached the touring players only a day before Mercer's suicide. Crawford had been enjoying his vacation time with Ada in San Francisco and his share of the tour proceeds—a healthy $600. But the news about his new baseball home did not please him. Sam told reporters he was sorry he had to leave the Reds. Expressing regret for signing with Detroit, he predicted that he would be homesick for Cincinnati and would miss his friends on the team.

In the wake of these sentiments, *Sporting Life* raised the obvious question: "If he loves Redtown so much why did he sign a prior contract with Detroit?" Thirteen years later, when interviewed by F.C. Lane for *Baseball Magazine*, Crawford provided a spin for his move to the American League. Contradicting his rueful statements at the time, the outfielder explained in 1916:

> It appeared to me, that the cause of the National League in its effort to dominate the situation was a lost cause. I stuck to them longer than almost any other ball player, but at the end I could see no reason why I should compromise my own future and at the same time be powerless to further the interests of my employers.... I remained with my [Cincinnati] employers as long as there was any prospect of their succeeding even at a considerable financial sacrifice to myself. When it seemed to me to be a certainty that further resistance was useless I saw no reason why I should jeopardize my own interests any further.

Very little of that statement rings true when compared with how the events actually unfolded in 1902-03. The "considerable financial sacrifice" claim, for example, ignores the hefty $5,000 salary Crawford had secured from the Reds. And the fact that it was baseball magnates, and not Sam himself, who made the final decision is also omitted from this later explanation.

But Sam did have a choice in August 1902, when he signed a contract with Detroit and set the ensuing controversy in motion. Did he really intend to jump to the American League at that time? If not, what did he hope would happen? Crawford's actions a year earlier provide a likely explanation. Prior to the 1901 season, he had signed a contract with Connie Mack to play for Philadelphia in the AL. He used that deal to leverage a higher salary from Cincinnati for the season. When signing with the Tigers, Crawford possibly had the same plan in mind. That is, in effect, what happened when he garnered a hefty raise from Herrmann just a couple weeks after inking the Detroit deal.

What ensued after the second signing is where events differed between the two cases. Mack gave up his claim to Sam fairly quickly in early 1901, when he was not as prized of a commodity after a so-so rookie season. By the summer of 1902, in contrast, he was a top slugger, and Detroit would fight tooth and nail to bring him into the fold. Crawford eventually declared his preference for Cincinnati, but with his name on two legally binding documents, events spun out of his control and others made the decision for him.

It thus seems that Sam, even when signing with Detroit, hoped to stay in the Queen City. That said, his move does not appear to have been merely a bluff. He played hardball with Herrmann over a period of tense negotiations. Had Cincinnati not countered with a competitive offer, Crawford was willing to jump to the American League as a Plan B. Through much of the 1902-03 offseason though, it appeared that his first choice to stay a higher-paid Red would play out. But even off the field, baseball is unpredictable.

And so Crawford's time with the Reds came to an end. In just over three seasons in Cincinnati, he batted .312 with 60 triples and 27 home runs. Sam's youth (age 22) and imposing .474 slugging average require no further explanation for why his two suitors fought so doggedly to claim him.

With the battle over, a new chapter in Crawford's baseball career would now begin.

Chapter 7

Tiger King

The end of a long relationship often leaves hard feelings among the former lovers—especially the jilted party. "I never really loved you anyway" and similar expressions of bitterness are not uncommon. The Crawford-Cincinnati divorce was no exception. When it appeared likely that Sam was out the door, sportswriters sympathetic to the Reds sharpened their knives. "His [Crawford's] work last season did not increase his popularity," one scribe wrote, "for it seemed at times that he was playing carelessly." Another writer said the Reds were not complaining about their right fielder's departure. "'Wahoo Sam' is not a brainy player," he wrote, "and could not participate in the teamwork planned by Kelley." Cincinnati correspondent Ren Mulford Jr. joined in the Sam-bashing by disparaging his skills as a run producer and team leader. He continued by writing, "The lad from Nebraska is not yet a finished inside man and he has much to learn of the science of helping a runner on first to advance."

Rejected paramours also tend to point out how quickly they have moved on to someone else—someone better. For Cincinnati that was the recently-incarcerated Mike Donlin. One writer jabbed that Sam lacked the "ginger" displayed by Turkey Mike, who would represent an upgrade in right field. Mulford expressed similar views: "Those [fans] who know how much grit, pluck and determination there are in the Donlin sand box," he wrote, "are not afraid of the comparison [with Crawford]."

The breakup of an engaged couple often requires the return of a ring. In Crawford's case, he had to return the $1,300 Garry Herrmann paid him for signing with the Reds the previous August. "As a returner of checks Crawford will lead both leagues when he pays up with Cincinnati," *Sporting Life* quipped, "as last fall he returned a draft for $1,000 to Detroit." In March, Sam mailed a check for the required amount. His divorce from Cincinnati was now final.

Sam and Ada arrived in Detroit early in the spring of 1903. With 285,000 residents, the city was nearly the same size as Cincinnati. Like the Queen City, Detroit featured thriving immigrant communities, with many of the newcomers hailing from Germany, Poland, and Ireland. A center of industry and commerce, turn-of-the-century Detroit was a major producer of cast-iron stoves, cigars, ships, and pharmaceuticals. Henry Ford established the Ford Motor Company in June 1903. Detroit would soon emerge as the heart of the automotive industry.

The Crawfords traveled about their new hometown looking for a flat. Sam knew that local writers were aware of his expressions of regret at leaving Cincinnati. After arriving in Detroit, he told the press that he was tickled to be there and eager to play for the Tigers. It is uncertain how much his feelings had actually changed by this point, but either way he had the good sense to try to start off on the right foot.

Crawford and his new teammates gathered in the Detroit office of Samuel Angus on Sunday, March 15. The Tigers owner gave a pep talk, encouraging his men for the upcoming season. Angus wanted to remove the bad taste of the previous campaign's seventh-place finish. With the new talent that had arrived, many fans and writers predicted the '03 Tigers would be the city's best team since 1887, when the Detroit Wolverines won the National League pennant.

After leaving Angus's office, the players boarded a train car reserved for them and traveled to Shreveport, Louisiana, for spring training. Ada accompanied Sam on this trip south. The Tigers stayed in Shreveport for two weeks, during which they enjoyed favorable weather, impressive facilities at the Shreveport Athletic Association's clubhouse, and splendid hotel accommodations at The Inn. Crawford soon impressed his new employers with his "midseason form." Interestingly enough, reporters covering the Tigers at Shreveport referred to Sam, just a month shy of his 23rd birthday, as one of the "older men" on the team.

Crawford's new Detroit colleagues included several familiar faces. Tiger outfielder Jimmy Barrett had debuted with Sam in Cincinnati in September 1899. Shortstop Kid Elberfeld also played for the Reds at that time. Once ejected from three games in little more than a week, the scrappy "Tabasco Kid" brought a quick temper and cyclonic throwing arm to the Detroit infield. Veteran Tigers backstop Deacon McGuire had caught for Brooklyn during Crawford's Cincinnati days. Hard-throwing Wild Bill Donovan had similarly defected from the National League to provide a formidable arm at the top of Detroit's pitching rotation.

Leading the Tigers into battle was manager Ed Barrow. This name would become famous in baseball history, though not for his work with Detroit. Years down the road, Barrow, as Boston skipper, encouraged Babe Ruth's transformation from pitcher to outfielder. Later joining the New York Yankees front office, Barrow played a leading role in building the Bronx Bombers dynasty of the 1920s and 1930s. With Detroit in 1903, however, the Tiger manager was more known for his hot temper, withering criticisms, and physical confrontations with his players.

After leaving Shreveport at the end of March, the Tigers traveled through the wind-swept South engaging local teams in exhibition contests. After a series against the Montgomery Black Sox, the team headed north for games against Louisville and Evansville. Detroit's favorable record in this exhibition tour increased optimism for the upcoming campaign.

The Tigers opened their 1903 season at home against Cleveland on April 22. More than 16,000 fans crammed into Bennett Park to watch this contest. Located just west of downtown at Michigan and Trumbull in Detroit's Corktown neighborhood, Sam's new baseball home was one of the league's smallest and oddest shaped ballparks. A rickety wood grandstand extended from home plate about halfway down the left field line, leaving the rest of the seats uncovered (two more grandstands would later be added). Cobblestones that once covered the floor of a hay market poked through the ground to cause erratic bounces, much to the chagrin of fielders. The trapezoidal-shaped outfield measured 308 feet at the left foul pole, 324 feet at the right foul pole and 390 in straight away center. But the left field wall and the right field wall ran straight, meeting at a 90-degree angle in left center 490 feet from home plate. Because of the ballpark's unique positioning, lefty batters like Crawford endured the sun shining at them from left field in the late afternoon. Full-color signs painted on the outfield walls advertised such products as Bull Durham tobacco and Stroh's beer.

Exceeding Bennett's regular 8,500 seating capacity, overflow fans occupied the deepest parts of the outfield for Crawford's first game as a Tiger. Playing in left, he "fielded finely," recording three catches and an assist. After drawing a walk in the eighth, Sam scored the tie-breaking run in Detroit's 4-2 victory over Cleveland ace Addie Joss. Taking the collar the next day, Crawford ripped a double in the season's third game for his first hit as a Tiger. His team, meanwhile, swept the opening series.

Sam was in a new league facing many pitchers he had never seen. Similar situations in the past had not stopped him from hitting, and this time was no different. Starting with that first double, he reeled off a nine-game hitting streak—five of them were multi-hit games. Along the way he hit his first triple as a Tiger on April 29th against White Sox hurler Davey Dunkle. The Wahoo barrage continued in May. On the 13th, Crawford rapped four hits in a 7-1 home win over New York. Two days later at Bennett Park he tagged his first home run as a Tiger off Long Tom Hughes, who would win 20 games for Boston that year.

Unfortunately, few other Tigers could match Sam's consistency. The team had bolted out of the gate, winning six of its first eight. But Detroit then lost eight out of nine. After a hot streak in mid-May, the big cats climbed into a tie for first place on May 24 with a record of 16-12. They then dropped seven of their next eight to fall all the way down to sixth place.

Around this same time, a vocal feud between Barrow and Elberfeld had reached the breaking point. The manager accused his shortstop of "loaferish conduct" and deliberately playing poorly. Elberfeld wanted out of Detroit and Barrow wanted him gone. They both got their wish a few days later when the Tigers dealt the Kid to the New York Highlanders.

Parting ways with the "Tabasco Kid" did not immediately improve Detroit's fortunes. The team dropped seven out of ten games on an East Coast road trip. But on June 19, the Tigers opened a home stand in which they won seven of eleven. This reawakening elevated them to fifth place at 27-30. To keep their pennant hopes alive, the players would need to become road warriors. Starting with a Fourth of July doubleheader in Philadelphia, the Tigers would play their next 15 games in the East. The trip included stops in Philly, Washington, New York, and Boston.

In contrast to a century later, hopping from city to city as a major leaguer was not so glamourous in the early 1900s. Players back then traveled in sleeper trains illuminated by gas lights. Crawford described travel conditions as "pretty rugged" as he recounted life on the road:

> The hotels weren't the best in the world, and the trains had coal-burning engines. So you'd wake up in the morning covered with embers. They had fine little screens on the train windows, but the cinders would still come through.

Conditions at home were not so glamorous for Crawford and his teammates either. The Bennett Park clubhouse stood in dead center field. After games, players had to wait their turn at the clubhouse's one showerhead. With no laundry facilities, players crammed their reeking, sweaty wool uniforms into metal cannisters for storage until the next game. Most ballparks at the time had a clubhouse for only the home team. Visiting players had to change into their uniforms at the hotel beforehand, and then travel to the game in a horse-drawn trolley.

On-field medical attention for spike wounds typically consisted of applying a wad of chewed tobacco to the afflicted area and then wrapping it in a handkerchief. Teams back then did employ a trainer. But according to Crawford, his main job was to give rubdowns with a substance called "Go Fast," a mixture of Vaseline and tabasco sauce. As Sam recalled, the experience "made you feel like you were on fire."

These modest accommodations reflected the status afforded ballplayers around the turn of the century. While the top talents in the game attained a level of celebrity with their fans, society as a whole still did not regard playing baseball as a respectable occupation. Many old-stock upper and middle-class Protestants took an especially dim view of the players at this time. As Crawford describes:

> We were considered pretty crude. Couldn't get into the best hotels and all that. And when we did get into a good hotel, they wouldn't boast about having us. Like, if we went into a hotel dining room—in a good hotel, that is—they'd quick shove us way back in a corner at the very end of the dining room so we wouldn't be too conspicuous.

Waitstaffs often did not afford ballplayers the best service. While dining with his teammates at a hotel in St. Louis, the Tigers sat ignored at their table for 20 minutes. Taking matters into his own hands, Kid Elberfeld grabbed a plate and tossed it high in the air. It shattered on the tile floor with a crash that resounded through the quiet dining room. Though the Kid solved the problem of being ignored, his action did little to improve the reputation of ballplayers.

It should be noted that the ballplaying fraternity had plenty of members who enthusiastically contributed to their negative stereotypes. Major and minor league rosters were filled with known drunkards, brawlers, gamblers, and the like. Their unruly behavior often brought fines, suspensions, arrests, injuries, and debt. A profligate lifestyle sometimes ended in tragedy.

On July 2, 1903, Detroit concluded its homestand with a 1-0 victory over Washington. Senators outfielder Ed Delahanty, one of baseball's top hitters over the past decade, sat out the game. In the weeks prior, Big Ed had quarreled with his manager, drank to excess, and displayed increasingly erratic behavior. The next day, when the Tigers headed east for their lengthy road trip, Delahanty abandoned his own team and boarded a train to New York. During the journey, he smoked heavily, downed five whiskies, broke the glass on an emergency tool cabinet, stumbled into an already occupied berth, and threatened passengers with a razor. After the conductor ordered Delahanty off the train at Fort Erie, Ontario, he walked across the International Railway Bridge over the Niagara River. After scuffling with a night watchman who tried to stop him from crossing, Big Ed disappeared into the darkness. He then stumbled or intentionally jumped (gambling and binge drinking had left him heavily in debt) off the bridge into the Niagara River. His body was found a week later several miles downriver.

Detroit played well on its road trip, winning nine of the 15 games. A personal highlight for Crawford came on July 18, when he ripped a couple hits, including a triple, off the already legendary Cy Young. The Tigers soon climbed back to .500, ten-and-a-half games behind league-leading Boston. Winning six of eight in late July propelled them into fourth place, but that was as close as Detroit would get. The Tigers played .500 ball in August before falling into a mid-September tailspin. Sam still provided fireworks, including a five-hit barrage with two doubles and a triple against New York on August 16. But

Barrow's boys limped to the finish line, ending the season in fifth place with a 65-71 record.

For Crawford, it had been a successful first year in Detroit. His .335 batting average, a personal best, was second highest in the American league, behind only Napoleon Lajoie. Sam led the AL with 25 triples and drove in 89 runs. His .489 slugging average was fifth best in the league. After just one season, Crawford had established himself as the top hitter on the Tigers.

Sam and Ada returned to Nebraska after the season ended. When visiting his parents and three siblings in Wahoo, Sam likely had plenty of baseball stories to tell. His younger brother Step had a few of his own diamond tales to share in return. Now 18, Step had followed in his older brother's footsteps by pitching for the Wahoo town team. In a game against Prague, he had struck out 15 batters. His hitting prowess also reminded people of his big brother. After Step homered in a win against Fremont, the local newspaper titled its article about the game, "Just Like Big Sam."

After earning a healthy $4,500 the previous season, Sam had a little extra money in his pocket. That offseason he invested a few of his dollars in land near Wahoo for cattle raising. Crawford's modest outlay in no way reflected a potential career change. Back in Detroit, however, major changes were taking place over the winter.

Running low on capital, Samuel Angus had already grown tired of owning a baseball team. His business manager Frank Navin, a former insurance company bookkeeper, found him the exit he desired by convincing William Clyman Yawkey to buy the Tigers. The richest man in Michigan, Yawkey had amassed great wealth through lumber and iron. Just before the deal closed, however, the 69-year-old Yawkey died of a heart attack. Navin then convinced the lumber baron's 28-year-old son, William Hoover Yawkey, to buy the team. The younger Yawkey named himself club president and promoted Navin to secretary-treasurer. Barrow would return as team manager.

These front office changes in Detroit meant that Crawford would now deal with the tightfisted Navin in his upcoming contract negotiation. When Detroit's offer arrived in the mail, Sam was not pleased. With the end of the Great Baseball War, team owners now felt free to cut the salaries of their players. For 1904, the Tigers offered Crawford $1,500 less than he had received the previous season. He refused to sign the contract.

While most of his fellow players faced the same predicament, Sam could have postponed his loss of income. A year earlier, before baseball's peace agreement, Detroit had offered him a three-year deal at $4,500 per season. Thinking the war would continue and salaries would rise, Crawford signed for just one year. With the war over, he could no longer use a rival league as negotiating leverage. Bound by the reserve clause, Wahoo Sam would play for Detroit or he would not play baseball in 1904.

Hoping to end his star player's holdout before spring training, Ed Barrow engineered a compromise. In late February, Crawford agreed to accept a $1,000 pay cut for the 1904 season. The press praised the Detroit skipper for his work in smoothing over the breach with his disgruntled outfielder. "Crawford himself has met the club's terms half way," *Sporting Life* reported, "realizing that organized base ball prevails; that war-time salaries are over, and that no place remains for outlaws."

With the contract dispute settled, Sam reported on time for the team's trip to Shreveport. The Tigers spring training in Louisiana ran from March 9th to the 24th. Crawford once again impressed with his early bat work. The team as a whole broke camp in good physical condition. Inclement weather, however, washed out many of the exhibition games scheduled for the trip north in late March and early April. As with most clubs, optimism buzzed about Tigers Nation that spring.

Detroit opened its season on the road with a 7-2 victory over St. Louis on April 14. Crawford contributed two hits and a stolen base to the cause. His bat cooled after that, leaving him with a meager .238 batting average after five games. He would sit out the next game in freezing Chicago after a crop of boils afflicted his right arm. The team doctor lanced the painful red bumps and placed Sam's arm in a sling. The condition was severe enough to keep him out of the lineup for ten games. During this stretch Crawford received even worse news.

On Thursday, April 21, after the team arrived back in Detroit, a telegram arrived informing Sam that his father had died that morning. Steve Crawford had fallen ill a week earlier. Suffering for several days from paralysis of the bowels brought on by liver and bladder issues, he died at his home on North Orange Street in Wahoo at the age of 61. Steve was buried next to his sons Tracy and Willie in Sunrise Cemetery east of town. Even though he was out of the lineup, Sam did not attend the funeral in Nebraska. The team doctor refused to let him travel, maintaining that his injured arm required careful treatment.

Crawford returned to the lineup on May 2, ripping a double and a triple in a 6-2 Tigers win over Cleveland. Three days later, Boston's 37-year-old Cy Young pitched a perfect game in Washington, retiring all 27 hitters in order. In his next start, on May 11, Young faced Detroit. The veteran again worked his magic, shutting down the Tigers for six innings. Because he had pitched nine hitless innings (seven of them in a relief appearance) before the perfect game, Young now had a string of 24 consecutive no-hit innings (still the MLB record). Crawford finally ended the streak with a double in the seventh inning. Detroit could not score though, eventually losing 1-0 in 15 innings. Young tossed all of those frames to continue a shutout string that would run to 45 consecutive innings. No wonder they named a pitching award after him.

Crawford appeared to be heating up when he pounded out eight hits in a three-game series in New York in mid-May. He then fell into a slump, going five for 34 the rest of the month. Barrow dropped his flailing outfielder to seventh in the lineup for a few games, hoping to shake things up. It did not work. Crawford's average lingered at a subpar .233 in mid-June.

Sam's struggles coincided with an overall team decline. After a .500 April, the injury-plagued Tigers bottomed out with an eight-game losing streak in May. By the end of the month, Detroit languished in seventh place, ten games below .500. The team was never able to get back on track in 1904.

The same could be said for Crawford, though he did have his moments that summer. On June 17, he rapped two hits off Rube Waddell, though his old friend got the last laugh by picking up the win. On July 18, Sam smashed a home run, a double, and two singles in a victory at New York—he liked hitting in the Big Apple that year. The next day, he rapped three hits off Jack Chesbro, who was on his way to setting a modern single-season pitching record with 41 wins. Though Wahoo did not maintain this consistency at the plate, his defense remained on track. "Crawford is fielding better than at any time in his career," sportswriter John R. Robinson reported in mid-summer.

Sam's durability remained another positive during his otherwise down year. Despite the time he missed in April, he still played in 150 of his team's 162 games (Detroit played 10 tie games in 1904 that did not count in the standings). Staying healthy remained a strength for Crawford throughout his career. Starting in 1901, he played at least 130 games in 15 consecutive seasons.

Sam's streak is even more remarkable considering the style of play common to baseball in the early 1900s. As an outfielder, he faced less risk of being spiked than the infielders. But getting hit by a pitch and running the bases brought plenty of potential for injury. When umpires were not looking, infielders would trip, elbow, hip-check, shove, and kick opposing baserunners. Fights, on and off the field, were more common then. Fans sometimes stormed the diamond to join in the fracas. Beyond the confines of the ballpark, hangovers and STDs accounted for even more missed time among Deadball Era players.

A nondrinker devoted to his wife, Crawford avoided the off-field problems that plagued many of his teammates. A commitment to conditioning provides further explanation for his durability. He avoided cigarettes during the season, went to bed early, and remained active throughout the year. During the off-season months, he hunted, golfed, and roller skated at an Omaha rink to stay in shape. Every year at spring training, his discipline and work ethic stood out among his peers. Walking five miles each day and forgoing his noontime meals, Crawford amazed reporters with his ability to shed pounds in the weeks leading up to the start of the season.

In a later season, Frank Navin elaborated on the disciplined habits of his star outfielder from Nebraska:

> No manager was ever worried about Sam's condition or his failure to report in excellent shape. No owner was ever worried that Sam wouldn't do his best work at all times and under all circumstances.... The neighbors around his home all say that Sam is as good as a clock to them. At 9 sharp the lights in his house go out. There is a regularity and method in all that he does. He never drinks, and as he has no other habits which could remotely be criticized, he sometimes smokes a little in the winter-time. But his conscience evidently troubles him, for he always gives up the pernicious practice long before spring training time and never relapses from the beaten path of rectitude until the active season is over.

Though Sam maintained his disciplined lifestyle, the summer of 1904 tested his patience. Occasionally, the frustrations cracked through his restrained demeanor. During a drubbing by the Athletics in June, Umpire Charles King ejected Crawford in the seventh inning for protesting a call too vigorously. Sam had gone hitless in four at-bats that day. In mid-September Ban Johnson suspended Crawford for two games for again arguing with an umpire.

As the Tigers continued to struggle, frustrations spread throughout the club. Relations soured between Navin and Barrow. In late July, the manager resigned with his team still mired in seventh place. On his way out, Barrow pointed to a lack of hitting for the Tigers failings. He singled out two specific players to throw under the bus. "Thirty games would have been won if Crawford and [Charlie] Carr had hit the ball at critical times," Barrow charged. "On their records they should have done this, but they didn't, and the games went to the bad." The outgoing manager's comments were a classless way to leave town. As for his charge that the two players cost the team 30 games, Crawford and Carr actually combined to contribute a positive offensive WAR (wins above replacement) for Detroit in 1904 (2.5 for Sam and -0.5 for Charlie).

Veteran second baseman Bobby Lowe took over in the interim as player-manager. In early August, the Tigers won seven of eight, showing they still had some fight left in them. But later in the month, they started a losing streak that stretched to eleven games. Following another skid in late September, Detroit closed out the season dropping six of its last seven decisions in October. As bad as they were, however, the 62-90 Tigers could not catch the 113-loss Senators in the race for last place.

The numbers were not pretty for Crawford, who concluded his worst season thus far in the majors. He batted .254 and slugged .361, a decrease of 81 and 128 points respectively from the previous season. Despite this overall decline, there were a few bright spots for Sam. He posted 16 triples, just three below the league lead, stole 20 bases for the first time as a big leaguer, and led his team with 73 RBI.

As the scribes recapped Detroit's disappointing 1904 season, Crawford's offensive failings consistently appeared on their list of reasons for the team's decline. In December one writer quipped that the Tigers manager lay awake at nights wondering if Sam would regain his batting eye.

Back in Omaha that winter, Crawford indirectly offered a reason for his subpar season. He called for the elimination of the foul-strike rule, which he believed reduced his batting performance by 30 percent. Counting foul balls as strikes (but not a third strike), removed an advantage for hitters, but did not have as weighty of an impact as Sam suggested. Given that he had completed three productive seasons (1901-1903) with the rule in place, the foul-strike explanation can be dismissed. A more likely reason for Sam's diminished output was the lingering effects from his arm ailment in April. The passing of his father early in the season also may have affected his performance.

Whatever the reason for his decline in 1904, it was certain that Crawford would work hard to improve in the winter months. One can again imagine him counting the days until spring. Come April, he would be raring to return to action at Bennett Park.

Unfortunately, off-season developments took a displeasing turn for Crawford. Navin, who had no qualms about dropping huge sums at the track, set about slashing Tigers expenses. For 1905 he moved the team's spring training from Shreveport to Augusta, Georgia, because a hotel in the latter city promised him lower rates. The miserly Navin actually talked about scrapping the spring trip to the South, grousing that the benefits were not worth the expense. Though he maintained that the players could work out just as effectively indoors in Detroit during the spring, he did not follow through on this radical cost-cutting measure.

Known as the Great Nickel Nurser, Navin prided himself on keeping player salaries in check. Coming off a down year, Crawford was a prime target for a pay reduction. In a letter sent in January, Navin reminded Sam that with just one exception, "you were the lowest hitter in the American League of the regular outfielders." The contract accompanying this correspondence offered $2,700 for the season, an $800 cut from the previous year. Crawford, who had received $3,500 his last year in Cincinnati and $4,500 his first year in Detroit, understandably did not comply with Navin's request to quickly accept this "very liberal offer."

Management told the Tiger players to report to Detroit on March 5. The next day they would travel via the Michigan Central Railroad south to Georgia. Holding firm, Crawford did not board this train. Several players across the league, including two other Tigers, similarly balked at the low figures on their contracts that spring.

As Crawford continued his holdout, rumors emerged that Detroit was planning to trade him to Washington for Malachi Kittredge, a 35-year-old catcher who had batted .242 the previous season. *Sporting Life* reported that the deal was likely to go through. It is unknown if this rumor had any impact on Crawford, but soon after it surfaced, he accepted Navin's offer and wired team officials that he was on his way to Augusta. With the reserve clause in place and no agents arguing their case, few players in this era made much headway in their disputes against the owners. Despite the considerable pay cut, Wahoo Sam's salary was still more than double the average annual pay of a skilled craftsman ($1,200) at the time.

Crawford would be playing for a new manager in 1905, his eighth different skipper in the big leagues. Former minor league outfielder Bill Armour had managed Cleveland for the previous three seasons. Though the team had posted a winning record each of those campaigns, the front office fired him because he did not get along with star second baseman Napoleon Lajoie. Navin jumped at the chance to hire Armour to manage the Tigers. Perhaps the team secretary-treasurer admired the 35-year-old skipper's sense of style—like Connie Mack, Armour wore a suit and tie in the dugout.

When Detroit's first baseman Charlie "Piano Legs" Hickman failed to impress in spring training, Armour decided to move Crawford to the position. Sam was not enthused by the shift. "The outfield suits me," he replied when asked about the change. "I've played there all my life, and find that it agrees with me." Armour nonetheless continued with the experiment. Remaining the professional that he was, Crawford put in the work to learn the new position. Though handling grounders and short-hops were a challenge, he soon impressed reporters with his ability to catch high throws and "find the bag while on the run."

During their time in Georgia that spring, the Tigers played five games against the Augusta Tourists, a Class C minor league team. Playing right field for the local nine was a skinny 18-year-old kid who was a bit overzealous on the basepaths. This was the first time Crawford crossed paths with Tyrus Cobb. Given that Sam played first, the two players likely engaged in some banter when Cobb reached base during the games.

The Tigers not surprisingly schooled the minor leaguers in a "master class" on baseball. Before the team packed up to head north, Wild Bill Donovan and second baseman Germany Schaefer took time to share a few pointers with Cobb. It is unknown if the outfield prospect made any impression on Crawford. Cobb biographer Al Stump describes a lengthy spring training conversation between the two in which young Ty seeks advice from Wahoo Sam. Stump, however, tended to exaggerate, fictionalize, and make up events. Given that he places the exchange at a 1904 preseason exhibition game in Augusta, a town the Tigers did not visit that spring, the Crawford-Cobb conversation he recounts likely never occurred.

Detroit started the 1905 season on a promising note, winning five of their first seven contests. The team then skidded into a five-game losing streak. This hot-and-cold trend continued over the following weeks. A month into the season, the Tigers treaded water in the middle of the American League pack with a .500 record.

Crawford shined as one of Detroit's brightest lights in the early season. Quickly learning his new position, he earned accolades for his skills at first base. Sportswriter W.A. Phelon described his defensive play as "beautiful," while noting that he could handle both high and low throws. Armour praised Sam for the hard work he put into learning the position, adding that "he has mastered it so that he can handle himself as well as anyone on the bag." Crawford's successful transition even drew favorable comments from AL vice president Charles Somers.

Even more encouraging was the return of Sam's thunderous bat. By early June, he was batting .344, only four points behind league leader Wee Willie Keeler. The reemergence of Crawford's hitting prowess followed his adoption of the slap-hitting, choked up batting grip used by Keeler. As Detroit scribe Paul Bruske reported, "Sam started in to learn the choke hold on the bat in the South this spring and has kept at it until he now uses a regular Keeler grip." Despite the change, Crawford still generated deep drives. On a road trip in mid-June, he bashed three home runs in a five-day span—an astounding power display for a batter using a choked-up grip during the Deadball Era.

On June 13, the same day Crawford started his home run barrage, Armour shifted him back to right field. Hickman's struggles with the sun while playing outfield necessitated the change. Though Armour, a known tinkerer, would later shift him back to first for a few games, Sam played most of the rest of the season in his preferred outfield habitat.

Unfortunately, as the summer weeks passed, both Crawford and the Tigers fell into decline. By mid-August, Sam's batting average had dropped all the way to .264. Following a skid that saw them lose nine of ten, Detroit had descended to sixth place in the standings. Inconsistency plagued their pitchers, injuries ravaged their outfielders (except for Sam), and Piano Legs Hickman quit when he tired of Armour's criticisms. The *Detroit Free Press* noted that at Bennett Park the applause was "frequently stronger for the visitors than for the home team." After a disputed call went against them in a game on August 15, the Tigers refused to take the field, prompting angry fans to chase umpire Bill Sheridan out of the ballpark. Detroit had to forfeit the game, taking another loss.

Desperate for help, Armour sent out Henny Youngman to find new talent. After an unproductive trip to Massachusetts, the scout headed south to check out the prospects in the Sally League. In Augusta, Georgia, he met a team manager who raved about his speedy young outfielder. After watching the kid in three games, Youngman had seen enough. He wired his boss about the youngster and the Detroit Tigers bought Ty Cobb from

Augusta. He was originally intended to finish out the rest of the season with his minor league team, but Armour paid an extra $200 (out of his own pocket when Navin balked at the added fee) to have the Georgia prospect join the team immediately.

Cobb made his major league debut on August 30 before a crowd of 1,200 at Bennett Park. He doubled and walked in Detroit's 5-3 victory over New York. Playing right field, Crawford likely did not pay too much mind to the new guy over in center. Few expected an 18-year-old from a Class C minor league in the South to make much difference at the major league level. Maybe the Georgia kid would stick around for a while, or maybe he wouldn't. For Sam, this was not a momentous day in baseball history. Trotting to the clubhouse after the game, he had no idea the impact that this redheaded newcomer would have on the rest of his career and his life.

Following Cobb's arrival, Detroit started playing better. They actually played great. The team won eight of ten in early September and posted a 21-11 mark for the entire month. Ending the season five games above .500, the once embarrassing Tigers had climbed all the way to third place in the standings.

Though Cobb was a fixture in the lineup the final five weeks of the season, it is hard to claim that his bat was the catalyst for the team's turnaround. Despite some stellar moments, he hit only .240 during that span. The recent death of his father, who was accidently shot by his mother, likely accounted for some of this diminished performance. Cobb nonetheless brought energy and an aggressive style of play to his team. His dynamic presence perhaps played some role in boosting the flagging spirit of the Tigers.

Batting cleanup just ahead of Cobb in the lineup, Crawford rebounded at the plate during the stretch run of the season. He finished the 1905 campaign with a solid .297 batting average, fourth best in the AL and just nine points below the league leader. His .430 slugging percentage was third best in the Junior Circuit. With offensive numbers down across the league, Sam tied for second in total hits and placed fourth in the AL with 75

RBI. Not only was Crawford still the top Tiger, he had reestablished himself as one of the premier sluggers in the major leagues.

Sam and Ada again returned to Omaha for the winter. As he continued his roller-skating regimen to stay in shape, the *Omaha Daily Bee* reported that he looked "bigger and stronger than ever." Crawford looked for a bigger and stronger salary to match his physique. But once again, he was disappointed by the offer that arrived in the mail.

Though a free spender in his personal life, Navin remained frugal as ever when dealing with players. Seemingly unimpressed with Crawford's improved performance the previous season, he offered his right fielder the same $2,700 salary. Wahoo Sam neither signed nor returned the contract and ceased communications with the club. Several other Tigers balked at their contracts too, but Crawford's holdout lingered the longest. With the date for spring training fast approaching, the disgruntled outfielder faced a fine of $100 if he did not report on time.

The Tigers headed south to Augusta with no Crawford. The team risked losing its best overall player. That player in turn risked fines and losing the opportunity to play baseball. The two sides finally came to an agreement. Sam signed for $3,000, a modest $300 raise, and reported to training camp little more than a week late.

With Crawford back in the fold, Armour had his right fielder. Matty McIntyre, an Ed Barrow acquisition who had started the previous two seasons, would play left field. Jimmy Barrett was still hobbled by the torn knee tendons that had shelved him for most of the previous season. The Tigers would soon ship him off to Cincinnati. That left an opening in center field. One of the men battling for the job was the highly-touted Davy Jones, a fleet-footed fly chaser acquired in the offseason from minor league Minneapolis in the American Association. The other option was that kid from Georgia who showed some potential the previous September. Similar to Crawford's experience in Cincinnati in 1900, Ty Cobb was sent to the bench in favor of an older player. Armour tabbed Jones to start in center on Opening Day.

Optimism abounded in Detroit at the start of the 1906 season. Paul Bruske reported these spring sentiments but tempered expectations with his own prediction for the team:

> The Detroit team starts the season in excellent spirits, with the greatest enthusiasm and in very fair physical condition. Local interest was higher than ever in the exercises of opening day, every seat in the grand stand being sold for days, and fully half the standing room in center field, to say nothing of the big bleacher. While I share the common belief that Detroit has the best team she has ever boasted since the American League was formed, I do not expect to se [sic] the club finish higher than third and think it will have all it can do to remain in the first division through the race.

During spring training, Crawford again changed his batting style. Abandoning the Keeler choke grip he had used the previous season, Sam moved his hands down the handle and went "back to the long bat and long swing." Since arriving in the majors, this was the second time he had adopted and then abandoned the slap-hit technique.

Returning to his natural power-hitting style yielded promising early results. He batted six for 18 in his first five games with two extra-base hits. In the third game of the year, he hit a mammoth blast over the center field wall at Bennett Park. The near 500-foot drive was only the second time a home run had cleared the center field fence at that ballpark.

Late in the fifth game of the season, played on April 21 at Chicago, Crawford strained a muscle in his leg. He would be shelved for a week, opening the door for Cobb to join the starting lineup. The young Georgian made some mistakes but hit well enough to remain an everyday player. When Crawford reclaimed right field on April 29, Armour shifted Cobb to center and benched Jones.

Defying the preseason reports of their improvement, the Tigers fell into a familiar pattern in the 1906 season. The team stumbled around .500 through April, before heating up to win eight of nine decisions. A cold streak then followed. At the end of May, Detroit's 18-17 record left them in a familiar fifth place spot in the standings.

Like his team, Crawford struggled to maintain consistency throughout the spring. His batting average cooled to .268 by early June. Few doubted that the Nebraska slugger would soon get back on track though. His former boss Garry Herrmann told reporters that he wanted Sam back. With the Reds fading in the standings, their president said Crawford was the best outfielder Cincinnati ever had, and he would pay $10,000 to get him back.

Detroit's woes continued when the team opened June by dropping two of three to St. Louis. And the Tigers had worse problems than their mediocre record. Though batting a robust .311, their 19-year-old star prospect from Georgia endured harsh treatment at the hands of his teammates. While veteran ballplayers at the time typically hazed rookies, Cobb endured a longer and more brutal period of abuse than was the norm.

The persecution had started in spring training when Matty McIntyre cursed out Cobb and tried to stop him from taking batting practice. After the Georgian pushed his way to the plate to take his cuts, he returned to the clubhouse to find that his specially-made black ash bats had been sawed into pieces. In the following weeks, Cobb's teammates destroyed his hats, tied his clothes into knots, hid his uniform, pelted his head with wet newspaper wads, and locked him out of the bathroom. Though McIntyre remained the ringleader in this campaign, catcher Boss Schmidt escalated the bullying to violent levels. The burly backstop, known for being able to pound a nail into a block of wood with his bare first, mixed it up with Cobb on multiple occasions. One time without any warning, Schmidt just sucker punched Ty in the face, leaving him laid out near the bench.

It is unclear how much of a role Crawford played in the hazing. Cobb stated that Sam was not friendly to him during his first year in Detroit. As a professional with a reserved temperament, Crawford likely did little, if any, direct persecuting himself. But he also did nothing to stop the tormenting of his young teammate. From Sam's point of view, all rookies go through this ritual. They should just take their medicine, laugh it off, and move on. But Crawford said that Cobb himself made it worse. As Sam later recalled:

> Cobb took it [the hazing] the wrong way. He came up with an antagonistic attitude, which in his mind turned any little razzing into a life-or-death struggle. He always figured everybody was ganging up against him. He came up from the South, you know, and he was still fighting the Civil War. As far as he was concerned, we were all damn Yankees before he even met us.

Armour initially did not intervene to stop the hazing. By late June, however, with dissension spreading to other players and affecting the team's on-field performance, he took action to stop the harassment of his top rookie. Targeting the ringleader of the hazing, Armour suspended McIntyre for what he officially labeled as "indifferent play." The players, of course, knew the real reason.

McIntyre's week-long sentence ended the open torment of Cobb, but tensions remained and the ostracization continued. Making matters worse, injuries ravaged the Tiger roster by mid-summer. The team floundered through July with an 11-15 mark. And at the end of the month, they would lose their star rookie. Weeks of abuse had taken their toll on Cobb, whom Armour sent home on July 19. The manager officially cited "stomach trouble" as the reason for his outfielder's hiatus. Gastrointestinal issues could have been a contributing factor, but it also may have been a nervous breakdown that shelved the Georgia Peach. Whatever the reason, he would not return to the team for a month-and-a-half.

Despite the team-wide turmoil, Crawford's bat heated up over the summer. He rapped four hits in a home win over Cleveland. In a game against the A's, he doubled and stole a base in a Tiger barrage that drove Waddell from the mound in the third inning. In a later contest against the same opponent, he doubled home the game-winning run off Waddell in the 10th inning. Always nice to catch up with old friends.

Crawford's production increased interest in his services among other American League clubs. One rumor had him going to Boston. Chicago president Charley Comiskey made an offer to Navin to bring Sam over to the White Sox. Detroit management wisely decided to hang onto their slugging outfielder from Wahoo.

Near the end of August, a train carrying the Tigers collided with another train near Buffalo. Several players incurred bruises after falling from their Pullman berths, but fortunately the incident resulted in no serious injuries. Navin nonetheless sought to bolster his thin roster by signing star 1880s and 1890s slugger Sam Thompson. The 46-year-old outfielder had not played in the majors for years, but as a key member of Detroit's 1887 championship team, he offered a chance to revive the sagging attendance numbers at Bennett Park.

Cobb returned to the team on September 2. In both games of a doubleheader the next day the Tiger lineup featured Thompson in right, Crawford at first, and Cobb in center. Despite the presence of a past, present, and future baseball legend, Detroit dropped both games to the Browns.

Though Cobb played well, his return revived tensions in the Tiger clubhouse. The team skidded through two losing streaks in September before rebounding to win nine in a row late in the month. That included a three-game sweep of the Highlanders, which helped the White Sox claim the pennant. Detroit dropped four of its last five to close out the disappointing season in sixth place with a 71-78 record. After the next to last game, Cobb punctuated his frustrating rookie campaign by brawling with teammate Ed Siever in a hotel lobby. After the fight ended with Siever lying in a bloody heap, Cobb walked away. But then moments later, he returned to deliver a final kick to the unconscious pitcher's face.

Crawford provided a bright spot in Detroit's otherwise dismal 1906 season. He batted .295, with 72 RBI and a career-high 24 stolen bases. His .407 slugging average led the team and his 16 triples were third best in the league. Wahoo Sam was still the Tigers' top offensive weapon, but the team needed more production from other players if it was ever going to contend for a pennant. Back-to-back 20-game winner George Mullin gave Detroit a top-of-the-rotation pitching ace. Wild Bill Donovan had a down year, but he too could dominate from the mound. As for hitters, that rookie Cobb showed promise by batting .316 over two-thirds of a season. But could the Tigers overcome the divisiveness that seemed to accompany the fiery young Georgian?

Chapter 8

Battling for Championships

Per usual, Sam and Ada spent the off-season in Nebraska. The star slugger took advantage of the mild weather of late fall and early winter to traverse the paved boulevards of Omaha in his new $750 Cadillac. A local reporter called him "a perfect picture of health, being twenty-five pounds lighter" than when he had left Nebraska the previous spring.

Back in Detroit, meanwhile, a new manager prepared for the upcoming 1907 season. Bill Armour's approval ratings had declined with the sixth-place finish. Never a fan of being shifted to first base, Crawford was among those Tiger players who had lost faith in the well-dressed skipper's baseball acumen. Friction grew between Armour and the front office as well, prompting Frank Navin to make a change. With a month left in the 1906 campaign, the Tigers president announced that Hughie Jennings would take over as manager after the season.

The shortstop for the rowdy Baltimore Oriole teams that won three NL pennants in the 1890s, Jennings had gained a reputation as one of baseball's more eccentric characters—and that is saying something for that time period. Not afraid to take his lumps, he remains the MLB career record holder for getting hit by a pitch. While studying law at Cornell, Jennings once unwittingly dove into a darkened swimming pool that had been drained of water. As Tigers skipper, he encouraged his players (and earned his nickname) by shouting "Ee-Yah" from the first base coaching box. He accompanied these yells by tossing grass in the air, blowing a whistle, and dancing about. In an attempt to distract opposing pitcher Rube Waddell, he even brought children's toys and a dog with him to the coaching box.

In early March, prior to spring training, Crawford and some of his teammates spent a few days at Hot Springs, Arkansas, to get an early start on preparing for the 1907 season. After bathing in the famous spas of the resort town, Sam and the others reported to Augusta, Georgia, for the official start of spring training. There, unfortunately, it did not take long before the troubles of the previous season carried over into the new one.

Jennings liked Sam, but he initially was not too keen on the Georgia Peach. This assessment did not change when, a week into spring training, Cobb engaged in a physical altercation with an inebriated ballpark groundskeeper who had gotten too familiar with him. Happening upon the scene, Boss Schmidt intervened, resulting in yet another fight with Cobb. Schmidt said that he was trying to stop Ty from choking the groundskeeper's wife, who had joined the fray. Cobb denied that he assaulted the wife. Schmidt's accusation lost some credibility after Jennings later revealed that he had encouraged his catcher to draw Cobb into an incident that would convince Navin to trade him.

After accounts of the brawl appeared in newspapers, Jennings' plan seemed to be working. Several Tiger veterans (Sam is not listed by name but could have been one of them) expressed discontentment with Cobb. The Georgia Peach himself asked to be traded, seemingly confirming that his days as a Tiger were numbered. But then Navin intervened. Recognizing Cobb's potential for greatness, the Detroit president encouraged Jennings to work things out with young Tyrus. When offers from other teams for Cobb proved uninspiring, Jennings dropped his trade efforts.

Thwarted in his plan to send away the Peach, Jennings had to find a way to preserve club harmony if the Tigers were to compete. A couple weeks after the groundskeeper incident, Schmidt again brawled with Cobb before a spring training game. And tensions remained between left fielder Matty McIntyre and the young Georgian. With the two outfielders going after the same fly balls, their feud could continue to flare all season long. Jennings came up with a solution. He moved Crawford into center field to keep McIntyre and Cobb separated. Though Cobb had accused Crawford of encouraging their teammates to saw his bats, there had thus far been less ill-will between the two. Plus, Sam was known as a team player who did not let personal feelings override his professionalism. If any of the Tigers could coexist in the outfield next to Cobb, it would be him.

George Mullin tossed a shutout against Cleveland on Opening Day at Bennett Park. The chilly 40-degree weather, however, took its toll as both Crawford and Cobb caught colds. Sam shook off the effects of his illness to hit safely in the first ten games of the season. During this early hot streak, he told a reporter that he named his bats. His favorites were Horace, Emma, Julia, Grace, and Minnie. After umpire Jack Stafford ejected Crawford on May 1, Sam and his wooden "friends" fell into a little slump. This downturn did not last though, and his ash gang soon got back to business. By mid-June, he was batting .314.

Despite their springtime dissension, the Tigers started strong. A five-game winning streak in late April put them at 8-5 at the end of the month. The wins continued in the following weeks. The team's 20-14 record at the end of May landed them in not-so-distant third place. This collective success, as well as Jennings' outfield experiment, had eased clubhouse tensions. The new manager was gaining popularity with his players and Detroit fans, the latter finding great enjoyment in his on-field antics. Bennett Park denizens displayed higher-than-usual levels of enthusiasm this season, as seen on May 22 when they swarmed the field after a controversial call, forcing umpire Billy Evans to seek police protection.

The Tigers spent the first three weeks of June on a 19-game road trip. Though they held their own during this stretch, Washington blasted them 10-0 on the 15th. That might sound like a bad day for all the Tigers players, but for one of them it was actually a great day. Back in Detroit, Ada gave birth to Sam's first child. Crawford would meet his daughter Virginia a week later when the team finally returned home.

The new papa and his teammates continued their success in the following weeks. By mid-July, Sam's batting average had climbed to .342, second highest in the American League. Personal mid-season success was not unusual for Crawford. The teams he played for, however, usually faded in the summer heat. But 1907 was different. Rather than dropping back to the middle of the pack, the Tigers posted a torrid 19-9 mark in July. With just two months left in the season, they found themselves in the thick of a four-team pennant race.

On August 2, the Tigers played a doubleheader in Washington. Before the first game, Senators manager Joe Cantillon warned the visitors he was going to start a "big apple-knocker" against them. Upon sighting the lanky 19-year-old hurler from Idaho, the Tigers commenced a barrage of taunts. One player mooed like a cow, while another shouted, "Get the pitchfork ready, Joe—your hayseed's on his way back to the barn." They quickly changed their tune when the kid started blazing in his fastballs. Cobb said the pitches "hissed with danger." The young pitcher kept the Tigers off-balance all game. In the eighth inning with the contest tied 1-1, Crawford connected with a drive that zoomed over the shortstop's head. The ball bounded against the left field wall, allowing Sam to circle the bases. Detroit held on to win by one run. And that is how the baseball world first met Walter Johnson, the pitcher Sam later described as the fastest he ever saw. Over the next 20 years, Johnson would win 417 games and 12 strikeout titles, with an astounding career 2.17 ERA.

After surviving their encounter with the Big Train, the Tigers stayed hot in August. They closed out the month with a seven-game winning streak to climb into first place, one-and-a-half games ahead of Philadelphia. Chicago and Cleveland were not far behind as the four-team race remained tight. Battling for a major league pennant for the first time, Crawford continued hitting. On September 8, he belted a home run in Chicago that contributed to a key road win. More timely hits followed down the stretch run as his average remained well over .300.

On Friday, September 27, with little more than a week left in the season, the Tigers led the A's by just a half-game. The team then traveled to Philadelphia for a crucial three-game series. Connie Mack sent future Hall of Famer Eddie Plank to the hill, while Jennings countered with Wild Bill Donovan. Nearly 18,000 raucous fans crammed into Columbia Park (which had a capacity of 13,600) for the series opener. Neither ace had his best stuff. Crawford drove in two runs with a double and a single to help Detroit hold on to a 5-4 victory. Anxious Detroiters hung on every update throughout the game, following the wire reports posted on bulletin boards at hotels, saloons, and stores across the city.

Rain washed out Saturday's contest, and with Sunday baseball illegal in Philadelphia, a doubleheader was scheduled for Monday. But the teams would play only one game that day, and it would end in controversy. Crawford again occupied center stage in an important event in early baseball history.

Swarms of fans—24,000 of them—packed the ballpark, lining both foul lines and the deepest parts of the outfield. This Philly horde delighted when the Mackmen jumped out to a 7-1 lead after six innings. In the top of the seventh, with the bases loaded, Crawford drilled a shot off Rube Waddell into the overflow crowd in the outfield for a ground-rule double. The two RBI were part of a four-run outburst that brought the Tigers back into the game. In the ninth inning, with his team down two runs, Crawford led off with a single against his former teammate. Cobb, batting cleanup, followed by driving a Waddell fastball over the right field wall to tie the game. Chirping and gloating for most of the afternoon, the over-capacity crowd now stood in stunned silence.

Both teams scored in the 11th, and the game remained tied as inning after inning passed. In the 14th, A's first baseman Harry Davis hit a fly ball to deep center field. Crawford backed to the edge of the crowd and settled under the fly. Just as he was about to make the catch, a Philadelphia police officer stepped from the roped-off throng and jostled his arm so he misplayed the ball. As the crowd cheered Davis's apparent double, Jennings stormed from the bench demanding that home plate umpire Silk O'Loughlin rule the batter out due to interference. O'Loughlin did not see what happened from his vantage point behind the plate, so he deferred to the other umpire on the field, Tom Connolly. Crawford and other Tigers crowded around the arbiters, pleading their case. With a better view of the play, Connolly ruled for Detroit and declared that Davis was out. More arguing followed from the A's. The already tense crowd appeared on the verge of a riot. Then a fight broke out between Tigers first baseman Claude Rossman and Philadelphia coach Monte Cross. The melee had the unintended benefit of distracting the irate spectators and preventing mass chaos.

The game continued with neither team able to score. After 17 innings darkness descended upon the ballpark, forcing the umpires to halt play. The AL's most important regular season game of the year thus ended in a tie. That result benefitted the Tigers by depriving their rivals an opportunity to gain ground. Mack and Philly fans remained bitter for years, blaming O'Loughlin for costing them a crucial victory.

The Tigers followed their endurance battle in Philly by sweeping four in Washington and taking another in St. Louis. Not counting the draw, that gave them ten straight wins. Philadelphia, on the other hand, lost to Cleveland and Washington (with Walter Johnson pitching) during the last week. When the dust settled, Detroit had captured its first AL pennant. Sam Crawford was headed to the World Series.

Following the tense pennant race, few baseball observers would dispute the assessment of Chicago scribe W.A. Phelon that Cobb and Crawford had carried the Tigers. Cleveland catcher Jay Clarke concurred, declaring that Sam was "the hardest man to pitch to in a pinch." Crawford's season numbers for 1907 were the best he had posted in four years: .323 BA, .363 OPB, .460 slugging, 17 triples, 81 RBI, and a league-leading 102 runs scored. In batting average, slugging, and total bases Sam finished second in the league behind only Cobb.

Supporting this potent one-two punch in the Detroit lineup were Rossman and Davy Jones (McIntyre missed most of the season after suffering a broken ankle in May). Wild Bill Donovan (25 wins), Twilight Ed Killian (25 wins), Wabash George Mullin (20 wins), and Ed Siever (18 wins) gave the Tigers a formidable pitching corps. Add in the team's strong fielding and Jennings' managerial magic and Detroit rooters had plenty of reasons for optimism heading into the World Series.

The Tigers next faced the NL champion Chicago Cubs, a team hungry to avenge its World Series loss to the White Sox the previous year. Winners of 107 games, the Cubs lineup boasted the famous Tinker to Evers to Chance double-play combo. But the real power behind the Chicago juggernaut was its pitching staff. The team deployed five starters who could absolutely dominate a game: Mordecai "Three Finger" Brown (1.39 ERA), Orval Overall (1.68 ERA), Carl Lundgren (1.17 ERA), Jack Pfiester (1.15 ERA), and Ed Reulbach (1.69 ERA). The 1907 World Series would be a matchup of Detroit's "irresistible force" offense versus Chicago's "immovable object" pitching.

Outside Detroit and Chicago, few burgs across the nation were more excited about the World Series than Wahoo, Nebraska. Businesses in the town shut down during the October games. Town leaders established a telegraph connection with the *Omaha Bee* so game reports could quickly reach the people of Crawford's hometown. Pandemonium broke out whenever their hero, the first Nebraskan to play in a World Series, delivered a hit.

The Series opened in Chicago, where more than 24,000 fans crowded into West Side Park. As he did for most of the season, Crawford batted third and played center field. Undaunted by the elevated stakes of his first-ever World Series game, Wahoo Sam rapped three hits that day, including a big one in the eighth inning. With the Tigers trailing 1-0, Crawford singled off Overall to drive in two runs. After the throw to the plate got past Cubs catcher Johnny Kling, Sam scampered all the way to third. When Cobb then grounded back to the pitcher, Crawford got caught in a rundown, but he made it back to third when Kling threw wide. Sam later scored on Rossman's sacrifice fly.

Detroit took a 3-1 lead into the bottom of the ninth. With Donovan cruising, it appeared that Game 1 was in the bag. But Chicago loaded the bases with just one out. A ground ball plated a run and left the Cubs with runners at second and third with two outs. Donovan just needed to retire pinch hitter Del Howard to end the game. And Wild Bill seemingly did just that when the batter swung and missed at strike three. But the ball got away from catcher Boss Schmidt, allowing Howard to reach first and the tying run to score. The teams played three more scoreless innings before darkness ended the game in a tie.

The Tigers never recovered from the gut-punch of Game 1 slipping away. Cub pitchers held Detroit to only three runs over the next four games. Chicago won each of those contests and the Series. Like his teammates, Crawford did little after the first game. Receiving a steady diet of low curve balls from Pfiester, Reulbach, Overall, and Brown, he batted just two for 16 after Game 1, finishing at .238 for the Series. Cobb similarly struggled at .200.

Despite the World Series disappointment, Detroiters considered the season a major success. The stress and exhaustion of the tense pennant battle partially excused the Tigers' poor October showing. Fan support remained high, and the team was banqueted formally and informally. Owner Bill Yawkey generously added $15,000 to the World Series losers' pot, so each of his players took home a share of $1,945.96. The sizeable bonus removed much of the sting of the postseason defeat for Crawford and his teammates.

For the first time, Sam and Ada would not spend the winter months in Nebraska. Though they still returned to the Cornhusker State for a visit, they now made Detroit their year-round home. As parents of an infant daughter, they wanted to put down roots in a single locale. Sam's mother Nellie by this time no longer lived in Wahoo. Earlier in 1907 she had married a Mississippi farmer named Duncan Patterson and moved to a farm near Fayette in his home state. Crawford's two brothers remained in Wahoo, maintaining the family ties with his hometown.

During the off-season, Sam and Ada went house hunting in Detroit. They found a nice two-story abode on Hague Avenue in the city's North End neighborhood, about four miles north of Bennett Park. A farming community during the previous century, North End in the early 1900s became an aspirational neighborhood that attracted politicians, business leaders, and other successful professionals. In subsequent decades, many African American families settled in the neighborhood as part of the Great Migration. A thriving music scene emerged, and the North End gained notice as the home of several Motown legends, such as Smokey Robinson, Aretha Franklin, and Diana Ross.

Settling into his new house delayed Crawford's arrival at spring training by a week. For 1908 the team shifted its training venue to Arkansas, where it spent three weeks in Hot Springs. After that, the players headed to Little Rock to begin team play in late March. An exhibition tour with stops in Louisville, Evansville, and Terre Haute followed.

Detroit scribes and fans alike displayed much optimism for their Tigers, the defending American League champions. And Crawford stood as a centerpiece of the team's prosperity.

Jennings called him "the perfect ball player of the present day." *Detroit Times* sports editor Paul Bruske concurred in a glowing preseason tribute to the slugger:

> Sam can hit with the best of them. He can play any of the outfield positions as few of the best are able to do. In throwing men out from the field he is virtually in a class by himself.... His speed on the bases is remarkable for one of his tremendous stature.... His presence on the Detroit club has always been an influence to harmony, team work and conscientious attention to the business in hand. There is not a man in his profession who does not respect and like Sam Crawford.

Crawford would soon be called upon to use his influence for harmony when Ty Cobb refused Navin's contract offer and threatened to play for an outlaw team. Tigers fans shuddered at the prospect of losing one of their top two offensive weapons. As negotiations stalled during these anxious times, Crawford invited Cobb to join him for a ride in his automobile. During this jaunt, Sam gave his teammate "fatherly advice" about the hazards of jumping to an outlaw league. Cobb soon ended his holdout and signed a contract for 1908. The press credited Crawford for playing a key role in bringing the young Georgian back into the fold. Calling Sam "a strong friend of Cobb," *The Detroit Times* reported that "the sage things that he [Crawford] said to the youngster had much to do with Ty's coming to reason."

An alarming episode soon overshadowed the good feelings that followed Cobb's signing. A few days before the Tigers were to leave Hot Springs, Crawford received word that his wife had a serious illness. He left training camp and returned to Detroit. A few days later, the newspaper reported that Ada's health had improved and that Crawford would soon rejoin the team. The press did not name the illness that had afflicted Ada.

Starting a season for the first time as defending AL champions, the Tigers stumbled out of the gate, dropping five of their first six games. Crawford belted a 10th-inning home run to beat Cleveland on April 25 to provide a rare highlight in an otherwise dismal April. At the end of the season's first month, the team sat in last place with a 3-9 record. Bruske blamed the pitching for the Tigers slow start, though rookie knuckleball sensation Ed "Kickapoo" Summers was a bright spot in the rotation.

Detroit finally got going in May with a six-game road winning streak that brought their record up to .500. Injuries and inconsistent play, however, continued to hamper the team in the following weeks. A loss to the New York Highlanders on June 9th dropped the fifth-place Tigers to 22-23. Crawford, for his part, did not enjoy a strong spring, batting just .250 up to this point.

On June 12, Detroit held a pregame flag-raising ceremony to celebrate the previous season's AL championship. Among the luminaries in attendance were Ban Johnson, Sam Thompson, former Detroit pitcher Charles "Lady" Baldwin, and former Detroit catcher Charlie Bennett. After the latter had lost both his legs from accidentally slipping under a passenger train in 1894, Detroiters named their ballpark that opened a couple years later in his honor. The 10,000 fans at Bennett Park (seating capacity had been increased in the offseason) went home happy on flag-raising day after the Tigers defeated New York 5-2.

Crawford's bat finally started heating up after he slammed home runs in back-to-back games against Boston. Defensively, he once again shifted to first base after an injury to Rossman. Though he still preferred the outfield, Sam provided "brilliant first basing" for his team. *The Detroit Times* raved that he was best in the league in timing his toss to first when the pitcher had to cover the bag.

On June 23, Crawford and his teammates drove Ed Walsh from the mound in the sixth, en route to a 6-2 victory. It was a rare off-day for the White Sox hurler, who would win 40 games that season. Sam, like most AL batters, did not like trying to hit Big Ed's spitballs. "I think that ball disintegrated on the way to the plate and the catcher put it back together again," Crawford said. "I swear, when it went past the plate it was just the spit went by."

Walsh, for his part, did not enjoy pitching to Sam, whom he considered the toughest hitter to face in a pinch. He described one occasion when he used all his strength and cunning to pitch Crawford an unhittable spitball that went in so fast it could hardly be seen. "But it came back a good deal faster than it went," Walsh said. "I heard a sharp sound like the crack of a rifle, and that ball came sizzling through the air over my head." Walsh's manager Fielder Jones offered a similar assessment of Sam. "None of them can hit them quite as hard as Crawford," the White Sox skipper said. "He stands up to the plate like a brick house; there's no moving him away from it."

As the summer got hotter, so did the Tigers. They won 10 of 12 in mid-June, and took 10 of their first 11 in July. A nine-game winning streak later in the month vaulted the big cats into first place. Crawford contributed to this run by raising his batting average to .287, an increase of 37 points in seven weeks. Tigers fans eagerly looked forward to another pennant run.

Ty Cobb, however, continued to do Ty Cobb things. Yes, he remained a potent weapon, batting well over .300 and frustrating opposing fielders with his daring baserunning. But his off-field actions were a distraction. In June, Cobb grabbed headlines by engaging in a street fight with an African American worker laying asphalt. Though the subsequent assault charge resulted in a suspended sentence, Cobb had to pay his adversary $75 to avoid a civil suit. In August, with the Tigers in the midst of a tense pennant battle, Cobb irked his teammates by taking off for a week to get married in Georgia. On the plus side, Cobb's feud with McIntyre had finally subsided. But a new dispute emerged when Crawford, back in center field after Rossman's return, objected to the young Georgian's habit of invading his outfield turf to chase fly balls.

Though Cobb's quarrel with Crawford did not burn with the intensity of his earlier feuds with teammates, it did not help with team harmony during a tight pennant race. For Cobb, difficult relations with other Tigers would be an ongoing reality. "Trouble was he [Cobb] had such a rotten disposition that it was damn hard to be his friend," Davy Jones said. "He antagonized so many people that hardly anyone would speak to him, even among his own teammates."

That summer Detroit fans engaged in a debate about which Tiger star was more valuable: Crawford or Cobb. Fans on both sides had plenty of ammunition to support their position. Crawford's advantages included hitting with men on base, power hitting, stronger arm, fewer errors, popularity with teammates, and an even temperament. Cobb's advantages included batting average, speed, aggressive baserunning, range, and quicker thinking. Perhaps surprising given their post-career standing in baseball history, in 1908 neither player had a clear edge in the question of who was better. The less disputed conclusion was that the Tigers needed both Crawford and Cobb in the lineup to compete for the pennant.

As with the previous season, the 1908 AL race would go down to the wire. On August 28, Sam hit an 11th-inning home run off Eddie Plank to beat the A's 1-0. But then a six-game losing streak followed, raising fears that a late-season collapse would derail the Tigers' chances. Making matters worse, Crawford injured his leg in a collision at first base on August 30, knocking him from the starting lineup for three games.

Crawford returned from his injury on September 3, not a moment too soon for Detroit fans. Similar to the previous year, his bat and glove played a key role in the stretch run developments. On September 10, Sam saved a one-run victory over Chicago by making a one-handed catch of a ninth-inning drive that would have plated the tying run. His hitting, meanwhile, improved to over .300 in September. The Tigers, however, dropped five of six in mid-month to fall from first. With just two weeks left in the season, Detroit trailed Cleveland by two games and Chicago by a half-game. St. Louis was just a half-game behind the Tigers in the tight four-team race.

On September 25, Crawford drilled two doubles to help his team garner a much-needed victory over Philadelphia. That triumph started Detroit on a 10-game winning streak to reclaim the top spot in the standings. On October 2, Cleveland ace Addie Joss pitched a perfect game against Chicago. With their pennant hopes fading, the White Sox rebounded the next day to take their revenge on the Naps. In Detroit, meanwhile, Donovan shut out the Browns to give the Tigers a one-and-a-half-game lead over Cleveland and a two-and-a-half-game lead over the White Sox heading into the final series of the season. Detroit held the upper hand in the standings but had to play its last three games in Chicago against a desperate White Sox team still fighting for the pennant.

In the series opener at South Side Park, Chicago southpaw Doc White surrendered just three hits to beat the Tigers 3-1. Both teams caught a break when Cleveland's game against the Browns that day ended in a tie after eleven innings. Detroit led the Naps by a game and Chicago by one-and-a-half games with two more to play. The next day, Ed Walsh used all his powers of expectoration to again shut down the Tigers. Cleveland, meanwhile, dropped the first game of a doubleheader in St. Louis to fall out of the race. But Detroit's lead over Chicago had dwindled to just a half-game. Anxiety gripped Tigers Nation at the prospect of the pennant slipping away.

One final game would determine the pennant. The night before, rowdy Chicago fans yelled and raised a ruckus outside the hotel where the Tigers were staying, keeping many of the players awake most of the night. The next morning, Jennings delivered a fiery pep-talk to rally his groggy troops for the upcoming battle.

White Sox skipper Fielder Jones gave the ball to Doc White. Jennings countered with Wild Bill Donovan. Crawford had never played in a regular season game with such high stakes. All of his teammates could say the same. McIntyre singled to lead off the game. Rookie shortstop Donie Bush then struck out, bringing Crawford to the plate. Wahoo Sam drilled a double into the overflow crowd of White Sox fans. Cobb followed with a triple, plating two runs and knocking Doc White from the game. The visitors scored two more runs in the first inning and never looked back. Crawford tallied four hits in the 7-0 victory. Chicago fans poured onto the field after the game, some of them crying over the loss and some of them congratulating the Tigers on winning the pennant.

When the heat was on, Jennings' boys once again rose to the occasion. Back at the hotel, the Tigers whooped and shouted their manager's trademark cry, "Ee-yah!" The jubilant skipper told his players they would each receive a new tuxedo. The next morning, a crowd of a thousand greeted the team as their train arrived in Detroit. The players then rode in open cars to the Detroit City Hall to receive a grand reception.

The Tigers' dynamic duo continued their dominance of the American League offensive categories. Crawford's .311 batting average and .457 slugging average were both second only to Cobb, as were his 80 RBI, 184 hits, and 270 total bases. Sam did win the AL home run crown with seven round-trippers. In so doing, he became the only player to lead both major leagues in home runs—a distinction he would have all to himself until Fred McGriff accomplished the feat in 1992.

Detroit would again face the Chicago Cubs in the World Series. The Cubs had barely eked out the NL pennant by winning the season's final game against their rivals, the New York Giants. This contest was made necessary when Giants second baseman Fred Merkle had earlier cost his team a win by not touching second base on a teammate's apparent game-winning hit ("Merkle's Boner"). As with the previous October, Chicago would deploy a murderers' row of pitching, led by 29-game winner Three Finger Brown, 24-game winner Ed Reulbach, and 15-game winner Orval Overall. The Tigers hoped to counter that mound arsenal with Donovan, Mullin, and rookie knuckleballer Ed Summers, who led his team with 24 wins and a 1.64 ERA.

Unfortunately for Detroit, the 1908 World Series started much the same way as the preceding Fall Classic. In Game 1 the Tigers carried a one-run lead into the ninth at Bennett Park, before Summers yielded six straight hits. When the carnage ended, the Cubs had plated five ninth-inning runs to claim the opening victory. Overall then shut down the Tigers in Game 2. Crawford went 0 for 8 in these first two contests. In Game 3 at Chicago's West Side Park, Sam tasted his first World Series triumph when Detroit prevailed 8-3. Playing center field, Crawford contributed two hits and an RBI. For a moment, the Tigers had a glimmer of hope. But then Brown and Overall tossed back-to-back shutouts to end any doubt as to which team was the best in baseball in 1908. Sam rapped two hits in Game 4, but in the fourth inning Chicago catcher Johnny Kling picked him off second to derail a potential Tiger rally. With defeat imminent, only 6,210 subdued fans showed up for Game 5 at Bennett Park, the smallest crowd in World Series history. Crawford again batted .238 for the Series.

Low attendance numbers limited the losers' take to just $870 per player. Having bought nearly half the team's stock shares from Yawkey, Navin was now the Tigers president and in full control of the club's business affairs. So unlike the previous year, there would be no bonus coming from team ownership. After a postseason banquet and reception at Detroit's Hotel Pontchartrain, the Tigers returned to Chicago to play an exhibition game against the World Champions. Nearly 7,000 showed up to watch Detroit prevail in this meaningless game 8-3. Crawford had two hits, including a triple. Two days later the teams played again in Terre Haute, Indiana, in front of a sizeable crowd. The extra money from these two exhibition contests bumped each Tiger's postseason bonus to $1,100.

Though his team disbanded in Terre Haute, Crawford was not through playing baseball in 1908. He returned to Wahoo the following week and helped the home team beat Fremont 2-1. Before his first at-bat, townspeople presented him with a "fine set of cut glass." While in Omaha, Sam met up with Guy Green, the organizer of the Nebraska Indians team he had briefly played for a decade earlier. After spending a month in Nebraska, Crawford returned to Detroit for the remainder of the offseason.

Since one-year contracts were the norm for major league ballplayers in this era, Crawford and the Tigers had business to discuss. Staying on good terms with the boss, Sam and Wild Bill Donovan visited team offices on December 24 to wish Navin a Merry Christmas. It is not known if that gesture helped with negotiations (or if it was intended to) that offseason. In any event, Crawford's salary finally again reached the $4,500 he had received during the Great Baseball War. He remained the highest paid Tiger in 1909, just ahead of Cobb who signed for $4,000.

Drawing such a robust income allowed Sam to indulge his automobile interests. Cars were still in their first decade as a consumer option, but Crawford had already become an enthusiast. Each year he bought a new machine. This offseason he acquired a 1909 Chalmers-Detroit model. When not motoring the roads of Detroit in his latest purchase, Sam could be spotted taking long walks in his crimson sweater. These hikes, like skipping his noon meal, were part of his annual springtime regimen to get in shape for the upcoming season.

Despite the success of the previous two years, Navin once again changed the venue for the Tigers' spring training. He apparently was not given to superstition like many of his players. In March 1909 the team reported to San Antonio, Texas, for three weeks of training. Before leaving, Crawford ordered two dozen bats from A.G. Spalding & Bros. The slugger provided exact specifications, including a heavier head to help him reach the right field bleachers in Cleveland that Naps ownership had moved back during the offseason.

In Texas, Sam, ever the fan of short hair, convinced Davy Jones to join him in shaving his head for spring training. The former barber later convinced Donie Bush and newly-acquired third baseman George Moriarty to let him apply the clippers to their scalps as well. A more harmonious and jovial atmosphere prevailed among the Tigers that spring. This included Cobb, who took Crawford and two other teammates for a drive in a new automobile that a fan had loaned him. The two-time defending AL champs looked sharp in Texas, raising expectations that a third pennant would be coming their way.

The consistent production and steadying presence of Crawford stood out as a major reason for the optimism surrounding Detroit. The press noted that he remained humble about his own accomplishments, while praising the contributions of his teammates. Known for his quiet nature for most of his career, Sam had become a more vocal leader during the previous season, exhorting his fellow fielders to stay on their toes. Recognizing Sam's status as the AL's top power hitter, Paul Bruske hailed him as the "king of sluggers."

Detroit's early season play did nothing to dissuade predictions of a third straight pennant for the Motor City. Mullin pitched a one-hit shutout on Opening Day, and the Tigers won 12 of their first 15 games to bolt to an early lead in the standings. Crawford's hitting provided plenty of fuel for this acceleration. By the middle of May he was batting .314. Earlier that month, he belted a mammoth shot that cleared the center field wall at Bennett Park, reportedly the longest drive ever hit there.

The following month, Crawford hit a ball that did not travel quite so far. In the sixth inning of a scoreless tie, Sam batted with one out and runners on first and third. His old friend Waddell, now pitching for St. Louis, threw a curve that did not break. With the ball headed toward his neck, Crawford twisted his body and backed away. In so doing, his bat moved into the path of the ball, which ricocheted onto the field in fair territory. Though both Sam and Rube were too startled to react, McIntyre bolted home to score on what in effect became a sacrifice bunt. That fortuitous tally turned out to be the only run scored in the game, indicating how well things were going for Detroit at this point.

In many ways, the club's 1909 season followed the script of the previous two summers. The team continued racking up wins through June. In July, after an 18-inning scoreless tie against Washington on the 16th, Detroit took nine of its next twelve. But again there were rumors of friction in the Tigers clubhouse. *Sporting Life* reported that the veterans had grown resentful of Jennings' preferential treatment of the younger players. Rossman, moreover, had lost favor with management due to his defensive lapses and fading batting eye. The Tigers would soon part ways with the first baseman, even though he had been hailed as the team's third best hitter just a season ago.

And Ty Cobb of course still created headlines that Navin and Jennings did not like to see. In August, the Georgia Peach raised the ire of Philadelphia fans and Connie Mack for spiking A's infielder Frank Baker while sliding into third. The incident sparked concerns about Cobb's style of play and even brought some death threats from Philly fans, until newspapers printed a photograph of the play showing that Ty did not deliberately target Baker.

A worse episode followed a few days later. Returning to his hotel in Cleveland after midnight, Cobb argued with a bellboy. The hotel watchman intervened and soon traded blows with the Peach. As the adversaries fell to the floor grappling, Cobb pulled out a pen knife and slashed the hand of the watchman. The latter backed away and drew his gun to keep the ballplayer at bay. With his other hand, the watchman grabbed his nightstick and struck Cobb over the head. Other hotel employees then intervened to end the fracas. Two days later, a Cleveland court issued an arrest warrant for Cobb, causing him to steer clear of Ohio the rest of the season.

In another familiar pattern for Detroit, Jennings shifted Crawford to first base. He would play a total of 17 games there that season. On August 20, the Tigers traded Rossman to the Browns in exchange for Tom Jones, a first baseman known for his defensive prowess. This acquisition allowed Sam to return to center field for the stretch run. In another move, Detroit sent infielder Germany Schaefer to Washington for second baseman Jim Delahanty. With this trade, the Tigers said goodbye to one of the game's top showmen. A flashy character who entertained crowds with his baseball antics, Schaefer would later etch his name in baseball history by stealing first base. This unusual episode started when he was on first with a teammate on third. He stole second but did not draw a throw from the catcher to give the man on third a chance to score. On the next pitch, Germany startled everyone by running back to first. A pitch later, he broke for second again, finally drawing the throw he had hoped for before.

Crawford's bat remained hot through the summer, with his batting average remaining well over .300. Early in August, however, he was slowed by what he called a "lame leg." Playing through the ailment, he remained a constant in Jennings' lineup during yet another tense pennant race. When Detroit dropped seven of nine in early August, Philadelphia passed them for the top spot in the standings. On the 19th, Donovan shut out the White Sox on three hits. That gem started Detroit on a 14-game winning streak that vaulted the Tigers back into first place by Labor Day. After getting ejected in the first game of a doubleheader that holiday, Crawford sat out the second contest. In spite of Sam's absence, Detroit still swept the twin bill at Bennett Park.

The Tigers held a four-game lead over the A's when they opened a series in Philadelphia on September 16. This would be Cobb's first appearance in the City of Brotherly Love since the Baker spiking incident. Given the threatening letters he had received, the city sent 100 policemen to maintain order at Shibe Park. Though a tense atmosphere pervaded the ballpark, the game passed with no violence directed at Cobb. Davy Jones nearly got into a scuffle with A's outfielder Danny Murphy, but officers prevented any punches from being thrown. Philadelphia won the contest 2-1. Mack's boys went on to claim three of four in the series to move to within two games of Detroit in the standings.

The Tigers then headed to Washington, where they split a doubleheader with the Senators. The next day, Crawford bashed two triples, a double, and a single in his team's 8-3 victory. The big cats were uncaged again, winning seven of eight. On September 29, Crawford drilled a three-run first inning homer to kick off what would become a doubleheader sweep at Boston that all but ended the race. When the A's dropped two to Chicago the next day, it became official—Detroit had won its third straight pennant. Just as in the previous two years, the Tigers came through in the final leg of a close race.

Once again, Crawford turned in a magnificent season. He batted .314 with 97 RBI and a league-leading 35 doubles. Despite a sore leg in late summer, he stole 30 bases for the first time in his career. Sam's .452 slugging average was second only to Cobb, who reached an even higher level of brilliance by winning the AL triple crown (.377, 9 HR, 107 RBI). Similar to 1907 and 1908, this one-two punch gave Detroit just enough firepower to hold off its rivals. When reflecting on the 1909 race a few months later, Jennings said "If Cobb or Crawford had been out of the game for a week at a time last season the Tigers probably would have lost the pennant to the Athletics."

October excitement again spread throughout Tigers Nation. Optimism increased in the Motor City at the prospect of avoiding the Cubs juggernaut. But the 110-win Pittsburgh Pirates represented a formidable foe. Howie Camnitz (25-6, 1.62 ERA) and Vic Willis (22-11, 2.24 ERA) led an imposing pitching corps for the NL champs. And Pirate shortstop Honus Wagner was the top offensive player in the Senior Circuit. Crawford later called Wagner the greatest all-around player he ever saw. "He was a wonderful fielder," Sam said, "terrific arm, very quick, all over the place grabbing sure hits and turning them into outs."

As with the previous two World Series, baseball exuberance again permeated Wahoo. Townspeople gathered in front of a bulletin board that displayed the results of game action conveyed via telegraph. As popular as ever in Nebraska and Detroit,

Crawford was even gaining fans in the enemy territory of Pittsburgh. Arriving at the Forbes Field gate before one of the games, he gave two tickets to a couple of boys who could not afford the admission price.

Despite his arsenal of veteran arms, Pirates manager Fred Clarke tabbed rookie Babe Adams (12-3, 1.11 ERA) as his surprise starter for Game 1. Adams relied on curveballs and off-speed pitches, a style known to frustrate the fastball-pounding Tigers. George Mullin, a 29-game winner, took the ball for Detroit. Nearly 30,000 fans, a new World Series record, filled the seats and ringed the playing field at Forbes Field. After a shaky first inning, Adams shut down the Tigers, and Pittsburgh prevailed 4-1. Batting cleanup behind Cobb, Crawford went one for four.

Detroit battered Camnitz, who had been ill with quinsy, to even things up with a 7-2 victory in Game 2. Sam doubled and scored in the contest. For Game 3, the series shifted to Bennett Park. First-inning errors—one of them a wild throw from Crawford—buried the Tigers in a 5-0 hole. Detroit tried to rally late, but fell 8-6. Sam went hitless in five at-bats. The thermometer barely topped freezing the next day for Game 4. Clad in yellow and black Tiger colors, a chilly, yet enthusiastic, Bennett crowd roared its support as Mullin tossed a shutout to even the Series.

Crawford brought the thunder to Forbes Field for Game 5, delivering three hits and a stolen base. In the sixth he doubled home Cobb and then scored the tying run. Two innings later, he blasted a long home run off Babe Adams into the center field bleachers. In chasing this dive, Pirate centerfielder Tommy Leach crashed into the fence, breaking the boards and tumbling over the barrier in a summersault. This solo shot was too little, too late though, as the Pirates battered Tiger starter Ed Summers to prevail 8-4. In Game 6 the next day in Detroit, Crawford's first-inning RBI double and ninth-inning defensive skills at first base helped the Tigers again even the series.

Detroit won the coin toss to secure home-field advantage for the deciding Game 7. More than 17,000 fans crowded into Bennett Park, most of them Tigers fans anxiously awaiting their first World Series championship. Dark clouds hovered above on game day, and a frigid biting wind swept the ballpark. Jennings gave the ball to Donovan, even though the hurler was known to perform better in warmer weather. Wild Bill lived up to his name on this occasion, hitting a batter and walking six in three innings. Though Donovan worked out of trouble to surrender just two runs, Jennings replaced him with Mullin in the fourth. Wabash George unfortunately had nothing left in the tank after pitching three complete games over the previous week. Pirates starter Babe Adams, on the other hand, was sharper than ever, tossing a six-hit shutout. Crawford and Cobb went hitless in the 8-0 rout.

It had been Detroit's best showing in a World Series thus far. The same could be said for Crawford, who batted .250 with four runs scored and three RBI over the seven games. The press, however, labeled his performance another postseason failure. With four extra base hits though, he slugged a robust .464 over the seven games.

Had such awards existed at the time, Babe Adams, with his three wins, would have been named the Series MVP. Wagner would have placed second in the voting with a .333 batting average, six RBI, and six stolen bases. The Flying Dutchman's performance far outshined Cobb, who batted .231 with two stolen bases. For the Peach, Sam, and their teammates, it was a third straight postseason disappointment. But they again received the consolation of another sizeable financial bonus— each Tiger took home $1,274.76 from the losers' pot.

Soon after the dust settled from Game 7, rumblings emerged that Navin was upset with Jennings over his handling of his pitchers against Pittsburgh. A civic group known as the "Citizens of Detroit" was more forgiving, holding a postseason banquet at the Hotel Pontchartrain to celebrate the team's accomplishments. Following the banquet, twelve of the Tigers

(Crawford and Cobb not included) traveled to Havana for a series of games against two top Cuban teams.

Despite his disappointment at again losing a World Series, Navin recognized that a team that annually won pennants was a money maker. He moved quickly to secure the services of one of the major reasons for the Tigers' success. Barely a week after Game 7, the team president summoned Crawford to his office. Their conversation lasted about two minutes, after which Wahoo Sam signed a two-year deal for $5,000 a season.

The results of the final game notwithstanding, it been another good season for Crawford. With ten years' experience, he remained one of the top stars in the majors. He played on one of MLB's best teams, an annual pennant contender, and had a healthy income locked in for at least two more years. He was living his childhood dream.

Chapter 9

The Hardest Hitter in the Game

As a centerpiece on the three-time American League champions, Crawford soon found a way to profit from his celebrity status. Following the season, he became a spokesman for Chalmers-Detroit—an appropriate gig for a star athlete in the Motor City. In January 1910, he and racer Joe Matson demonstrated the features of the company's latest models at Detroit's annual automobile show. A true car enthusiast himself, Crawford proved an effective pitchman for his employer's four-wheeled products.

A couple months later, Sam and his wife and daughter spent a week in Dundee, Nebraska, visiting Ada's parents. Crawford then joined his teammates in St. Louis to head south to San Antonio. This year, the Tiger veterans did not have to report for spring training until March 15, two weeks after the rookies arrived in Texas. Hughie Jennings wanted to work with the youngsters on their own before training began with the entire team.

With Detroit's core players returning, Crawford and his teammates had reason to be hopeful about winning another pennant. Similarly optimistic, Frank Navin had made improvements to Bennett Park for the upcoming season. One of the most notable changes was the addition of new bleachers in left field, which reduced the dimensions of that part of the outfield. As Paul Bruske noted, however, this change would help the visitors more than the home team, since the top two Tiger sluggers were lefty hitters. Crawford and Cobb would still need to launch mammoth blasts to reach the distant right field stands.

A nagging ailment presented troubling news for Sam's 1910 prospects. At some point that spring, he had injured his ankles while sliding. He later admitted that this part of the game had often caused him to hurt himself. Crawford asked to leave training early, but Jennings refused his request. The ankle ailment nonetheless cast doubt on Sam's status for Opening Day.

These concerns, fortunately, proved to be unfounded. Unleashing the fury of his bat, Crawford opened the season by driving in four runs on four hits. Detroit, however, disappointed the 14,000 at Bennett Park by falling in extra innings to the Naps. Though they lost again the next day, the Tigers rebounded to win eight of their next nine. After treading water through most of May, Detroit reeled off 11 straight victories to close within a couple games of first place. It seemed that Tiger fans could indeed look forward to a fourth straight pennant come fall.

Crawford delivered solid production during this stretch. He was batting .292 in late June, while driving in bushels for runs from the cleanup spot. Sportswriters observed that Sam was playing well and displayed "a lot of speed in spite of two bad ankles." While noting the Nebraskan's wheels, *The Detroit Times* supported Jennings' decision to move Crawford to right field for this season so the faster Cobb could play center.

One of the season's highlights for the team came on a road trip to Washington, D.C., where President William Taft attended a game. After the contest, the Tigers passed before the president's private box. Jennings introduced each player as he shook hands with the chief executive. Two years earlier, Taft had defeated Nebraska's William Jennings Bryan to reach the White House. It is unknown if the president knew of the tonsorial connection between one of the players he greeted that day and his recent political adversary.

Another highlight for Sam came in Cleveland in early July. Crawford had long irked Naps officials by driving balls over their right field fence. In the off-season, team secretary Ernest S. Barnard ordered the construction of a 20-foot high wall topped by a 25-foot high screen. Observing this 45-foot-high barrier before his team's home opener, Barnard said, "I guess we've got this Crawford man crossed up now."

In April, when the Tigers had first visited the ballpark that season, Sam paused to examine the new screen. "So that's Barney's dream?" he said. "I'll show him." That day the Detroit slugger drove a ball into the screen about six feet from the top. Three months later, Sam belted a terrific blast off Cy Falkenberg that cleared the screen and disappeared behind a house across the street from the ballpark. Cleveland fans cheered for several minutes after the unprecedented feat.

A late June swoon had dropped Detroit six games off the pace. On July 8 the Tigers opened a crucial four-game road series against the league-leading Athletics. Here, Jennings's boys had an opportunity to narrow the gap in the standings. But the Tigers dropped all four contests at Shibe Park to fall ten games back. Though nearly half the season remained, the Philadelphia massacre dashed Detroit's pennant hopes for 1910. Connie Mack's roster bristled with talent, led by star infielders Eddie Collins and Frank Baker, plus a powerful mound corps that boasted Jack Coombs (31 wins on the season) and future Hall of Famers Chief Bender and Eddie Plank. The A's had too much firepower to be caught. Detroit finished with a respectable 86-68 record, but 18 games out of first.

Crawford's bat cooled a bit over the second half of the season, but he still drove in runs with his timely hitting. His best game of the year came on October 2, when he rapped five hits against St. Louis. Overall, Sam turned in another solid campaign, batting .289 with a league-leading 19 triples and 120 RBI (no other AL player topped 100). Despite the lingering ankle issues, he stole 20 bases. Crawford's productivity batting behind Cobb helped the Peach lead the AL with 106 runs scored.

Speaking of Cobb, the volatile Georgian once again added to the drama and disharmony dogging the Tigers. In August, police officers had to restrain him from charging into the stands to assault an African American fan who had insulted him. That same month, he quarreled with Davy Jones over missed signs. A more significant feud developed when Cobb started riding 22-year-old shortstop Donie Bush. This hazing eventually raised the ire of Crawford, who threatened to slap Ty's face if he kept it up.

Though Cobb let up on Bush, many of his teammates, Sam included, stopped speaking to him. But Crawford still had plenty to say *about* him. Late in the season, Sam told the press that Detroit's failure to win the pennant was the result of management allowing too much freedom to Cobb, who put his personal quest to win the batting title (and the Detroit-Chalmers automobile that went with it) ahead of team goals. This hitting race ended in a controversy that resulted in both Cobb and Napoleon Lajoie being awarded cars. Major League Baseball recognized Cobb as the batting champion for that year, though subsequent stat corrections show that Lajoie had a higher average by the barest of margins. The latter's claim to the title is compromised, however, by the St. Louis Browns allowing him to tally several uncontested bunt hits on the season's final day. Historians and fans have been debating the true winner of the 1910 AL batting title for more than a century.

In explaining Detroit's team failure as "too much Cobb," Crawford said that the Georgian "finally became unbearable" after the club allowed him to do whatever he pleased. Many Tigers fans sided with Wahoo Sam in this dispute. In his first at-bat at Bennett after the interview appeared in the paper, fans vigorously applauded the veteran outfielder. The press picked up on Crawford's Cobb theory as well, though a few writers pointed to Sam's declining batting average as a factor in Detroit's third-place finish.

The news was not all bad for Crawford and the Tigers in the fall of 1910. In late September, word arrived that a mining venture organized by William Yawkey and Frank Navin had struck copper veins in Arizona. The shares that Sam and several teammates had bought for $3 apiece soared to a value of $50.

In November, Crawford joined many of his Tiger teammates on a trip to Havana for a dozen exhibition games against two top Cuban teams. Cobb joined this squad a couple weeks later to play in the final five games on the island. While there, Sam and Ada sent a letter to Navin describing what a great time that they and the other Tigers were having in the warm weather. The barnstorming Detroiters won seven, lost four, and tied one game against the Cuban teams. They won four of five after Cobb's arrival. Playing for the hosts were a few African American players from the states, including John Henry "Pop" Lloyd, a star shortstop considered by many to be Honus Wagner's equal, and Bruce Petway, a strong-armed catcher who thrice gunned down Cobb attempting to steal. With the color barrier imposed by major league owners, this was one of the few opportunities for Sam to compete against black and Latino ballplayers. Crawford batted .360 in the series, while Lloyd led all hitters with a .500 mark.

Like usual, Crawford spent the winter counting the days until the next baseball season. Whispers that he had lost a step with age (he was 30), further fueled his desire to return to the fields of green. He remained active in Detroit's cold weather months shoveling coal into the furnace and snow off the walk. Though he hated mosquitos, he eagerly arrived at the Tigers' new spring training location in Monroe, Louisiana, in early March. Working out and dieting at Hot Springs the month prior, he showed up to camp at a lean 184 pounds.

With his ankle troubles behind him, Sam displayed impressive speed. When Jennings timed his players' sprints to first base, Wahoo dazzled observers by matching the marks of his fastest teammates. Rumors of his age-related decline motivated Crawford to work out with extra vigor. Jennings noticed, remarking "the way the big boy is going at his training this year is a great big element in confirming my belief that the Detroit club is going to have another corking good year."

An unpleasant bit of old business remained, however, with Crawford's ongoing feud with Cobb threatening to disrupt the team's progress in the new season. Jennings, Navin, and team captain George Moriarty all tried to negotiate a peace between the two outfielders, but to no avail. During the spring exhibition games, the non-speaking teammates would not exchange signals while at-bat and let fly balls drop between them in the outfield. Progress occurred when Davy Jones and Donie Bush agreed to bury the hatchet with Cobb. Crawford's grudge lasted a little longer, but at the start of the season he reluctantly shook hands with the Peach. This gesture marked a tenuous truce that did not include verbal communication, though the teammates soon resumed exchanging signals during games.

A sad event tempered the excitement of Opening Day when the baseball world learned of the death of Cleveland pitcher Addie Joss from tubercular meningitis. Just 31 years old (he was born six days before Crawford), Joss had been one of the American League's most dominant pitchers over the previous decade. Crawford sent a message of condolence on behalf of his team to Cleveland. Later that summer, a group of American League players, Sam included, played an all-star game to raise money for Joss's widow and his two children.

Detroit burst out of the gate in 1911 with the hottest start in club history. The team looked unstoppable that spring, winning 21 of its first 23 games. By late May, the Tigers led the league by nine games. It appeared the AL race could be over by the Fourth of July. Though the big cats cooled off in June, they still held first place by five-and-a-half games in mid-July. The pennant still seemed well on its way back to the Motor City.

Crawford's lava hot start played a big role in his team's success. Wahoo opened the season with six hits in his first two games, and his bat continued to sizzle in the following weeks. At the end of April, he was batting over .400. As a compliment to his excellent hitting, Sam stepped up his speed game as well. He stole bases with unprecedented frequency, even sliding headfirst on occasion, and beat out grounders that normally would have been outs. Bruske commented that Crawford was displaying the "rejuvenation of a man who has always been a star in his batting and fielding, and has now added the base-running accomplishment to round himself out."

Defying the critics who labeled him an "old man," Crawford continued his dominance throughout the season. His exploits even attracted attention in the halls of Congress. When the Tigers traveled to Washington, D.C., to play the Senators, Congressman Charles Lobeck convinced his Nebraska colleagues James Latta and Charles Sloan to join him at the ballpark to watch Crawford, whom he had seen play in Wahoo years earlier.

The hits continued to rocket off Sam's bat. When he made solid contact, observers described the sound as a rifle shot. He blasted six multi-hit games in a single week in early summer. By late July, he batted in the .380s. Cobb, meanwhile, assaulted AL pitching with even greater ferocity, hitting well over .400 at this point.

The earlier acrimony between Crawford and the Georgia Peach had subsided, providing no ill-effects on either player's performance. By late season, the teammates were apparently on speaking terms again. During a game in Cleveland in September, Cobb twisted his knee, requiring him to head to bed as soon as the team reached the hotel. *The Detroit Times* reported that Crawford was one of the first teammates to visit Ty's room to check on the ailing star.

Although internal dissension did not hamper Detroit's pennant chances, the Tigers' east coast rivals created plenty of problems. In late July, the Highlanders delivered a gut punch by sweeping four games at Bennett Park. The first-place Tigers still nursed a game-and-a-half lead over Philadelphia near the end of the month. But on a lengthy road trip east, Detroit dropped three of five to the Athletics, four of five at Boston, and three of five in New York. Limping home after this disastrous run, the Tigers trailed Philadelphia by a game-and-a-half. With seven weeks remaining in the season Detroit was still very much in the race, but Jennings' boys could play no better than .500 the rest of the way. This allowed the Athletics to steadily increase their lead, winning the pennant by 13-and-a-half games over second-place Detroit.

Jennings blamed Tiger pitching as the primary reason for his team's late summer slide. The numbers support his claim. Detroit hurlers turned in a 3.73 team ERA, second worst in the American League. The Tigers offense, on the other hand, posted the second highest batting and slugging averages in the league.

Crawford continued his torrid pace all season, finishing with a .378 batting average and a .526 slugging average—both career highs. He drove in 115 runs, stole 37 bases, and rapped 217 hits, third most in the AL. Cobb posted even more phenomenal numbers, batting .420 and slugging an astounding .621 with 248 hits, 127 RBI, and 83 stolen bases. While Detroit's top two offensive weapons enjoyed spectacular seasons, it should be noted that offensive production increased across the board in 1911. Following the introduction of a livelier ball with a new rubber-coated core, drives shot off bats with greater velocity. The batting average for the entire American League in 1911 was .273, a full 30 points higher than the previous season. Runs per game increased from 3.6 to 4.6.

Crawford turned in a solid defensive year as well. His .975 fielding percentage was second highest among outfielders. He recorded 16 assists and 180 putouts, the latter mark trailing Harry Hooper by just one for the lead among right fielders. All told, the new and improved Sam Crawford removed all doubt as to whether he had been slowed by age.

Following the season, Crawford became a theatergoer. In December, he joined several current and past teammates in attending a vaudeville performance by the always entertaining Germany Schaefer. A few days later, Sam visited the Lyceum Theater in Detroit to watch Cobb perform in *The College Widow*, a popular comedy written by George Ade. Wahoo's attendance provides more evidence that a détente had been reached between the two outfielders. In something of a surprise, former Cobb foe Matty McIntyre was among the other ballplayers at the theater that night. Perhaps absence had made Matty's heart grow fonder since he had been sold to the White Sox prior to the 1911 season. After the performance, Cobb's current teammates presented him with a handsome traveling bag to show their appreciation for his amazing season.

It had been a great year for Crawford—arguably his best as a major leaguer. Though his team had faded in the stretch run, he still played for a contender. The next year would be his 10th in a Tiger uniform. Looking forward to smashing more baseballs off more hapless pitchers, Sam signed his 1912 contract for $5,000 in late December.

Coming off his best season statistically thus far, Crawford's baseball abilities and his popularity among Detroiters were never higher. Some observers, however, still seemed to think that ballplayers of his age—early 30s—were fated to decline. Jennings even said that if Sam drank, he would have been out of baseball years ago. "When a man gets into the thirties he finds that it is almost impossible for him to reduce much [weight]," the Tigers skipper said. "If he has been in the habit of drinking and putting on weight in the winter he will soon get slow."

Still avoiding the bottle and unhealthy foods, Crawford again chiseled himself into shape for the upcoming season. During the spring exhibitions, he told reporters that "the ball looks bigger than ever." Even more ominous for American League pitchers, Wahoo was wielding a heavier bat than usual.

The greater heft of Crawford's weaponry was not the only change for the 1912 season. Sam and his teammates now had a new baseball home. Just a few days after the previous campaign had ended, workers razed Bennett Park. In that same location at "The Corner" of Michigan and Trumbull a new concrete and steel edifice arose. Workers completed the modern stadium in time for Opening Day in April. The majestic new baseball plant featured covered stands that extended down both foul lines to the outfield fence. With a reconfigured playing area, home plate no longer faced the sun, but now, unfortunately for Sam, the rays shined directly into right field in late afternoon.

The $300,000 stadium boasted a roomy playing area with outfield dimensions of 340 feet in left, 400 to center, and 365 to right, meaning it would not easily surrender home runs. On the other hand, batters appreciated the green panel in center that provided a favorable backdrop for seeing pitches. The yellow-painted seats could accommodate more than 23,000 fans. A huge scoreboard beyond the left field wall kept those in attendance updated on other games, while a large U.S. flag flapped atop a 125-foot pole standing in deep center. Originally called Navin Field, the stadium would be the home of the Tigers until the end of the twentieth century.

Detroit opened the 1912 season in Cleveland on April 11. After splitting a four-game set against the Indians, the Tigers traveled to Chicago. The team arrived in the Windy City on the 15th as the nation reeled from the news that the British luxury liner *Titanic* had slammed into an iceberg and sunk in the Atlantic Ocean. The Tigers split their two games against the White Sox and then headed to Detroit. A capacity crowd filled Navin Field on April 20 for the Tigers home opener. Cobb stole home in the first inning to tally the first run at Detroit's new ballpark. Crawford ripped three hits, including a double, to help the hosts prevail 6-5 in eleven innings.

The home opener victory was one of the few April highlights for the Tigers, who then lost six of their next seven games. A month into the season Detroit sat mired in sixth place, three games below .500. Crawford struggled as well, batting just .226 during the early weeks of the campaign. There were signs that Wahoo would soon turn things around. His stolen base total was among the league leaders. On May 10, during his first series at newly-opened Fenway Park, he hit what turned out to be a game-winning three-run homer past Harry Hooper in the ninth.

The Detroit Times opined that Sam would soon be hitting his stride again.

The next day, the Tigers traveled to New York looking to pick up some momentum at the expense of the struggling Highlanders. Detroit won three of four in the Big Apple, but it was an off-field incident involving one of the players that made headlines. And of course that player was Ty Cobb.

Throughout the series, a loudmouth fan in an alpaca coat had been continuously riding Cobb. Named Claude Lucker, this man unleashed a flood of taunts that stood out from the normal abuse hurled down from the Hilltop Park stands due to their persistence, vulgarity, and racial slurs. Cobb asked New York team officials to remove Lucker, but to no avail. Between the third and fourth innings of the last game of the series, one of the Tigers—maybe Davy Jones, maybe Crawford, or maybe someone else, sources vary—asked Cobb if he was going to let that loudmouth get away with calling him those names. Throughout his life the Georgia Peach placed a high priority on defending his honor—he would take no more of this insolence.

Cobb darted from the dugout, jumped the railing, and charged up the stairs. He then tore into Lucker with his fists and feet. A nearby fan tried to stop the attack by yelling that Lucker had no hands (he was missing all the fingers on one hand and two fingers on the other). Continuing his assault, Cobb allegedly responded, "I don't care if he has no feet." By the time umpire Silk O'Loughlin and a park policeman pulled Cobb away from his victim, Lucker lay bleeding from repeated punches, kicks, and spike cuts. O'Loughlin ejected Cobb, who received an escort back to the dugout from his teammates. When the Peach later crossed the field to the clubhouse, he received a mix of boos and cheers from the New York fans.

It so happened that Ban Johnson attended this game. The AL president suspended Cobb for an indeterminate number of games and announced he would be levying a fine. Viewing Cobb's actions as justified, the other Tigers rallied to their teammate's defense. After playing their next game in

Philadelphia without Cobb, they sent a telegram to Johnson demanding his reinstatement or they would boycott their next games. As the team leader, Crawford placed his name at the top of this message that concluded with, "If players cannot have protection, we must protect ourselves." When Cobb's suspension remained, the Tigers refused to play their next game—the first players strike in baseball history.

With the game still going on as scheduled, Jennings and his coaches scoured the sandlots of Philadelphia to find college and semipro players to field a team against the Athletics. Not surprisingly, the Mackmen trounced the scrubs 24-2. In the wake of this embarrassment, Johnson threatened to fine each of the Tigers $100 a game if the strike continued. Not wanting his teammates to incur this financial hardship, Cobb urged them to return to the field. The Georgia Peach and Johnson meanwhile reached a compromise settlement. The AL president reduced his suspension to 10 days (six games total) and set his fine at $50. The other Tigers would have to pay $50 each for the game they sat out. Cobb returned to the lineup on May 26 to help Detroit win 6-2 in Chicago.

The Lucker incident demonstrated that by 1912, the Tigers, Sam included, may not have viewed Cobb as a friend, but they accepted him as their teammate. And they would not tolerate an outside party treating him unjustly. The departure of the anti-Cobb leaders Matty McIntyre, Boss Schmidt, and Ed Siever from the Tigers had furthermore helped improve clubhouse harmony by this time.

In contrast to the Lucker incident, Detroit's on-field performance failed to attract many headlines that summer. After briefly poking their heads above .500 in late May, the Tigers dropped nine of eleven in June. They treaded water for the next few weeks, before posting a disastrous 9-19 mark in August. Jennings' crew lost nine of their last ten to finish the 1912 season in a distant sixth place. Pitching once again proved to be a weak spot, with Detroit hurlers recording the second highest ERA in the league.

Though his team struggled, Crawford heated up in the summer months. A four-hit game against the White Sox at Navin Field in late June pushed his average above .300. This mark climbed even higher as the hits continued flying off his bat. In mid-August he homered into the center field bleachers at Hilltop Park to claim the nearly unwinnable box of cigars offered by a neighborhood tobacco store to any hitter who could reach those distant seats. At Navin Field in September, he hit an inside-the-park home run against the eventual pennant-winning Red Sox. That same game also featured an inside-the-park homer from one of Boston's top young stars, Tris Speaker.

Crawford concluded yet another strong campaign by batting .325 and slugging .470. He accumulated 21 triples and topped the 100-RBI mark for the third straight year. Even more impressive, the 32-year-old stole a career-best 41 bases. Cobb again dominated the AL offensive leaderboards by slashing .410/.458/.586 (batting, on base percentage, slugging). Even an attempted mugging in August that left him with a stab wound in his shoulder did not slow down the Peach.

Crawford had again defied the pundits who whispered that he might be losing a step. This ongoing top-level productivity, combined with his team's inability to garner postseason pennant bonuses, convinced him that it was time for a raise. Meeting with Navin in a lengthy conference in early December, Sam expressed his wishes for a higher salary. The bald and bespectacled team president frowned at his ballplayer with a stern countenance. To paraphrase his response, the poker-faced Navin told Crawford he would get no raise and like it.

Not giving up, Sam pointed out that the club planned to move him to first base next season. He argued that the first sack was the most difficult position to play and more susceptible to injury, thus warranting more money. Navin, who also faced a raise request from Cobb, countered by pointing out that the sixth-place Tigers, even with their two superstars, were not drawing enough fans to support their requests. "We won't pay

Cobb and Crawford what they ask," Navin told the press, "simply because we can't."

Crawford responded by stating, "no more pay, no work." With Sam threatening to hold out, trade rumors started circulating. One possible deal had Navin sending his outfielder to the White Sox in exchange for Ed Walsh. The Detroit president quickly squashed this speculation, saying that Sam would be staying with the Tigers. The impasse continued.

A few days after Christmas, Crawford traveled south to New Orleans, where he worked as a representative for a Detroit business called Peerless Weighing Machine Company. With neither Sam nor Navin showing any sign of budging, 1912 ended with the possibility that Wahoo Sam had played his last big league game.

The advent of a new year did not bring the two sides any closer to a resolution. Navin remained firm, stating in early January that "I have told Crawford and [pitcher Jean] Dubuc just how much I can pay them next season, and, on my honor, I will not raise this offer a cent." The Tiger president later added that Sam was already one of the four top-paid outfielders in the American League, and thus should not object to the $5,000 offered by the club. Navin further stated that he was not worried at the prospect of Crawford sitting out all year, pointing out that the team finished in sixth the previous season with the slugger—how much worse could it get without him?

To increase their bargaining power, Crawford, Cobb, Dubuc, and catcher Oscar Stanage joined forces, agreeing that they would not sign unless all their demands were met. The quartet became known as the holdout clique. As the impasse lingered, the press reported that Crawford wanted $7,000 for the 1913 season. Cobb meanwhile demanded $15,000. Navin admitted that Tyrus might be worth that much to him during a pennant-winning season when the club made more money, but not now when the team was in decline. This point also applied to Crawford.

Not backing down, Sam publicly expressed interest in continuing his work selling scales in New Orleans. According to the Peerless company president, Crawford earned more than $1,600 in salary and commissions for three months work. It seemed that if baseball did not work out, scales provided a viable career alternative. At the same time though, Sam prepared for future diamond action. While in New Orleans, he played for a semipro team called the Braquets. He predictably dominated at that level, winning a diamond stickpin as the league's best player.

Jennings undercut his outfielder's cause by stating that Crawford's baseball training indicated that he was not really serious about leaving the game. Sam responded that he just wanted to be ready in case circumstances changed to facilitate his return to baseball. He also hinted that he would not object to a trade to another team.

The day before the Tigers were due to report to New Orleans, Crawford returned to Detroit with his wife and daughter. He told reporters that Peerless had made him a long-term offer to continue working in the scales business. Fellow holdout Cobb provided support by publicly stating that Crawford deserved the raise for which he asked.

Spring training started without Sam, but the Tigers made no concessions. Stanage broke ranks and signed for no pay increase. Crawford then dropped his demand to $6,000, but with no effect. Concerned about the impact that granting raises would have on salaries across the board, Ban Johnson and other AL owners encouraged Navin to remain firm, which he did. With the very real prospect that he would soon be out of Major League Baseball, Sam blinked. On March 20, he signed his contract for $5,000, not a penny more than he had received each of the previous three seasons. Frustrated at his defeat, Crawford blasted Ban Johnson in the press. Sam criticized the AL president for limiting the income options of ballplayers, and charged that Johnson "had things so fixed that he can railroad any player he does not like into the minor league...." A member of the recently-formed Base Ball Players' Fraternity, Crawford suggested that the union would soon make its voice heard.

Following Sam's return to the fold, a Tigers official proclaimed that no holdout player ever receives an increase. Dubuc caved as well, but Cobb's holdout continued. The volatile star missed the first week of the season. And then another. With the Georgia members of Congress suggesting an investigation of baseball's antitrust exemption, Navin finally offered him a contract for $12,000, a $3,000 increase from the previous season. Cobb signed, though with time missed the amount he would be paid for 1913 was $11,332.55. Still more than twice the amount that Crawford received.

On one hand, Sam was still earning a comfortable living well above the national average. Steelworkers and other manufacturing professions made less than $1,000 annually at this time. The average salary for a decent, established ballplayer hovered around $3,000. Compared to other top veteran stars in the game, however, it seemed that Crawford was a bit underpaid. Hal Chase, a good defensive first baseman but not Sam's equal with the bat, drew $6,000 from the Cubs. Walter Johnson, the top AL pitcher, signed for $7,000 in 1913. Christy Mathewson, the best NL hurler, garnered $8,000.

Though Navin was able to get his band back together, the Tigers stumbled out of the gate. A nine-game skid early in the season erased the hopes of all but the most optimistic Detroit rooters that the 1913 squad would contend for the pennant. *Sporting Life* reported that the other American League teams were using the Tigers as a football. By early July, Detroit had sunk 20 games below .500 to wage a not-so-spirited battle with St. Louis for sixth place.

In the wake of his spring holdout battle, Crawford did not start strong. He batted .260 through the first month of the season. Some scribes assigned blame for Detroit's spring decline on Wahoo's lack of hitting. In early May, Jennings shifted him to first base. Feeling that he was not allowed adequate time to prepare for that position, Sam expressed his disappointment with the move. The Tiger skipper soon moved Wahoo back to the outfield. Crawford played a total of 13 games at first base in 1913. The usually tightfisted Navin surprisingly paid him an extra $750 for these few games at the first sack. This bonus was likely a way for ownership to ease the discontent of one of its star players, while still publicly maintaining that the team did not concede any money during the holdout.

Though his team remained abysmal, Crawford started hitting as the temperature increased. By the end of May, his average had climbed to .275. By mid-July, he had broken into the .300 ranks. Along the way, Wahoo's mighty bat provided plenty of highlights. On June 11, he hit a grand slam in Washington. A couple weeks later, he hit a single, double, triple, and home run over the two games of a doubleheader against Cleveland. On July 14, he destroyed A's pitching with four hits and five RBI, including a game-winning ninth-inning triple. On August 2 in Washington, Crawford drilled three hits off Walter Johnson at a game attended by President Woodrow Wilson.

Though both Crawford and Cobb hit like usual in 1913, Jennings decided to reverse their order in the lineup. So Sam now batted third, and the Peach batted cleanup. This meant the speedier Cobb often found himself behind Crawford on the bases and was thus unable to fully display his running talents. And likewise, Sam's clutch-hitting bat had fewer opportunities to drive in runs. In August, Paul Bruske called out the Detroit skipper for this unusual strategy:

> The writer has always maintained that Manager Jennings' present batting order places Ty where his talents are by no means available to their maximum extent.... When Detroit was winning pennants, Ty batted in the third position, and Crawford fourth. Each man was where he belonged. Ty could bunt or hit and run, or slug. Cobb on first and Crawford at bat was a proposition fitted to make any pitcher quail.... Now, when both hit together, it still takes a drive or two to get a run around for Crawford, though more than fairly fast for a big man, is nevertheless an obstacle to any sensational stunts which Ty might try.

Jennings' questionable lineup juggling likely did not have much impact on the Tigers season. With a pitching staff that posted the league's worst ERA, Detroit was not going to contend regardless of where Crawford and Cobb batted in the order. As it was, the team finished in sixth place for the second consecutive year.

Sam Crawford again contributed a typical Sam Crawford year. Playing in all 153 of his team's games, he batted .317 with a league-leading 23 triples. His 298 total bases led the AL, and his .489 slugging was fifth-best. Without Cobb batting ahead of him, Sam's RBI total dropped to 83. Only Frank Baker topped Crawford's nine home runs in the Junior Circuit.

Though the Tigers were not World Series bound, Sam still had plenty of baseball left to play in 1913. White Sox owner Charlie Comiskey and Giants manager John McGraw had organized a grand tour to promote baseball around the world. Though the two teams that would play each other retained their Chicago and New York names, star players from other clubs filled out the rosters. The only Tiger to make the trip, Crawford became a member of the White Sox for this set of global exhibition games. The players would wear red, white, and blue stockings and U.S. flags on their uniform sleeves.

The White Sox and Giants kicked off their World Tour with a game in Cincinnati on October 18. From there, the two teams played each other in Chicago; Ottumwa, Iowa; Sioux City, Iowa; Blue Rapids, Kansas; and St. Joseph, Missouri, where Sam tagged Christy Mathewson for four hits. Years later, the legendary Giants hurler said Crawford was the greatest batter he ever faced. On November 5, the tourists played in El Paso, where an airplane was driven onto the field to further entertain the crowd. Sam climbed in the plane (flying machines had been in existence for only a decade) and went for a ride with the pilot. Unphased by his aerial sojourn, Sam returned to earth to complete another four-hit game.

The tourists next headed west through Arizona and California. The teams then worked their way up the West Coast to Portland, where the White Sox prevailed 2-0. Since rain washed out the next day's game in Seattle, the U.S. leg of the tour finished with each team winning 15 games. It had been a profitable venture thus far, drawing large crowds and netting $97,240. Each player received back the $300 deposit he had paid to participate in the tour, plus an additional gift of $250. Comiskey, McGraw, and promoter Jimmy "Nixie" Callahan split all remaining profits, which by the end of the tour would turn out to be substantial.

On November 20, the tourists boarded the *Empress of Japan* and departed from Victoria, British Columbia. Several players' wives, including Ada, were among the 67 people that comprised the baseball party. The ship would sail across the Pacific, bound for Japan, the first overseas stop on the World Tour.

While crossing the Pacific, the *Empress* encountered rough waters and eventually crossed paths with a typhoon that rocked the vessel with 60-foot waves. Crawford and several other players got seasick. Stokers worked knee-deep in water that had poured into the ship's coal bunkers. With the wet coal allowing for only three functioning boilers, the vessel plodded along. After nearly two weeks on the ocean, the travelers delighted at the sight of the Japanese coast.

The Giants and White Sox played before enthusiastic crowds in Tokyo. After their Japan games, the tourists traveled to Hong Kong, Manilla, and Australia. Playing in Brisbane and Sydney in January when it was summer "down under," Crawford missed seeing snow. The teams moved on to Ceylon and then to Egypt, where they played two games in Cairo in early February. Ever the camera enthusiast, Crawford documented his global journey with many pictures, including an impressive shot of the pyramids.

The tourists next sailed to Italy, where they played in Naples and met Pope Pius X in Rome. In a private audience at the Vatican, the pontiff pronounced a blessing on the players, endorsing athletic sports "for the strengthening of the body" and the practice of religion to "strengthen the soul." From Italy, the teams went to Nice and Paris in France.

After finishing their contests in mainland Europe, the tourists crossed the Channel to play in England. On February 26 at Stamford Bridge, the famous Chelsea football (soccer) stadium in London, 20,000 spectators, including King George V, watched the White Sox defeat the Giants in 11 innings. Crawford provided one of the game's top highlights when he belted a two-run homer in the 10th to tie the game. As the king applauded heartily, Sam doffed his cap to the royal party. "If I live to be 100, I will never forget my sensations as I trotted around those bases and then looked up at the home plate to King George applauding me," Sam said. "I would not have missed this day if it had cost me everything I own to get here." *The London Daily Mail* told its readers that Crawford was "reputed to be the best batsman in the United States."

A couple days after the London game, the tourists traveled to Liverpool. There, they boarded the *Lusitania* for the voyage back home across the Atlantic. The "Tour to End All Tours" had been a financial and public relations success. McGraw summed it up by stating, "The most notable thing to me about the whole trip was the expression of national good feeling at all points we visited." For Crawford and the other players, the tour provided the opportunity of a lifetime. They saw the world on Comiskey's dime. It is a good thing the tour happened when it did. Only five months after it ended in March 1914, World War I broke out in Europe. The following year, a German U-boat sent the *Lusitania* to the bottom of the ocean, killing more than 1,000 passengers.

Among the touring players, Jim Thorpe drew the greatest attention at stops around the world. The Giants outfielder had become a global celebrity in 1912 after winning many track events and two gold medals at the Olympics. Many considered the Native American multisport star to be the greatest athlete in the world. Baseball, however, proved to be a challenge for him. Though impressed with Thorpe's speed, Crawford observed that he lacked fielding skills, hitting skills, and "that baseball instinct that is so necessary for a big league player." In the few dozen games Thorpe played for the Giants in 1913 and 1914, he failed to bat .200. He fared better a few years later, finishing his baseball career in 1919 with a lifetime .252 batting average.

The tourists arrived in New York on a chilly, misty morning on March 6. An enthusiastic crowd greeted them at the harbor. To celebrate the tour and its participants, a great banquet with 600 guests was held at the Biltmore Hotel. After this feast, Sam and Ada returned to Detroit and the home they had not seen in five months. They soon hit the road again, traveling to Omaha to visit Ada's parents for a few days. And then Sam had to report to Gulfport, Mississippi, for spring training. While in Nebraska, Crawford told a reporter that he had enjoyed the tour that was "full of thrills," but he was tired of traveling and glad to be back in the states.

While Crawford and the tourists were overseas, baseball drama had escalated in America. A new circuit called the Federal League emerged to challenge the established major leagues. Like Ban Johnson 13 years earlier, the outlaws declared war and started making offers to star players. One of their top targets was Crawford. As the tourists took in the sights of the Middle East and Europe, U.S. newspapers speculated on how the baseball war would impact big league rosters.

Even before the tourists had returned to the states, Federal League president James Gilmore sent wireless messages to Sam urging him not to sign with Detroit until he had seen their offer. Brooklyn's club in the new league emerged as the leading suitor for Crawford's services. The Tip-Tops were reportedly willing to pay $10,000 or even $12,000 to reel in Wahoo. Just a year after his failed holdout, Sam indicated that he might be willing to go with the highest bidder. He followed this up with two words: "money talks."

League executives on both sides eagerly awaited the return of the *Lusitania* to secure player signatures on contracts. Among the frenzied crowd at the dock were Ban Johnson and several MLB team presidents. A Federal League official allegedly shoved his way past a group of women to reach Crawford at the end of the gangplank. Offended by this ungallant behavior, Sam reportedly pushed the man against an iron railing and said, "Don't you talk to me, you rowdy bum!" While those were almost certainly not his exact words, the incident cast the new league in an unfavorable light for Sam. He already had some doubts about how the outlaw league would impact the national game. Spurning Federal League envoys, he met with Navin and signed a four-year deal that would pay him $7,500 annually through 1917.

While Sam gained a $2,500 increase over his previous year's salary, he did seem to leave money on the table. Did he commit a blunder by quickly accepting Navin's offer? Actually, no. Though the Federal League would have yielded at least $10,000 for 1914, the new circuit lost the baseball war and survived only two seasons. After the Federals went out of business in 1915, Sam would have had to return to MLB hat in hand at a much lower salary than his multi-year deal with Navin guaranteed for 1916 and 1917. By staying with Detroit and Organized Baseball, he backed the right horse.

Noting that Crawford played baseball and traveled the world through the off-season, some reporters wondered if the lack of a break from ballplaying would adversely impact the veteran's performance in the upcoming season. Sam assured them that it would not, explaining that the infrequent games on the tour were not high-pressure contests. His prediction turned out to be correct. Knocking the cover off the ball through the first month of the 1914 season, his batting average topped .400 in early May. This explosive production helped propel Detroit into first place.

Though Crawford's bat cooled a bit in the following weeks, he still led the American League with a .348 mark in early June. Back to the cleanup spot behind Cobb, Sam produced soaring RBI totals as well. Crawford and the Tigers further benefited from the emergence of left fielder Bobby Veach, a young slugger who provided a solid bat in the fifth spot in the order.

Newly acquired southpaw Harry Coveleski led an improved pitching corps that kept Detroit in the thick of the pennant race.

In mid-July the Tigers occupied second place, just a couple games behind Philadelphia. On the 16th of that month, Crawford drove in a run to help his team win 5-2 at Fenway Park. Taking the loss for Boston was a 19-year-old southpaw making just his second start in the majors. The kid likely did not make much of an impression on Sam, but he and the rest of the baseball world would soon learn a whole lot more about Babe Ruth.

Along with Crawford's bat, Ty Cobb's production helped fuel Detroit's early summer success. Unfortunately, the other side of Ty Cobb also came into play this season. In late June, his wife got into an argument with a Detroit grocer. Upon later learning of this, Cobb charged into the store with a revolver to demand an apology for his wife. The proprietor quickly grabbed a phone and obliged, seemingly diffusing the matter. But then a butcher at the store brandished a meat cleaver and ordered Cobb to leave. The two men put down their weapons and stepped outside to settle the issue with their fists. Though Cobb got the upper hand in the fight, he soon found himself in a paddy wagon. Even worse for the Tigers, the Georgia Peach had fractured his thumb while pounding his adversary's head. He would miss seven weeks, during which Detroit went 17-25. By the time Cobb returned to the starting lineup, the Tigers had dropped out of the pennant race.

Detroit finished the 1914 season in fourth place with a 80-73 record. Despite a disappointing second half, there were reasons for optimism in the Motor City. Coveleski (22 wins) and Hooks Dauss (18 wins) had replaced Mullin and Donovan as a formidable one-two punch at the top of Jennings' rotation. Veach and rookie first baseman George Burns displayed skill with the bat, and Cobb, after his return, won yet another batting title. A promising young outfielder named Harry Heilmann also appeared in a few dozen games with the Tigers that summer.

Crawford remained a bright spot for Detroit. He batted .317, stole 25 bases, and paced the AL with 104 RBI. His 26 triples tied Joe Jackson's American League record, a mark that still stands today. Displaying a more patient batting eye, Crawford drew a career-high 69 walks to boost his OBP to .388. Despite setting a record by playing 250 games the previous year (New Orleans, MLB season, World Tour), Sam did not miss a single game for the second consecutive season. Wahoo's stellar campaign netted him a second-place finish behind Eddie Collins for the AL Chalmers Award—the Deadball Era's version of the MVP. Notably, Crawford posted a higher WAR than Cobb in 1914. Had it existed at the time, that statistic would have bolstered the arguments of the sizeable minority of Detroit fans and sportswriters who argued that Sam was more valuable to the team than the Peach.

By the time the calendar flipped to 1915, Crawford had logged 15 full seasons in Major League Baseball. Soon to turn 35 years old, he had become one of baseball's venerated veterans. Many former teammates who had started their careers around the same time as Sam, like Jimmy Barrett, Noodles Hahn, and Matty McIntyre, were out of the game. The previous April tuberculosis had claimed the life of Rube Waddell, who was just 37.

Articles during the offseason noted Crawford's career accomplishments. With more than 2,650 hits, the milestone of 3,000—a mark thus far exceeded by only three players (Wagner, Lajoie, Anson)—appeared well within reach. Motivated to join their ranks, Sam declared that he would attain that record "or bust in the attempt." Having averaged 188 hits the previous two seasons, it seemed likely that, barring injury, Crawford would achieve the celebrated mark by the end of the 1916 season. With 91 career home runs, Sam also had a good shot at reaching the rarified air of 100 round-trippers.

In the spring of 1915, the press marveled at Sam's durability, longevity, and conditioning. *Sporting Life* noted that he had not missed an inning of baseball over the previous two seasons. "Sam takes better care of himself than any other player in base ball," declared Detroit trainer Harry Tuthill, "probably better care of himself than any other man in the country." The trainer explained that Crawford begins conditioning for the new season just after the beginning of the year. Noting that Sam avoided pastries, alcohol, and cigarettes, while following a regular diet and lifestyle, Tuthill predicted that Wahoo would play at a high level in the majors for at least five more years.

Following a late February visit to Omaha with Ada and Virginia, Sam reported to spring training in Gulfport. Though he did not play baseball over the winter months as he had done in previous off-seasons, he had found another activity to help him stay in shape. "Most of my recent slugging has been aimed at a little white ball out at the golf club,' Crawford explained. "I can hit it now, but I can't get it to go straight yet. But golf is a great game, and I am going to learn it, and learn it right."

Embracing his "respected team elder" status, Sam took on a more active teaching role at spring training. He spent as much time instructing the recruits as he did playing on the field. *The Detroit Times* reported, "Although it is not required of him, he is always giving suggestions about the proper use of the sliding pit, the correct way to swing a bat and a thousand and one little things that compel the rookies to admit that 'Wahoo Sam' is a regular fellow." The veteran from Nebraska also maintained his status as a master of Crokinole, a tabletop game played with a round board and small disks.

The Tigers broke out to another hot start, winning 18 of their first 25 games. Hitting on all cylinders, the team continued to pile up the Ws into the summer. After playing an exhibition game on June 25 in Grand Rapids, where the locals celebrated "Sam Crawford Day," Detroit won nine of its next 12 contests. Near the end of the month, the Tigers climbed within a game of league-leading Boston.

Cobb, Veach, and Crawford were all smoking the ball. Sam was hitting .325 at the midpoint of the season and battling teammate Veach for the league lead in RBI. With Dauss, Coveleski, and Dubuc taking care of business on the mound, Tigers fans stirred with excitement at the prospect of a pennant.

In mid-August, Jennings' boys won nine in a row to claim a half-game lead over Boston with a 73-39 record.

On August 24, these top two contenders opened a crucial three-game series at Navin Field. Boston took the first game behind the superb pitching of Ernie Shore. The second contest was tied 1-1 after 12 innings. The Red Sox then scored in the top of the 13th. With two outs in the bottom of the frame, Cobb doubled to put the tying run on second. Representing Detroit's last hope, Crawford stepped to the plate. He faced one of the toughest southpaws in baseball, Dutch Leonard, who a year earlier had set a single-season record with a 0.96 ERA. Undaunted, Sam smashed a terrific blast to deep center field. The drive would easily score Cobb and likely place Wahoo on third. Except that Tris Speaker "raced nearly into the next county" to make the catch and end the game. Detroit rebounded from that disappointment to claim the series finale.

The Tigers played strong baseball during the stretch drive. After winning six of seven in mid-September, they headed to Boston just two games out of first. The next four games at Fenway would determine the pennant. Dauss pitched Detroit to victory in the first game. During this contest, Cobb threw his bat at Boston pitcher Carl Mays, who had buzzed the Tiger outfielder with inside fastballs. After Cobb caught the last out of the game, Red Sox fans stormed the field. The defiant Georgia Peach walked slowly toward the rowdy mob before police officers and bat-wielding Tiger teammates cleared a path through the crowd for him.

In the three games that followed at Fenway, there were no more near riots. But there were also no more Detroit victories. By taking three of four, the Red Sox built a four-game lead in the standings that all but ended the pennant race. Fighting to the end, the Tigers won nine of their last twelve to tally 100 wins for the first time in franchise history. But they finished two-and-a-half games behind Boston. It was a heart-breaking result for the team, its manager, and their fans.

Crawford batted one for 16 during those four crucial September games at Fenway. That performance continued a larger slump that he had fallen into that month. Desperate to revive the slugger, Tuthill came up with an unusual diagnosis. "Crawford has gone stale simply because he hasn't any bad habits," he said. "And his staleness has affected his batting ability. I have instructed Sam to take a glass or two of beer after each game and thus make an effort to regain form." Tuthill elaborated that because Crawford did nothing worse than go to a moving-picture show, he was more susceptible to feel the strain of a long season. Beer was thus the recommended solution.

The suds therapy did not work and Crawford's average dropped below .300 by the end of the season. He had still completed an impressive campaign, leading the AL with 19 triples, finishing second with 183 hits, and tying with Veach for the RBI lead with 112. His 35-year-old legs carried him to 24 stolen bases. But Sam's batting had faded during the final weeks of a tight pennant race.

After battling for so long, to fall just short of the flag was a tough blow for Tigers Nation. Few felt worse than Jennings, who called the second-place finish "my biggest disappointment in Detroit." He would remember these sour feelings, and those he deemed responsible for them, the following spring.

A couple months into the off-season, rumors surfaced of a proposed trade that would have sent Crawford to the St. Louis Browns in exchange for a rookie first baseman named George Sisler. It would have been better for both Sam and the Tigers had that deal gone through.

Chapter 10

End of the Road in the Motor City

Though he had driven in 100-plus runs for the fifth time in six years, Crawford viewed his previous season's output with disappointment. Most irksome was his batting average, the overvalued metric of a batter's performance. Sam's 1915 mark ended a string of four straight .300 seasons. "One hit or, at most, two, would have altered all that ..." he said. "A few points difference, of course, may not mean much to anybody, but .300 sounds a lot better than .297." He actually batted .299, but the point remained the same.

In any event, 1915 was in the past. Crawford had plenty of reasons to look forward to the upcoming season. Having just led the league in triples for the sixth time, he remained one of the top power hitters in the game. His team was again a contender for the league title, making another trip to the World Series a real possibility. And he needed only 149 more hits to reach the celebrated 3,000 mark. Honus Wagner and Napoleon Lajoie had recently crossed the threshold, and Sam wanted to join that exclusive club. Given that he had tallied 183 hits each of the previous two seasons, Wahoo's prospects were looking favorable for 1916. *Baseball Magazine* added to this optimism by featuring Crawford on the cover of its February edition that year. This issue included several photos of Sam, a 14-page biographical profile, and an article that he himself wrote titled, "What I Think About Baseball."

Injury or benching posed the only major threats to Crawford reaching his career hit goal. The former is always a possibility, but Sam remained one of the best conditioned athletes in the game. Few players seemed more likely to stay healthy and in the lineup. Given his long rapport with Hughie Jennings, a prolonged benching also seemed out of the question. The Detroit skipper had recently penned a letter to *Baseball Magazine* praising Crawford:

> He is always ready and willing to give the best he has for his Team, and his record as a player and a man will stand beside that of the greatest men of the game. He has enjoyed success and rightly deserves it. He has enjoyed remarkable popularity all around the circuit.... He has always been a high class, intelligent player, has the respect of his fellow players, and his ability is feared by his opponents.

American League president Ban Johnson also held a high opinion of Crawford. When the baseball powers that be debated adding a player representative to the National Commission, Johnson nominated Sam as an ideal candidate. Johnson said that the Detroit outfielder "is not known as a trouble-maker, is not trying to dabble in a lot of things at once, is loyal to his employer, has the respect of his colleagues, and is admired by the whole athletic world." Crawford's rebuff of Federal League advances two years earlier had apparently garnered favor with the AL president.

Fellow Commission member Garry Herrmann, however, did not share Johnson's enthusiasm for Crawford. Still smarting over losing the player to Detroit 13 years earlier, the Reds president called him one of the game's most notorious contract jumpers. Herrmann vetoed Sam's nomination, and the whole idea of adding a player representative to the National Commission soon evaporated.

Crawford remained an active member of the Base Ball Players' Fraternity. Sam himself usually refrained from public comment about labor issues, though during his early years he did complain about not receiving a copy of his contract. With the demise of the Federal League after the 1915 season, major league owners moved to cut salaries again. Having signed a multi-year deal while the baseball war still raged to preserve his salary at $7,500 through 1917, Crawford was immune to this round of belt-tightening. He had learned from his mistake of signing a one-year contract during the previous war.

Because a hurricane had destroyed their regular hotel in Gulfport, the Tigers shifted the location of their 1916 spring training site to Waxahachie, Texas. Crawford reported on March 17, a few days after the other players—except for Cobb, who showed up even later. *Detroit Free Press* scribe Joe S. Jackson noted that Sam looked good, like usual, and did not need much preparation for the upcoming season. Crawford hit well during his team's tune-up games against the New York Giants. He appeared ready to deliver another productive campaign.

Batting fifth behind Cobb and Veach in the order, Crawford rapped hits in five of his team's first six games. After playing the sixth game of the year, a 3-1 win at Cleveland, Sam extended his major-league record of consecutive games played to 472. Unfortunately, a heavy cold and fever, contracted in the poor weather during the trip north from Texas, ended Sam's streak. Having not missed a game since the end of the 1912 season, Wahoo was the Cal Ripken Jr. of his day. But Crawford's more modest iron man record (Ripken's streak reached 2,632 games) would last only two years before it was broken by Eddie Collins.

Sam's illness, which *Sporting Life* called the grippe (aka the flu), settled in his chest and sidelined him for nearly two weeks before he made a pinch-hitting appearance on April 29. The next day, Jennings put Crawford back in right field. The lengthy ailment had taken its toll, however, and the hits came slowly for the weakened slugger. Jennings more frequently gave him days off or used him as a pinch hitter.

Crawford's bat slowly warmed through the first half of May, and his average climbed to .279. Jennings then made the startling pronouncement that Sam's days as a starter were over. With the emergence of 21-year-old Harry Heilmann, the skipper decided to play the younger man alongside Cobb and Veach as the Tigers' everyday outfielders. Jennings explained he made this move not because of Crawford's hitting, but because his speed and fielding had declined. Hughie then added:

> If Sam had taken my advice, he would still be a regular. Two years ago I noticed that Sam was slowing up and I wanted him to take up first base.... You would not notice that Sam was slow around first base. For that matter he is just as fast now as most first basemen. He can cover ground and make the short jumps, but when it comes to getting over distance in the outfield the legs are no longer able to carry him.

In late May, Jennings again wanted Crawford to move to first base for the rest of the 1916 season. Failing to read the handwriting on the wall, Sam resisted his skipper's plan. As Detroit's longest-tenured veteran, he felt that he should not be forced back to the infield to play a position for which he had not prepared. He furthermore disliked first base because errors made there incurred jeers from the stands and critical press comments that left him rattled and disgusted. Jennings, for his part, was disgusted by his player's resistance to his plan. Add in Crawford's slump during the previous season's stretch run, plus Heilmann's hot bat, and the 36-year-old veteran became expendable.

Jennings' move was not popular with the many Tigers fans who continued to vigorously cheer Crawford before his rare at-bats at Navin Field. *Baseball Magazine* ran an editorial questioning the benching of one of "the hardest-hitting batters on the circuits." Sam himself also considered his benching unjust. He believed his bat was still potent and had earned him a spot in the starting lineup. But hurting the slugger's case was another illness—a cold that settled in his back in early June. The pain from this lumbago grew so severe that Crawford could not even put on a uniform without assistance. The slugger acknowledged, "I am not in good shape yet, and consequently am not able to show my best work."

Aside from a few pinch-hitting appearances and a couple starts at first, Crawford sat out nearly the entire month of June. In early July, Cobb drew a suspension after throwing his bat into some empty stands at Comiskey Park. The Georgia Peach's absence earned Sam three games in right field, during which he rapped five hits, including two doubles. Despite this offensive flurry, Crawford returned to his sporadic pinch-hitting role for the next three weeks.

That summer Detroit again found itself in a tight pennant race. By late July, the Tigers trailed league-leading Boston by only a couple games. With Heilmann's bat cooling by mid-summer, Jennings looked for more offense to keep pace with the Red Sox. He soon found himself writing Crawford's name on the lineup card more frequently. Wahoo would reclaim his right field position for the final two months of the season.

On July 27, Crawford went three for three with a triple to help the Tigers beat Washington at Navin Field. It was his 300th career triple—a mark reached by no other big leaguer before or since. In the following weeks Crawford continued to deliver the offensive goods, raising his average to .313 by mid-August. His hot bat helped Detroit hit the accelerator during the stretch run. On September 17, the Tigers pulled out a ten-inning victory over Philadelphia. With 18 wins in their last 22 games, Jennings' boys had edged ahead of Boston into first place.

After dropping the next game to Philly, Detroit fell into a tie for the top spot in the league. That was the situation when the Red Sox came to town on the 19th for a three-game series at Navin Field that held major pennant implications. Excitement rippled through Tigers Nation at the prospect of returning to the World Series after a seven-year absence. The three weekday games drew 40,000 Detroiters to the ballpark to observe the climactic battles.

Boston submariner Carl Mays shut down the home team in the opener to deliver a 3-1 Red Sox victory. The visitors again prevailed the next day when pinch hitter Olaf Henriksen (a .202 hitter on the year) delivered a two-out single in the eighth to drive home the game-winning run. Boston then won the finale 10-2 behind a seven-hitter by Babe Ruth. Reminiscent of the previous September, the Red Sox sweep dashed Detroit's pennant hopes. Crawford batted .500 over the three games but committed a two-base error that helped Boston grab an early lead in the third game.

Not counting the one month he played for Cincinnati in 1899, Sam's 322 at-bats were his lowest season total as a major leaguer. He nonetheless showed that he could still wield a potent stick by batting .286 with a .401 slugging average. Despite starting in little more than half his team's games, Crawford placed seventh in the league with 13 triples. And he stole 10 bases, not bad for a player who was benched for being old and slow.

On the downside, Sam had in fact lost a step in the outfield. Sportswriters made comments about his lack of agility at tracking fly balls. In noting that Crawford recorded only 85 putouts during his 79 games in the outfield, *Sporting Life* remarked: "They must have been falling all around the old boy, game after game, and it can now be easily seen why Jennings set Sam on the bench."

Not everyone concurred about the decline of Wahoo Sam though. Joe S. Jackson thought he looked good enough to return to right field in 1917. Many Tiger fans felt the same way, spawning a postseason debate over whether Crawford's benching had cost the Tigers the pennant. Sportswriter William A. Phelon believed the answer to this question was yes. In evaluating why Detroit did not surge to the front of the pack early in the 1916 season, he wrote, "I'm now convinced that the answer is the absence of the Cobb-Crawford combination."

Despite spending nearly half of the season on the bench, Wahoo Sam remained one of the most popular Tigers.

Crawford's favorable standing with Detroiters convinced Wayne County Democratic Party leaders to recruit him to run for sheriff. After considering the opportunity Sam declined, expressing his preference to continue playing ball.

But questions now loomed over whether Crawford would have that opportunity. Yes, Detroit fans wanted him back on the field, but they were not the ones who would make that decision. With the talented Heilmann having gained another year of experience, could Sam convince Jennings that he still deserved to play right field? The veteran slugger thought he could. Without being hampered by the illnesses that had slowed him the previous campaign, Crawford believed his arm and legs would carry him to a successful season in 1917. He planned to head south in January to get an early start preparing for spring training.

A potential baseball strike grabbed headlines over the winter months. This issue arose when the Base Ball Players' Fraternity headed by David Fultz attempted to improve conditions for minor leaguers. Full pay for injured players and paid travel expenses to spring training were among the concessions that Fultz wanted. As a vice president in the Fraternity, Crawford was asked his viewpoint on the potential walkout. While expressing his support for Fultz, Sam remained noncommittal about whether he would actually lay down his glove and join the picket line on behalf of minor leaguers.

The National Commission and the owners took a hard line and rejected the Fraternity's demands. Fultz mobilized his troops for a strike, getting more than 600 players to sign a pledge to sit out the upcoming season. Adding to this threat was a report that the Fraternity had applied for a charter in Samuel Gompers's American Federation of Labor. But this proposed affiliation soon fell through and many players disregarded their pledges and signed contracts for the 1917 season. In the face of threats from the baseball establishment, few major leaguers wanted to risk their careers to advance the interests of their minor league brethren. The strike threat dissipated, and the defanged Fraternity faded away.

The status of the upcoming season was assured, but Crawford did not know how much of a part of it he would be. Sportswriters that spring reminded their readers of his declining outfield skills during the previous campaign. Harold Wilcox wrote that unless fly balls landed in Sam's pocket, they went for doubles or triples. He suggested that opposing batters would intentionally try to hit the ball into right to capitalize on Crawford's lack of speed. Wilcox also criticized Sam's lack of hustle on the basepaths, arguing that he had missed several infield hits because he did not run out grounders. Jennings seemed to agree with these assessments. Speaking to reporters at Waxahachie, he talked up 24-year-old rookie George Harper as a worthy successor to Sam.

Rejecting the negative assessments, Crawford worked hard at spring training to retain his spot in the starting lineup. He told reporters that his arm was stronger than it had been in a long time. He explained his low putout total the previous season by asserting that "a fellow can't get them if they aren't hit his way." Wilcox did not buy this defense, maintaining that Crawford made a mistake by refusing Jennings' request to play first base in 1916. The Detroit scribe and others viewed a shift to the first sack as the only way Sam could prolong his career. Thinking otherwise, Wahoo stuck to his guns to remain in right field.

Crawford's bat showed plenty of life that spring, knocking out four hits in a game against Fort Worth. He also hit well in the exhibition games against the New York Giants, though his fielding errors did not help his cause. The headlines soon shifted to Cobb, who engaged in another high-profile brawl. After enduring repeated taunts from Buck Herzog, Cobb spiked the Giants infielder during a steal attempt. Following a brief scuffle, the two agreed to settle their differences in a hotel room that evening. Cobb prevailed in that encounter, cutting Herzog's face and dislodging a couple teeth. After Giants manager John McGraw criticized Cobb's behavior, the Georgian declared he would not play against New York again that spring. Not wanting his star outfielder to get injured in a brawl, Jennings agreed to Cobb's request to work out with the Reds in Cincinnati.

On April 6, 1917, the United States declared war on Germany and entered World War I. While the global conflict would eventually impact baseball, the pending season would go on as scheduled. Jennings at this time declared he would not ask for waivers on Crawford. That answered the question of who Sam would be playing for in 1917, but how often he would play remained in doubt. The fact that Jennings had been considering waivers did not bode well for Wahoo's chances of cracking the Tigers starting lineup.

Sure enough, when Detroit opened its season at Navin Field on April 11, Crawford sat on the bench. Cobb, Veach, and Heilmann covered the Tigers outfield, while George Burns played first base. Sam pinch hit for catcher Oscar Stanage in the seventh inning but failed to reach base. Cleveland won 6-4.

The first week of the season passed with Crawford on the bench, limited to late-inning pinch hitting appearances. With Detroit flailing at 1-5, Jennings started Sam at first in Cleveland on April 17. Wahoo brought the thunder, slamming a home run and a double. Crawford started five more games at first base in April, but managed only two hits in 20 at-bats.

The good news was that Sam, having apparently withdrawn his objections to first base, was getting opportunities to play. The bad news was his bat stayed cold. Jennings started him a few more times at first base in early May. Unfortunately, the hits did not come, and Crawford's average loitered below .200. Wahoo went back to the bench, limited to sporadic pinch-hitting assignments for nearly a month. Unlike the previous season when he led the AL in pinch hits, he now failed to deliver in these opportunities. By the end of May, he had tallied just nine hits thus far in the season.

Crawford started the 1917 campaign needing just 57 more hits to reach 3,000. Even if he received half the at-bats of a regular season that total seemed easily attainable. But with game after game passing with Sam riding the pines, this goal seemed to be slipping from his grasp. Realizing the increasing unlikelihood of achieving his ambition, Crawford penned an article for *Baseball Magazine* that summer. He described the unpleasant experience of watching his long-sought-after goal fade away. Admitting that he was not as fast as he was earlier in his career, Crawford maintained that he could still cover ground and play competently in right field. He furthermore argued that he could still hit, explaining his low batting average as a product of his sporadic use as a pinch hitter. Sam closed his piece with an expression of support for Detroit management and a final plea for the opportunity to play:

> I am not criticising anybody nor anything accept [sic] the unusual succession of events which have brought me so near the realization of my dreams and then threatened to leave me just short of its attainment. For I am not through, I will not admit that I am through. I can still hit that old baseball. I can still play the game up to major league standard. I can still get those three thousand hits if only I have the chance.

In mid-June it appeared that Crawford might in fact get his chance when Jennings started him in four straight games (three at first base, one in right field). But Wahoo produced just one hit in 14 at-bats over those four contests. Though Sam delivered a pinch hit the following day, he returned to the bench. He received just three pinch hitting opportunities over the next ten days.

At the end of June, Detroit remained in the middle of the AL pack, hovering just above .500. On July 1, the team played a doubleheader at Sportsman's Park in St. Louis. From his usual spot on the pines, Sam watched his teammates prevail 5-0 in the opener. In the second game, Browns hitters battered Tiger starter Howard Ehmke. Trailing 10-2 in the seventh, Jennings sent Crawford to the plate to pinch hit with a man on base. Recalling his past glory days, Sam blasted a delivery from Allen Sothoron for a two-run homer. It was the 97th and last home run of Crawford's career.

Despite that brief flash of lightning, Sam's appearances became less frequent as the summer continued. Though Jennings had little use for Crawford, Cleveland owner James Dunn thought that the veteran slugger could still play. Dunn made an offer to acquire Wahoo. Given that Navin was paying Sam $7,500 to sit on the bench, one would think he would have welcomed the chance to unload the expensive pinch hitter. But the Detroit owner rejected Cleveland's offer. Crawford would remain a Tiger.

On July 24, the Tigers set out on a three-week road trip. Sending a definitive message about his view of Sam's usefulness to the team, Jennings left the veteran slugger behind in Detroit. This snub provided Crawford with a three-week vacation, during which he continued to draw his hefty salary.

Though his time as a Tiger had all but ended, this season provided one final highlight for Sam. The contract he had signed with Navin back in 1914 contained a clause promising him a testimonial game as his career in Detroit neared its end. Given the right to pick the date for his tribute, Crawford selected Saturday, August 25th. After the deduction of expenses, Sam would receive all ticket receipts from that game.

More than 7,000 fans showed up at Navin Field to pay homage to their hero on "Sam Crawford Day." Wahoo played right field and batted fifth in the lineup. It would be his last start in a Tiger uniform. Philadelphia starter Jing Johnson sent Detroit down in order in the first inning. Sam was due up second in the bottom of the second inning. Before his at-bat, civic leader Charlie Burton led a committee of fans onto the field. After a short speech, they presented Crawford with the gift of a diamond ring from his local admirers. When play resumed, Sam drilled a fly ball to deep right field—a triple here would be a fitting punctuation to his brilliant career in the Motor City. But alas, right fielder Charlie Jamieson tracked the drive to the wall, where he made a one-handed catch. Crawford went hitless in four at-bats, though he caught both chances that came his way in right. The gate from that day's game added $1,200 to his wallet.

Crawford batted only two more times after his testimonial game. Pinch hitting on September 15, he made the final out in a 2-1 loss to the White Sox at Navin Field. The next day, with Cleveland leading 8-3 in the ninth, Sam stepped into the batter's box with a runner on second. In what would be his 9,570th and last major league at-bat, he grounded out to pitcher Jim Bagby. A big league career filled with thunderous blasts ended with barely a whisper.

The numbers for Crawford's final campaign were not pretty. He hit .173 with four doubles and two homers in 104 at-bats. He logged no triples in 1917—the only such drought in his career. Though no one knew it at the time, his last hit came on July 17—a pinch hit double off fellow Nebraskan Win Noyes. That gave Sam a total of 2,961 hits, the fourth most in major league history at that time.

Detroit closed out the 1917 season in fourth place with a 78-75 record. Near the end of the campaign, the Tigers received waivers on Crawford from the other big-league teams. The club then granted an unconditional release, allowing him to become a free agent. Though Sam had previously announced his intention to move to Los Angeles, the door was not necessarily closed on his major league career. The Indians had recently had expressed interest in him. A few other teams similarly wondered if Wahoo still had some gas left in the tank.

In late October, Sam, Ada, and Virginia traveled to Nebraska. There, they attended a family reunion at his sister Zadia's house in Fremont. Their mother Nellie arrived from Mississippi to attend the gathering. After the reunion, Sam's younger brother Neal, a draftee, had to report to the Army. With World War I still raging, the United States was increasing its troop deployment to Europe.

Along with his wife and daughter, Crawford then headed to Omaha, where they spent a week with Ada's parents. During this time Sam paid a visit to his nearby hometown of Wahoo. The

Crawfords next traveled west to Los Angeles, where they planned to spend the winter. What Sam would be doing next spring was still to be determined.

The previous summer, while still a member of the Tigers, Crawford had taken the high road when publicly discussing his benching. Noting that baseball had been good to him, he told *Baseball Magazine* that he had no cause to complain on most accounts. He said he understood that Jennings was doing what he thought best by putting him on the bench: "The management is after results and if those results can be better obtained by having someone in my shoes, why the management would be foolish not to follow that plan."

A few months later in Los Angeles, Crawford offered a different opinion. No longer on Navin's payroll, he told a LA reporter what he really thought about his final season in Detroit. Sam blamed two men—Cobb and Jennings—for running him out of the Motor City. He pointed out that at his testimonial game in August, when all his teammates gathered around him at home plate, both Cobb and Jennings remained on the bench. The other players took notice of this public snubbing of their veteran teammate.

Crawford then said that Cobb was actually managing the Tigers, pulling strings to get Jennings to do his bidding. Sam maintained that Cobb had not liked him since they had butted heads over Donie Bush years earlier. In the spring of 1917, Cobb wanted Heilmann to start in right field instead of Sam, even though Heilmann himself wanted to play first base. Crawford further alleged that Cobb had arranged for the dismissal of other players from the team whom he disliked. Though aware of Cobb's enmity toward him, Sam said, "I never thought he would be able to 'get me,' however."

Crawford's comments gained national attention, prompting whispers that Detroit might trade Cobb. Navin quickly squelched these rumors, declaring that he would not trade or sell the Georgia Peach. Sam's criticisms raise the question of how well he and Cobb got along during his later years in Detroit. As illustrated by the 1912 Tigers strike, Crawford accepted Cobb as a teammate and did not stand for what he considered unfair treatment of him. But they were not friends. In 1913 *Baseball Magazine* noted that Crawford did not appreciate Cobb's tendency to encroach on his outfield territory when chasing fly balls. The periodical added, "Cobb is touchy, and hot headed, and impetuous, and Crawford, while of a far more even temperament and a mighty fine fellow, is not over and above fond of being left completely in the shade, being something of an outfielder himself."

Cobb for his part complained that Crawford did not communicate with him in the outfield. The Peach further alleged that Sam purposely fouled off pitches to prevent him from stealing second base. Wahoo denied the allegations, saying that he fouled off pitches in order to get one he could drive—a practice that Cobb himself commonly followed.

Yet, for all the discord, the top two Tiger outfielders respected each other's abilities. Crawford marveled at Cobb's "fast thinking" and "dynamite" baserunning skills. He considered the Georgia Peach to be one of baseball's all-time greats. Cobb likewise appreciated his slugging teammate's skills. He even admitted that Crawford was actually a better hitter than himself. Cobb said his higher average came from beating out infield hits and the harder work he put into breaking out of slumps, in contrast to Crawford who merely waited for his luck to change when slumping. The two teammates, moreover, did not let their cool personal feelings toward each other prevent them from working together on the basepaths to flummox their opponents.

Having vented his frustrations about his exodus from Detroit, Crawford turned his attention to the upcoming 1918 season. He made it clear to the press that he was not through with baseball, that he could still hit major league pitching, and that he wanted to collect those few dozen hits to put his career total over 3,000. With the slugger eager to "show Jennings up," rumors abounded through the off-season about Crawford's next baseball destination.

In January *The Sporting News* reported that Sam might be headed to Philadelphia to play for Connie Mack, who needed to replace several players lost to the military draft. A week later, rumors surfaced that Branch Rickey had made an offer to Crawford to play for the St. Louis Cardinals. In February, Sam sent a letter to his brother Neal, stationed at an army aviation training camp in San Antonio, stating that Cleveland had made him an offer. Crawford also reportedly had multiple opportunities to play for and/or manage a minor league team.

As a 37-year-old husband and father, Crawford was not subject to the draft, increasing his appeal to teams losing players to the military. And yet, the weeks passed without his signature on a contact. Earlier in the off-season, some scribes had speculated that his past activities in the Base Ball Players' Fraternity had caused magnates to want him out of the game. The multiple offers that came his way soon dispelled that theory.

Crawford's salary demands proved to be a larger barrier to his return to the big leagues. *The Sporting News* reported that he wanted between $8,000 and $8,500 to play in 1918. That was well above the top salary he had drawn as a Tiger. Even the most ardent Wahoo Sam supporter had to admit that his asking price was a bit excessive for a limited-range outfielder who had batted .173 the previous season. Cardinals manager Jack Hendricks remarked that Crawford negotiated as if he were still in his prime, telling reporters, "He talks about a 1918 contract in terms of a few years ago."

Crawford, nonetheless, stuck to his guns. As spring training approached, his negotiations with each big league club ceased. In late March, he signed a contract to play for the Los Angeles Angels of the Pacific Coast League. Reporters speculated that the minor league club likely would not pay him much more than $3,000 for the season.

This turn of events raises the question, why did Crawford make such unrealistic compensation demands, thereby shutting the door on a return to the major leagues? It was not a matter of need—he had received a robust $7,500 a year for his last four seasons with Detroit. Added to that, Sam owned real estate in Detroit and several profitable blocks of stocks and securities.

This suggests the possibility of pride as a motivating factor for Sam. Feeling disrespected by his dismissal from Detroit, Crawford wanted a salary befitting a star player with his tenure and stature. His asking price after all was still less than half the $20,000 that Cobb received. Following the humiliating bench campaign he endured in 1917, Sam would come back only if baseball made it worth his while. But what about his 3,000 hits? He certainly wanted to accomplish the feat, as his many statements on the subject indicate. But, as it turned out, there were other issues more important to him at this time.

These issues became apparent to the press in March 1918. Ada was pregnant, and the baby was due to arrive in the middle of the month—right around the time when spring training would begin. Leaving his 37-year-old wife just before her delivery was not an appealing prospect for Sam. Neither was moving his family again under these circumstances.

Sam and Ada's son, Sam Jr., was born on March 15 at the Crawfords' residence on 1954 Canyon Drive in Hollywood. The child's arrival ended the debate about Wahoo's immediate baseball future. *The Sporting News* reported that "rather than take a chance on the health of Samuel Crawford Jr., and Mrs. Crawford, the former Detroit slugger decided to remain in California." In the end, Sam chose family over the opportunity to continue his big league career.

Though his tenure in the major leagues had ended, Sam's time in baseball would continue. For the first time in 19 years, he would be playing in the minor leagues.

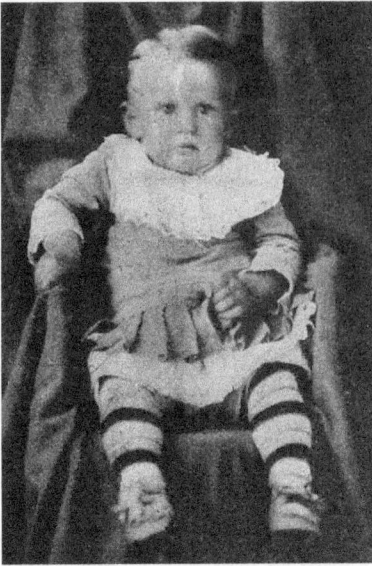

Sam Crawford at two years old, 1882.
Baseball Magazine

Sam Crawford (back row, second from left) in his first baseball uniform in 1896. His teammates included Amiel Killian (back row, third from left) and Ed Killian (back row, fifth from left). The oldest Killian brother, Tom (seated in middle), was team manager. Sam's brother-in-law Elmer Johnson (husband of Ada's sister Belle) is in the back row second from right. *Saunders County Historical Society*

Sam as a rookie for the Cincinnati Reds in 1899.
Baseball Magazine

Sam developed an interest in photography as a young man.
Baseball Magazine

After arriving in Detroit in 1903, Sam Crawford became one of the most feared sluggers in the American League.
National Baseball Hall of Fame and Museum

Sam's strong throwing arm recorded 20+ outfield assists in a season three times in his career.
Library of Congress

The Chicago Cubs battle the Detroit Tigers at Bennett Park during the 1907 World Series. *Library of Congress*

Detroit players leaving for spring training in San Antonio in 1909. Left to right: Harry Tuthill, "Bumpus" Jones, Matty McIntyre, Heinie Beckendorf, Davy Jones, "Twilight Ed" Killian, Sam Crawford, Ed Summers, George Winter, and Hughie Jennings. *Library of Congress*

Gripping the bat at the end of the handle and standing at the plate in a wide stance, Sam Crawford generated tremendous power with his swing. *Library of Congress*

Detroit Tigers in October 1909. Left to right: Ty Cobb, Davy Jones, Ed Summers, Wild Bill Donovan, George Mullin, Ed Willett, Sam Crawford, "Twilight Ed" Killian *Library of Congress*

Sam Crawford's 309 career triples stands as one of Major League Baseball's "unbreakable" records.
National Baseball Hall of Fame and Museum

Though primarily an outfielder, Sam Crawford played 151 games at first base in his major league career. *National Baseball Hall of Fame and Museum*

Sam Crawford and his daughter Virginia at their house in Detroit.
Baseball Magazine

Sam finishing and polishing his bats in his workshop in 1910. *Baseball Magazine*

Ty Cobb, Bobby Veach, and Sam Crawford formed one of the greatest hitting outfields in baseball history. *Baseball Magazine*

Sam studying the pitcher before his turn at the plate. *Baseball Magazine*

Sam and his daughter Virginia.
Baseball Magazine

Sam, Virginia, and Ada in
California in 1915.
Baseball Magazine

Sam with Virginia and his granddaughter Julie in 1940.
Julie Ann Johnson

Sam with his granddaughter Julie in the 1960s.
Julie Ann Johnson

Chapter 11

Los Angeles Angels

The Angels' signing of Sam Crawford grabbed sports headlines in the spring of 1918. Reporters praised team owner, LA socialite John F. Powers, for making the best move of any of the Pacific Coast League (PCL) magnates that offseason. The team had not generated this much preseason buzz since Powers had signed Frank Chance to manage the club a few years earlier. *The Sporting News* predicted that Sam would be a big draw for the league: "If the other clubs could line up as great a drawing card as Crawford will prove to be, the league should finish the season in a healthy condition."

Following the departure of Chance the previous season, former Cincinnati Reds outfielder Wade "Red" Killefer took the reins in Los Angeles as player-manager. Crawford knew Killefer from years earlier when the latter had played a few games with the Tigers as a utility man in the 1908-1909 seasons. Sam would get along well with his new skipper, who gained notice in the PCL for his fiery demeanor and keen baseball intellect.

The Angels opened their 1918 season at Washington Park in Los Angeles on April 2. Batting fourth, Crawford made an impressive PCL debut, rapping two hits, driving in a run, and throwing out runners at third and home from right field. Angels fans reportedly "howled like mad" when Wahoo came to bat.

The other star in the Los Angeles lineup, former White Sox first baseman Jack Fournier, also delivered an RBI hit, but the home team fell 7-5. The next day, Sam helped LA notch its first win of the season by stealing a base and scoring on a hit by Rube Ellis, another Angel with big league experience.

As the season progressed, Crawford showed that he could still play baseball at a high level. The Pacific Coast League was a AA level circuit, the highest classification for a minor league at that time—the equivalent of a AAA league today. Calling Sam a wonderful ballplayer, *The Standard* in Ogden, Utah, said that he "can throw, hit and run as well as most of them [in the PCL] ..." In mid-April Crawford displayed his trademark power for the Utah fans, hitting one of the longest home runs ever seen at Derks Field in Salt Lake City. He also impressed sports scribes with his defensive skills in the outfield. Noting his proficient glove and throwing skills, United Press correspondent H.C. Hamilton wrote, "No one ever did accuse Sam Crawford of being a flashy fielder until he got out on the Pacific coast—but he's all that now."

Following his revival in the PCL, many reporters opined that Crawford could have continued playing in the major leagues had he not wanted to remain closer to home following the birth of his second child. Sam's on-field production supported the case that he still had the talent to have remained in the bigs. By mid-May he was seventh in the league in total bases. When asked about his enduring abilities as a hitter, Crawford cited conditioning as the key factor. And to achieve top condition, he advocated sleep—specifically, the early to bed, early to rise schedule. "Even if one does not feel sleepy it is a good thing to go to bed early and rest," Sam said. "While stretched out on a bed all of the muscles are relaxed. They are given a chance to rebuild the strength which has to be used during the day."

Though slowed by an injury in May, Crawford remained in the lineup to help Los Angeles battle for the top spot in the league. Sports reporters continued their laudatory comments, writing that Crawford "is outhitting, outthrowing and outfielding all the young players in the league." He even drew cheers from opposing teams' fans when the Angels played at their parks.

As baseball teams across the nation battled for pennants, real battles continued to rage across Europe. In the spring and summer of 1918, the United States increased its troop commitment to the Western Front in France. Back home, the federal government urged citizens to support the war effort by purchasing Treasury Department bonds. A propaganda campaign used newspapers, rallies, posters, and slogans such as "Come Across or the Kaiser Will" to encourage citizens to support the cause. During a Liberty Loan drive in the spring of 1918, Crawford showed his patriotism by buying $3,000 worth of bonds. His generosity boosted the Angels' team contributions to $7,000.

Though the draft required all men between 21 and 35 years of age to register, the military had called few ballplayers in 1917. Aside from players practicing pregame military drills and a few other patriotic gestures, World War I initially had a limited visible impact on Organized Baseball. This changed in May 1918, when the federal government issued a "work or fight" order. This edict required all draft-age men (ballplayers included) to join the military or work at a job "essential" to the war effort. With baseball's claim that it was an essential industry rejected, players left their teams to join the service or work as shipbuilders, steel workers, and farmers.

Though Crawford's age exempted him, the government order covered most of the players in the PCL and every other professional baseball league. The widespread exodus of talent eroded fan interest and gate receipts. Major league magnates decided to end their season on Labor Day, just after the compliance deadline for players set by Secretary of War Newton D. Baker, who granted pennant-winning teams a two-week extension to play the World Series. All but one of the minor leagues followed suit by suspending their operations early.

With declining attendance taking its toll on club finances, PCL officials decided to end their season in mid-July. Separated in the standings by only a game-and-a-half, the top two teams, Vernon and Los Angeles, would play a best-of-nine postseason series to determine the league champion. Crawford's four hits helped his team prevail in the opener 7-5. He added two more hits, including a double, the next day as LA again beat the Tigers. The Angels continued this momentum to win the series five games to two.

Crawford batted .292 and slugged .379 with 14 doubles, seven triples, and one homer in the abbreviated season. Though very respectable numbers, especially when compared to his final year in Detroit, he did not dominate PCL pitching. Sam's early-season injury had slowed him for a while, hindering his overall season output. Fournier (.325) posted the best offensive campaign for the Angels, and Killefer (.295) matched Wahoo's production.

Following the cessation of the PCL season, Sam joined hundreds of other ballplayers in seeking a position that contributed to the war effort. He soon found employment with the Montebello Oil Company. Oil had been discovered in the hills east of Los Angeles the previous year. The Montebello fields would soon account for one-eighth of the crude oil produced in California.

The guns of World War I ceased firing on November 11, 1918, bringing an end to Crawford's brief career in the oil industry. Though peace returned, the nation remained in the grip of the Spanish flu pandemic in the final months of the year. That winter, as the deadliest wave of the disease finally passed, Sam announced that he was quitting baseball. After just one year in the PCL, the veteran of 20 professional baseball seasons said he would not return to the diamond. A newspaper in one of the Angels' rival cities agreed that it was time. While most of the press coverage of Sam's 1918 campaign was positive, the *San Francisco Chronicle* declared that the former Tiger had lost his appeal as a drawing card. The paper continued that Crawford looked tired, lacked pepper, and "showed as much enthusiasm for the sport as the hired hand bending over the well-known wood pile, saw in hand and disgust in his heart."

Deciding he had a few more logs to split, Sam changed his mind and signed a contract to play another season with the Angels. Did the rantings of an enemy scribe stoke his competitive fires? Possibly. Or maybe Crawford had been using his threat to quit as leverage to negotiate a higher salary. Or perhaps he just could not say goodbye to the game he loved while he was still able to compete at a high level. Whatever the case, Sam was coming back to knock the ball around for another campaign.

Crawford's bat looked especially potent at spring training in 1919, prompting predictions that he would wreak havoc on PCL pitching that summer. The early games in the season confirmed the prescience of these forecasts. Sam and the Angels burst out of the gate like gangbusters. On April 20, he went four for four in the first game of a double-header sweep of Vernon. Los Angeles held first place at this time with a 12-2 record, while boasting the league's top three hitters in Fournier, Crawford, and Killefer.

The next day, on Monday, April 21, Sam's mother Nellie Patterson died in Vicksburg, Mississippi, following an operation to treat a carcinoma. Sixty-four years old at the time, she died 15 years to the day after Sam's father had passed away. Nellie had been living near Fayette, 45 miles south of Vicksburg, for the past dozen years with her second husband, Duncan Patterson. She is buried in Fayette Cemetery next to her mother Sarah, who had died two years earlier.

A couple weeks after Nellie's passing, her children agreed to sell the Crawford house on North Orange Street in Wahoo. Sam's sister Zadia and her husband Arthur traveled in from Grand Island, Nebraska, where they now lived, to execute the transaction. Charles J. Fair, a department store manager, paid $2,250 for the property. A year later, the U.S. Census listed Fair as a 35-year-old widower living in the house with his four-year-old son, his mother-in-law, sister-in-law, and grandmother-in-law. The house where Sam grew up belonged to another family.

Crawford and the Angels remained hot through the spring of 1919. By early June, he led the league with a .379 mark. He also regained his power stroke, evidenced by the two home runs he drilled in a game against Portland in early July. The previous season, Crawford showed that he could still compete with the top minor leaguers in the country. In 1919 he proved that he could dominate at this level. His formidable bat raised questions about a possible return to the majors. Sam himself said no, telling *The Seattle Star* in July that he had played his last big league game. "The cold weather gets me," Crawford said, "and then I haven't the speed I once had." The slugger, moreover, had put down roots in Los Angeles with his wife and two children. Moving all the way across the country did not appeal to him. Plus, he had no monetary incentive to return to the bigs. Sam had saved his earnings while playing in the majors and was financially set for the foreseeable future.

On July 23, Crawford strained a ligament in his right leg while sprinting for an infield hit in Sacramento. The injury put him on the shelf for a week. Upon returning to the lineup, he picked up where he had left off, terrorizing PCL pitchers. As the season entered the home stretch Sam battled Salt Lake City outfielder Bill Rumler for the batting title. A fellow Nebraskan, Rumler had been one of the top pinch hitters in the majors a couple years earlier when he played for the St. Louis Browns.

The race for top batting honors came down to the last day. In a scenario reminiscent of the Lajoie-Cobb controversy of 1910, a conspiracy derailed Crawford's hopes of winning the batting title. Salt Lake City played its last game against Oakland, whose fielders made little effort to handle Rumler's grounders. He recorded four hits that day, three of them bunt singles, to edge Crawford in the batting race .362 to .360.

Similar to Sam, the Angels finished a close second in the pennant race. Though Los Angeles posted an impressive 108-72 record (the PCL played a longer season than MLB), the club trailed first-place Vernon by two-and-a-half games. The champion Tigers at this time were owned by comedy film star Fatty Arbuckle, though he sold his interest in the team the following year. Despite the disappointment of a second-place finish, Crawford could look back on a monster season in which he played in 173 of his team's 180 games. In addition to his stellar .360 batting average, he slugged .539 with 18 triples and 14 home runs. Fournier and Killefer complemented Wahoo's thunder by hitting .328 and .320 respectively.

The following season the 27-year-old Fournier jumped to the major leagues, where he emerged as a top slugger in the NL for several years—even winning a home run title in 1924. Vernon Tigers outfielder Bob Meusel, who batted .337 with 14 home runs in 1919, similarly advanced to the Big Show. He landed in New York, where he won a home run title as part of the Yankees' vaunted "Murderer's Row" with Babe Ruth and Lou Gehrig.

In October, Sam's former team, the Cincinnati Reds, won its first World Series championship. This victory over the heavily favored White Sox, however, raised questions about the legitimacy of the Series. Rumors abounded that the AL champs might have taken money from gamblers to throw the games. These rumors would escalate into a full-blown scandal the following autumn. A similar controversy would soon rock the Pacific Coast League.

An agricultural venture started to pay dividends for Crawford in the off-season. He and Killefer shared a 22-acre walnut ranch in the Los Angeles area. Despite these profits, Sam decided to continue his "day job" on the diamond. Even though he had just completed a long Pacific Coast League season, he did not wait until the next spring to return to the field.

The winter after the 1919 season, Babe Ruth traveled to California. While there, he staged exhibition games with some major league players hibernating on the West Coast and a few of the PCL stars. Having just set the single-season home run record with 29, the Red Sox slugger stood out as the top attraction for these contests. Ruth's aggressive salary demands and swirling rumors about his impending sale to the New York Yankees only added to his mystique.

In December, Ruth captained an all-star team set to play two games in Los Angeles against an opposing squad headed by Wade Killefer. Crawford played left field for the latter team. Sam had seen the Babe many times before, facing him in high-stakes at-bats when the Tigers battled the Red Sox for the pennant in 1915 and 1916.

Ruth homered in his first at bat in the opening game but later struck out twice as Killefer's team prevailed. The next day Ruth whiffed three more times. When he came to the plate in the ninth, the opposing outfielders—Crawford, Killefer, and NL home run king Gavvy Cravath—abandoned their posts to leave the entire outfield wide open. Not amused by this stunt, Ruth demanded that the fielders return. They did not move, prompting the crowd to howl with glee. Taking his at-bat, Ruth lifted a high pop up to left field. Though an easy out, Crawford continued relaxing in the shade of the fence. After the ball dropped, he retrieved it and threw it back to the infield. Standing on second, Ruth demanded an explanation for this indifference. "Thought you needed that hit to help your batting average," Sam replied. "You only had one hit and this makes two. We must uphold your reputation as a star." Though Killefer's team won again, Ruth recovered from this razzing to clout 54 home runs the following year in his first season as a Yankee.

Though Los Angeles stumbled out of the gate in 1920, Crawford continued to wield a devastating club. Now 40 years old, he drew accolades as one of the fastest players on his team. An order from his manager to never slide made his feats of speed even more impressive. At a game in San Francisco, he somehow stole home. A couple weeks later, he raced around the bases for an inside-the-park home run.

Crawford continued his barrage through the summer. Angel victories soon followed. By the end of June, the team had climbed into third place in the eight-team circuit. In the majors, meanwhile, Ruth rewrote the record book with his epic home run pace. Fans and reporters speculated that a "lively ball" was the reason for his increased power numbers. Crawford's name came up as one of those earlier sluggers who would be piling up the homers if they still played in the Big Show.

That summer Sam accomplished a home run feat unmatched by Ruth and possibly no other slugger in baseball history. Batting with the bases loaded, Crawford launched a drive deep into Washington Park's spacious outfield. Wary the ball would be caught, the runners stayed close to their respective bags. Sam, however, put his head down and charged around the bases. When the ball did hit the ground, Wahoo was flying around second toward third where he passed his slow-to-react teammate. Sam crossed the plate thinking he had hit a grand slam, but his "phantom home run" had in fact resulted in a triple play. The umpire ruled out all three men he had passed on the basepaths.

Crawford's bat remained hot through the stretch drive. During a seven-game home series against Portland in September, he torched the Beavers' pitchers for 18 hits in 33 at-bats. The Angels climbed into second place with a month left to play. But Los Angeles could not keep pace, finishing fourth—seven-and-a-half games behind the champion Tigers.

Though he missed the final series due to a charley horse, Crawford completed another estimable campaign. He led his team with a .332 batting average and a .505 slugging average. Along the way he belted 21 triples and 12 home runs. In the wake of this impressive performance, PCL fans voted Sam to the league's All-Coast Team.

Late in the 1920 major league season, allegations of a fix in the previous World Series dominated baseball headlines. A grand jury convened and the story came out that gamblers had bribed several members of the White Sox to lose the Series to the Reds. Though a jury acquitted the eight accused players, newly appointed commissioner Judge Kenesaw Mountain Landis banned all of them (the Black Sox) from baseball for life.

Around the same time, a similar scandal hit the Pacific Coast League.

In August 1920, rumors surfaced that Vernon Tigers first baseman Babe Borton had bribed Salt Lake City Bees outfielder Harl Maggert to throw games the previous season. When called before the PCL president, Borton spun a tale that he and his teammates had paid three of the Bees (Maggert, Bill Rumler, and pitcher Gene Dale), as well as players on Portland and Seattle, to lose games to Vernon in 1919. Borton told the president that his team had raised a slush fund to bribe opponents so Vernon would win the pennant. Further investigation cast doubt on Borton's slush fund story but did uncover his connections with a Seattle gambler named Nathan Raymond, the true source of Borton's bribe money. Similar to the Black Sox, the four accused players (Borton, Maggert, Rumler, and Dale) escaped court conviction but were banned from playing in the PCL. Noting that Vernon had won several thrown games in a close race, the grand jury investigating the matter concluded that the second-place Angels would have won the 1919 pennant had the contests not been fixed.

Crawford's former Detroit employers made news following the 1920 season when Hughie Jennings resigned after a disappointing seventh-place finish. "Ee-Yah" had just completed his 14th season as Tiger skipper—he was Sam's manager for 11 of those seasons. While they did not part on the best of terms, Crawford achieved his greatest baseball success on teams managed by Jennings. Frank Navin chose Ty Cobb as the next Tiger manager, a selection that likely did not stir any longings in Sam for a return to the Motor City.

As had become his regular off-season ritual, Crawford announced his plan to retire from baseball. Then as spring drew closer, he changed his mind and decided to play another year. He loved to hit baseballs, and as long as he was still good at it—one of the best in the league, in fact—he could not bring himself to quit. The return of far-ranging centerfielder Arnold Statz to help cover part of right field increased the appeal to Sam of playing another season.

As the Angels opened spring training at Elsinore, about 40 miles southeast of Los Angeles, the press took note of Crawford's longevity in the game. Soon to turn 41 years old, he would be starting his 23rd season in professional baseball. Noting his abuse of their hometown pitchers, *The Seattle Star* wrote that "the big boy can still run, field, and throw as Seattle fans who saw him in action last year will remember."

While some things stayed the same with the Angels, like Crawford's presence in right field, other things changed in 1921. Chiefly, John F. Powers sold a controlling interest in the team to chewing gum magnate William Wrigley, Jr. The new boss, who was also the majority owner of the Chicago Cubs, acquired a PCL team anchored by several former big-leaguers north of 36 years of age: Crawford, Killefer, first baseman Art Griggs, and second baseman Bert Niehoff. The club added to this veteran cast by acquiring Sam's former Tiger teammate, Oscar Stanage, to take over as catcher. To address its desperate need for speed, Los Angeles added fleet-footed Dixie Carroll to play left field.

When the games began, Crawford again displayed his prowess with the bat. By mid-season, he was batting .347 and still showing that he could reach the fences. The *Omaha Sunday Bee* declared that the 41-year-old Nebraskan could still return to the majors if he so desired. Content to stay in Los Angeles, Crawford remained his team's top offensive threat through the first half of the season. The Angels, however, lingered in the middle of the PCL pack.

In the second half, Griggs, batting cleanup just ahead of Sam, started to find his stroke. Niehoff and leadoff man Arnold Statz further bolstered the Angels attack. Doc Crandall and Vic Aldridge meanwhile emerged as a potent one-two punch at the top of Killefer's pitching rotation. Thirty-seven-year-old Tom Hughes, an alumnus of the 1914 World Series champion Boston Braves, contributed from the mound as well.

Los Angeles started to chip away at the dozen-game lead the San Francisco Seals had built over them. A hot streak in the stretch run vaulted the Angels into first place in late September, though the Seals would soon edge back into the top spot. In the final week of the season, Los Angeles won six of eight from Portland, while San Francisco stumbled against Seattle. Sacramento also remained in contention.

Heading into the final day of the season on October 1, three teams still had a chance to win the PCL title. The Angels led Sacramento by one-and-a-half games and San Francisco by two games. Each contender closed out with a doubleheader—LA just needed to win one of two to secure the crown. Crawford drilled three hits to help his team claim the opener and the pennant in Portland 12-3. The Angels fell in 11 innings in the meaningless second game. Sam went three for six in what would be the final game of his professional baseball career.

Crawford's potent bat proved a crucial factor in the Los Angeles pennant drive. Playing in 175 games, he batted .318 and slugged .463, with 10 triples, nine homers, and 10 stolen bases. Defying the doubters, Sam and his veteran teammates showed they could still get the job done. Their accomplishment impressed many sportswriters, including Philadelphia's Robert W. Maxwell, who admitted that he had earlier felt sorry for the old men playing for Los Angeles. The writer said they moved like truck horses at the start of the season, but "after they were thawed out, they played wonderful baseball and won the pennant."

In the four seasons after Hughie Jennings had little use for him, Crawford accumulated 799 hits and batted .331 for the Angels. Granted, this production came against minor league pitching, but the Pacific Coast League was the top bush circuit of the day. Some observers considered the level of play in the PCL equal to that of the American League and National League. Indeed, PCL rosters bristled with former and soon-to-be major leaguers. The circuit was not quite major league level in the early 1920s, but it was not far below.

Given Crawford's stellar four-year production in the PCL, he easily could have collected the 39 hits needed for 3,000 had he returned to the majors after his release by Detroit. He probably would have made a run at Lajoie's total of 3,252, though Wagner's MLB record (at the time) of 3,430 hits was likely out of reach. Sam would have held his own with the bat, but his continuance in the majors would have depended upon his tolerance for cooler climates and his manager's tolerance for subpar outfield play—or Wahoo's willingness to play first base. Had the designated hitter existed back then, Crawford may have played till age 50!

In the off-season following the Angels' championship, it appeared that Sam would be back in 1922. He stated that he hoped to play two more seasons to reach a quarter century in professional baseball. Reports surfaced early in the year that he had signed a contract with Los Angeles. But alas, these accounts proved to be premature. As players started reporting for spring training in March, *The Sporting News* revealed that Crawford had a clause in his contract making him a free agent if he and the Angels could not agree on a salary figure. And such disagreement between player and ownership did occur. Noting Sam's newfound freedom, the publication speculated on his future:

> Crawford, one of the greatest hitters in the game, has a ranch near Los Angeles. It is enough to keep him busy, but he likes to play ball and it would not be surprising to see him hooked up with some other Coast League club.

Indeed, it would not have been surprising for Crawford to sign with another PCL team. A likely candidate would have been the Vernon Tigers, the league's other LA team. Even San Francisco or Sacramento would not have been too far from home. But it was not meant to be—he did not sign to play for any team in 1922.

Wahoo Sam's playing days had come to an end.

Chapter 12

Coach

As shouts of "Play Ball!" echoed across the nation's ballparks in the spring of 1922, Sam Crawford found himself in an unfamiliar situation. For the first time since his early childhood in Nebraska, he would not be playing the game he loved. At age 42 he was old for a pro athlete but still a relatively young man. And so Sam had to answer the question: what's next?

Tending to his small ranch occupied part of his time that summer. But given Crawford's affinity for the diamond, it is no surprise that walnuts did not hold his full attention. Before the end of the year, he had returned to baseball.

In 1922 Jess Orndorff moved forward with a plan to establish a commercial baseball school. His idea followed the burgeoning specialization trend of law schools, dental schools, technical schools and other institutions that prepared young men for a specific profession. Orndorff, who briefly reached the majors in 1907 as a catcher for the Boston Braves, called his school the National College of Baseball. Enlisting Frank Chance as an advisor, Orndorff hired several former big leaguers for his faculty, including Rube Ellis, Frank Dillon, and "Death Valley" Jim Scott. The biggest name among the school's "professors" was Sam Crawford.

Orndorff broke ground for his facility in Burbank, California, on October 22. Hollywood film actress Edith Roberts christened the new field by breaking a bottle over a bat held by Crawford. The school would open for its first term on January 10, 1923. In its three-month courses, the school offered aspiring ballplayers individual instruction and intensive practice that was not available at overcrowded spring training camps. Orndorff claimed his school would quickly develop recruits by teaching essential points of the game, technical skills, and physical conditioning.

A few months later, during the summer of 1923, Crawford made news not for his professorial skills, but as a bat designer. Wahoo Sam had long been an enthusiast for the wooden clubs he wielded on the diamond—not surprising given that hitting a baseball was the aspect of the game he loved best. Gloves, on the other hand, held less importance to him. During his playing days, *The Detroit Times* reported that Crawford would use any cheap hand-covering, never paying more than a dollar for a glove. He claimed the cheaper versions worked just as well as the expensive ($2.50) gloves. Upon purchasing his leather, often a Draper-Maynard product, he would cut the padding out of the pocket to get the "feel" that he liked. After Sam was finished with a glove at the end of a season, he bequeathed it to teammate Matty McIntyre.

In contrast to his feeling about gloves, Crawford was hyper-particular about his lumber. *The Detroit Times* maintained that he would devote his entire fortune, if necessary, to buying the right bats. Sam wielded a heavy war club—his preferred Spalding models weighed 40 ounces or more. He ordered them specially made from the finest ash with certain modifications, such as a slightly lightened barrel and an enlarged knob. Upon receiving the new weapons, Crawford oiled, polished, and finished them in his workshop for the coming season. A pioneer in the practice of seasoning bats by soaking them in oil during the winter months, Sam became a respected authority on bat quality. Former Detroit teammate George Moriarty said that Crawford could assess the driving power of a bat with just "one glance at the run of the grain."

In the batter's box, Wahoo tightly gripped the lumber with his hands together at the extreme end of the handle. As the pitch came in, his shoulders unleashed their full driving power, while his wrists swept the bat around to smash the ball. Like most players of his day, Sam spent little time analyzing and breaking down his swing. "All I know is that I go up there with the determination to hit the ball and hit it hard," he said, "and if I am lucky I connect."

For Crawford, hitting came down to just a few simple rules: plant your feet firmly in the ground, watch the ball, ignore the chatter of the catcher, and keep your head clear of notions. "That's my system," Sam said, "and the more beef you put into the swing the farther she will go." Crawford hit many a pitch plenty far, especially when a hurler made the mistake of giving him one low and on the inside half of the plate.

Managers occasionally tried to convince Crawford to adopt the scientific slap-hitting style of the day but with little success. As Hughie Jennings recalled:

> Crawford could have improved his average and obtained many more hits had he shortened his swing, but it wasn't natural for him and you could never get him to do it. Once or twice he tried chop hitting and because he didn't get immediate results, he abandoned the effort. He always went back to his long swing, which was the way he learned to bat in his youth, out in Nebraska.

Retirement as a player did not diminish Wahoo's enthusiasm for the tools of the batter's trade. In 1923 he invented the so-called "quadrebuilt bat" (aka laminated bat). As its name suggests, the unique feature of this club was that it combined four different pieces of wood glued together. Noting that an ordinary one-piece bat naturally included weak parts of the wood, Crawford sought to eliminate those spots by constructing a bat with four sections, each of them of the highest-quality seasoned wood. The goal was to create a much stronger bat.

To test out this idea, Crawford sent a quadrebuilt model to the leading slugger of the day, Babe Ruth. The Bambino took to the bat with much alacrity, using it to break out of a slump with a barrage of hits and home runs. After Ruth used this weapon, which he named "Betsy Bingle," for a few weeks, the baseball powers that be investigated its legality. Given Crawford's stake in the company producing the quadrebuilt models, the impending decision held significant financial consequences. The new bats retailed for $8 each (in contrast to $2 for ordinary big league models), and with Ruth's endorsement, great profits could be coming Wahoo's way.

The Crawford bat did not violate specific rules on the shape, size, or weight of bats. Ban Johnson, nonetheless, labeled it a "trick bat" that used a foreign substance (the glue that held the pieces together) and banned its use. Yankees owner Jacob Ruppert argued that his player was being discriminated against and wired his protest to Johnson. The ruling nonetheless stood and Ruth had to stop using the bat. He again fell into a slump but eventually came out of it. Ruth finished the 1923 season with a career-high .393 batting average, 41 home runs, and 130 RBI. Given his hitting dominance over the following decade, it is safe to say that Johnson's ruling hurt Sam more than it hurt the Babe.

Though Crawford had recently ended his playing days and was just in his early forties, many of his former teammates and opponents were no longer around. As noted earlier, his Grand Rapids teammate Rube Waddell had died in 1914 from tuberculosis. Six years later, nephritis claimed the life of Matty McIntyre at age 39. Another former Tiger, Ed Siever, also died in 1920, succumbing to heart disease at the age of 44.

In October 1921 Jimmy Barrett died of a stroke. The speedy outfielder had broken into the majors with Cincinnati the same time as Sam in September 1899. Though Barrett played just one full season with the Reds, he and Crawford were again teammates in Detroit from 1903 to 1905. Finding success in real estate following his playing days, Barrett left assets valued at more than $400,000 to his wife.

One of the most entertaining ballplayers of the Deadball Era, Germany Schaefer, also died in his forties. Well known for his antics and quips, Schaefer yielded many stories from his playing days, including one that involved Sam. Years earlier, a Detroit clothing company offered a suit of clothes to the first Tiger to hit a home run in the season. One day, with the prize still unclaimed, Crawford hit a mighty blast that sailed into deep center field. As Wahoo rounded the bases, Schaefer, coaching third, waved him home. Sam, however, lost his wind in the final leg and got tagged out by the catcher. Detroit fans booed and jeered Schaefer, blaming him for their hero's demise at the plate. After Crawford trotted to right field for the next inning, Schaefer got his attention and yelled out, "I'm sorry, Sam, ole friend, about that suit of clothes; I'm awfully sorry! I got you the coat and vest, but, darned if I could get you the pants."

On February 1, 1928, Hughie Jennings died from meningitis at the age of 58. A coach for John McGraw's Giants after his departure from Detroit, Jennings suffered from bad sinuses and tuberculosis in the mid-1920s. With his passing, baseball lost one of its most colorful figures. In 1910 *The Detroit Times* printed a verbatim report of the skipper's chatter from the coach's box during a game, including these exhortations from when Crawford came to bat:

> Oh, o-h, oh! See who's here. Now, Sam, hit it easy. Don't kill anybody, Sam. I hate to say what's going to happen here in a minute. Wh-e-e! Um di di dum dum. Wah! (cautioned by umpire for chatting when bases are unoccupied.) I beg your pardon, Mr. Umpire. (Picks grass, shakes fist at ump and grins at the crowd.) Wow! Oh, say, if you ever hit that one, pal, they'd have to call out the police to find the ball. (Claps hands.) Now, Sam, hit this one as hard as you please. Wah! Be sure and touch every base when you go around, Sam. (Crawford flies out.)

The unfortunate circumstances of Crawford's final two seasons in Detroit should not obscure the fact that he and Jennings got along well for most of their years together. Crawford was the top star on the Tigers when Hughie first took the managerial reins. In August 1910, well after many in the baseball world hailed Cobb as the greatest player in the game, Jennings praised Crawford as nearly equal to Ty. As late as 1915, the skipper still held Wahoo in high regard, describing the outfielder as "a man of most exemplary habits, remarkable disposition, and is an example that it would be well for any man in any profession to follow."

Opposing managers also thought well of Crawford. When asked in 1922 to select an American League team of all-stars from his years as Philadelphia skipper, Connie Mack picked Sam as one of his two outfield substitutes—Ruth, Speaker, and Cobb were his top choices. Noting Crawford's many game-winning hits against his Athletics, Mack said "while I regretted to see him play his last game, again it was one of the happiest days of my life."

Mack, who would manage the A's for five decades, witnessed many changes in the game. An explosion of offense emerged as baseball's most dramatic transformation of the 1920s. With Ruth leading the charge, major league teams hit more home runs, hit for higher averages, and scored more runs than ever before. Fans and scholars have long debated the reasons for this hitting breakthrough. A leading theory for explaining the hitting deluge is the shift to a "lively" or rabbit ball. While it is true that MLB started using baseballs made with Australian, rather than American, yarn in 1920, the juiced ball theory has been rejected by most scholars and experts who have studied the issue. Instead, they credit Babe Ruth's success with full-strength power swings as the main reason for the transformation. Soon other hitters copied the Babe's style, abandoning the shortened chop-hit stroke to swing for the fences. The practice of swapping out befouled and discolored baseballs for new, cleaner balls during a game also improved hitting in the 1920s. So too did the abolition of the spitball.

With balls flying out of stadiums at an unprecedented rate, many observers wondered what the leading slugger of the preceding era could have done in the 1920s. Praising Crawford's perfect timing and smooth swing, umpire Billy Evans maintained that Wahoo's numbers would have rivaled Ruth's had he played in the later decade. Hughie Jennings agreed. "I have often thought what a pity it was that Crawford could not have been in his prime when the lively ball appeared," the skipper wrote in 1926. "He would have studded the base ball record book with some new home-run marks." Many Deadball Era players, including Cobb, concurred. The Georgia Peach argued that Crawford would have matched the slugging feats of Ruth and Lou Gehrig if he had the opportunity to hit the lively ball. Sportswriters expressed similar sentiments. Factoring in the closer outfield fences of the decade, Grantland Rice wrote in 1929, with just a bit of exaggeration, that Crawford would average 100 home runs a season were he still playing.

While fans across the nation discussed his home run potential in the Roaring Twenties, Sam himself forged a new tie with his fellow ballplayers by joining the Association of Professional Ball Players of America (APBPA), a charitable organization formed in Los Angeles in 1924 to help sick and indigent players. Within two years, more than 2,000 current and former major and minor league players had paid the $5 membership fee. Team owners and the Commissioner's office also contributed money to the cause. Still active today with more than 100,000 members, the organization continues its work of helping needy ballplayers.

The National College of Baseball in Burbank evidently did not succeed as Orndorff had hoped, because he soon moved his school to Los Angeles and changed its name. Crawford had found other employment by this time. In February 1924, he accepted an offer to coach baseball at the University of Southern

California. Sam joined the world of academia at a good time, since college enrollment would double during the decade. Though football occupied the throne as king of the campus sports, college baseball was increasing in popularity. Coaches of university teams averaged a salary of more than $5,000 a year in the 1920s, roughly the same as professors.

The USC baseball program had experienced sporadic success since the 1890s but had yet to hit its stride as a full-fledged university sport. Looking to take Trojan baseball to the next level, Crawford added more games to the schedule and sought to improve his team by playing tougher competition. He was a driving force in the formation of the California Intercollegiate Baseball Association. Functioning as a division in the Pacific Coast Conference, the CIBA originally included USC, Stanford, University of California, University of Santa Clara, and St. Mary's College. In December 1927 Crawford was elected president of the CIBA.

During Sam's tenure, Southern Cal started playing its home games at the recently-built Los Angeles Memorial Coliseum. The coach soon abandoned this large venue after his outfielders complained that they could not see batted balls against the background of the Coliseum's seats. Sam feared that his players could get beaned by fly balls they could not track.

In 1926 *The Sporting News* quipped that Sam, as a coach, had not uncovered any new Crawfords at USC. While that statement was true, he did advance the ballplaying skills of his team. A few of his most talented charges gained opportunities to reach the professional ranks. John Henry Hawkins, a football and baseball star at USC, signed a contract with the St. Louis Browns in 1926 but failed to report. Upon Crawford's recommendation, John McGraw invited Hawkins to Giants spring training the following year. Commissioner Landis, however, ruled that St. Louis still held legitimate claim to the big first baseman. Hawkins was sent to Browns training camp, but he did not land a roster spot.

Another of Crawford's ballplayers, Red Badgro, achieved greater success in professional sports. After Sam's tutelage helped him lead USC in hitting, the burly outfielder played for Muskogee in the Western Association, Tulsa in the Western League, and Milwaukee in the American Association. He soon advanced to the Big Show with the St. Louis Browns but lasted only two partial seasons in the majors. A three-sport star in college, he instead found his niche in the National Football League. Dominating on both sides of the ball for the NFL's New York Giants, Badgro later gained induction into the Pro Football Hall of Fame.

One of Crawford's most successful baseball "finds" during his time at USC was actually not one of his own players. High school pitcher Lou Almada overwhelmed prep hitters in Los Angeles in the mid-1920s. In the summer of 1926, he attracted national attention by striking out Babe Ruth in an exhibition game at LA's Wrigley Field. Crawford saw the feat and secured a spot for the young southpaw at Giants training camp the following spring. Despite the Mexican-born youth's considerable skills, he struggled against major league hitters at spring training. After Almada was plunked by a line drive, McGraw assigned him to a Giants farm team. But he quit the organization and returned to the West Coast, eventually signing with the Seattle Indians of the Pacific Coast League. Switching to the outfield, Almada starred in the league for eight years, retiring with a career .304 batting average. His younger brother Mel became the first Mexican-born player in the majors when he signed with the Boston Red Sox in 1933.

In nearly every year since the first decade of the 1900s, a college team in either America or Asia would cross the Pacific to play a series of games against host teams on the other continent. Sometimes the teams met in the middle by playing in Hawaii. In the summer of 1928 USC took its turn in this exchange when Crawford and his team traveled to East Asia. The Trojans won 15 of the 27 games they played against teams in Japan, Manchuria, and Korea. Tokyo's Waseda University team, however, bested USC six games to five. Crawford hailed the trip as a success, especially for its promotion of good relations between the Japanese and the Americans. As she did on the World Tour 15 years earlier, Ada accompanied her husband on the four-month trip to Asia.

On June 5, following the end of the 1929 college season, Crawford resigned as coach of the Southern Cal baseball team. During his six seasons at the helm, his teams compiled a 59-46-3 record. More important than the wins and losses of his own teams was the long-term impact that Crawford had at USC. Inheriting a rag-tag team with little direction, Sam developed Trojan baseball into a program poised for great success. In so doing, he laid the foundation for the future of Southern Cal baseball.

The year following Crawford's resignation, his successor Sam Barry led the Trojans to a CIBA championship with a 25-5-1 record. The former University of Iowa coach built upon Sam's work to take USC baseball to the next level. From 1930 to 1941, Barry's teams claimed five CIBA titles and 219 total wins. And the best was yet to come for Trojan baseball.

For their first five years in California, the Crawfords lived at 1954 Canyon Drive in the Hollywood Hills. The house sat just two miles south of the "HOLLYWOODLAND" sign erected in 1923 to advertise a new housing development. The "LAND" part was removed in the 1940s after the famous sign came to symbolize the heart of the American film industry.

The now-iconic white letters atop Mount Lee would have been visible from the Crawfords' neighborhood on Canyon Drive. They did not enjoy their view of the sign for long though. In 1923 the family moved to Pico, a community a dozen miles southeast of downtown Los Angeles. This location was closer to Sam's walnut ranch and some of the other properties in the area he had acquired.

Crediting the warmer temperatures as a factor in his late-career success in the PCL, Crawford continued to enjoy the southern California climate after his playing days had ended. Golf remained a favorite activity. He even competed, participating in events such as the annual APBPA golf tournament. In the 1925 edition of this tourney, he lost to Vernon Tigers pitcher Clyde Barfoot in the quarterfinals. Other players in the tournament included Sam's former Angels teammate Arnold Statz and former Los Angeles manager Frank "Pop" Dillon.

Though he had moved away from Hollywood, Sam could not escape the call of the growing movie industry. By the mid-1920s, Buster Keaton had established himself as one of the top comedy film stars of the day, along with Charlie Chaplain and Harold Lloyd. An enthusiastic baseball fan, Keaton liked to stage impromptu games during shooting breaks. In 1927 the actor played a young man attempting to win the heart of a young lady by starring on various college sports teams. The main character's clumsiness and lack of athletic skill generate the laughs. Of course, one of the sports he attempts is baseball. And so the film, titled *College*, needed a coach. Who better to play this part than the real-life coach of the USC Trojans?

Crawford appears in a handful of scenes in the baseball section of the 66-minute movie. The advent of "talkies" had not yet arrived, so he has no spoken lines. But not surprisingly, he looks every bit the part of a college baseball coach. During a tryout, Keaton's character finagles his way into a practice game with the other college players. Diamond hijinks ensue.

Keaton displays impressive physical talents portraying his comedically unathletic character. Trips, flops, and pratfalls abound throughout the movie, which provides a glimpse into the athletic endeavors on a college campus in the 1920s. Though the film was not a hit, it did provide Crawford with an opportunity to kick Keaton in the rear end.

Virginia was 20 years old and Sam Jr. was nine when their father made his big screen debut in September 1927. Having graduated high school a couple years earlier, the elder child would be soon moving out of the Crawford household in Pico. In

1929 Virginia married Arthur Johnson, a young man later described by his daughter as "movie star handsome with high cheekbones, a great shock of wavy brown hair, and a Tom Cruise smile long before anybody'd ever heard of Tom Cruise."

Appropriately enough, the new member of the Crawford family loved sports. A teacher at Wilshire Junior High in nearby Fullerton, Johnson coached every boys sport the school offered—baseball, basketball, football, tennis, and track. Crawford liked his new son-in-law, who in turn enjoyed hearing about Sam's playing days. Virginia at this time worked as a salesperson in a dry goods store. The newlyweds' home in Fullerton in Orange County was about 15 miles southeast of Pico.

In April 1930, Crawford celebrated his 50th birthday. His income from his years as a professional ballplayer, college coach, and walnut rancher, along with a few dividend-yielding investments, had accumulated into a substantial net worth. His bank account did not match that of millionaire Ty Cobb—who collected hefty baseball salaries through the 1920s and owned profitable Coca-Cola and GM stocks—but Sam was well-off. According to the 1930 U.S. Census, the house Crawford owned in Pico was worth $35,000. That was about six times the value of an average house in the United States that year.

During his playing days, Sam gained a reputation for wisely managing his money. His financial skills would be tested in the coming years as the nation fell deeper into the quagmire of the Great Depression.

Chapter 13

A Man in Blue

At the onset of the new decade, Crawford found himself without a full-time "day job." He had resigned his coaching position at USC, just four months before the stock market crash of 1929. The growth of the Roaring Twenties came to an abrupt end and the nation plunged into the worst economic downturn it had ever experienced. The Great Depression would continue through the 1930s, a period marked by bank failures, plunging stock values, and soaring unemployment.

Crawford likely believed his healthy financial status would enable him to weather the storm, which most Americans viewed as a short-term development. That was the pattern that economic downturns had followed thus far in the country's history—they lasted for a few years, then the economy rebounded and prosperity returned. Sam and everybody else would soon learn that this one was different.

In 1930 Crawford appeared in another movie, *They Learned About the Women*, a baseball-themed musical starring the popular vaudeville duo Van and Schenck and the Oscar-nominated actress Bessie Love. This time, however, Sam was just one of many background ballplayers in the film's baseball scenes—a small and uncredited part. Other past and current big leaguers appearing in the movie included, Ernie Orsatti, Irish Meusel, Jim Thorpe, Bucky Harris, and Mike Donlin, the outfielder who had replaced Crawford in Cincinnati in 1903. *They Learned About the Women* drew tepid box office returns, though it did provide inspiration for the 1949 film *Take Me Out to the Ball Game*, starring Frank Sinatra, Gene Kelly, and Esther Williams.

After the second, and last, chapter of his brief movie career, Crawford opened a hot dog stand in Whittier, a neighboring town just a mile southeast of his Pico residence. He reportedly pursued this venture not because he needed the money, but for the diversion it provided to fill his idle hours. Around this time, he took up bicycling, showing that conditioning and fitness remained a priority for him in middle age.

In October 1932, Jess Orndorff announced plans for a barnstorming tour the following spring. For this trip, he assembled a roster of former major leaguers, including Chief Meyers, Harry Hooper, Bill Wambsganss, Jim Thorpe, and Mike Donlin. Having worked with Orndorff a decade earlier at the National College of Baseball, Crawford joined the tour as well. These "old-timers" were set to play a 55-game schedule starting in California in April 1933. They would square off against local semi-pro teams across the country. Seeking publicity for his National Baseball School, Orndorff encouraged boys in each city to come to the ballfields to receive free instruction from the players before the games. Young fans could even gain free admission by bringing a copy of *The Sporting News*, which the former big leaguers would autograph upon request.

After commencing in California, the tour made its way east to Utah in early May. Unfortunately, that was the end of the road. Citing the challenges presented by unfavorable weather in their early stops, the Old-Timers' club disbanded in Salt Lake City. In addition to the weather, the generous free admission policy and the difficulty of drawing a decent gate during an ongoing depression doomed the financial prospects of the tour.

Returning home to Pico, Crawford found an opportunity to remain active in baseball through one of the many government agencies created to help people during the Great Depression. In

1933 California established the State Emergency Relief Administration to distribute federal and state money for unemployment relief. Similar to some of the other New Deal-era agencies, SERA allocated funds for baseball leagues. Sam coached a SERA team in nearby Montebello. Former Cubs infielder Marty Krug also helmed a club in the same league.

Meanwhile, in Major League Baseball, the fortunes of Crawford's former employers had improved significantly by mid-decade. Besting the Ruth-Gehrig Yankees by seven games, Detroit captured the AL pennant in 1934—the first flag for the Motor City since 1909. The resurgent Tigers of the 1930s boasted a potent lineup with four future Hall of Famers: Hank Greenberg (1B), Charlie Gehringer (2B), Goose Goslin (LF), and Mickey Cochrane (C, manager). Schoolboy Rowe (24 wins) and Tommy Bridges (22 wins) led a formidable pitching staff that posted the league's second lowest ERA.

Crawford supported his former team from a thousand miles away, following their drive to the pennant in the newspapers and on the radio. With the Tigers' success in 1934, the press reflected on the stars of their flag-winning teams from a quarter-century earlier. Some writers wondered if Sam would travel to Detroit to attend the World Series games at Navin Field. The answer was no. Noting his continuing support for the team, the Associated Press reported that "lack of wherewithal alone is keeping him away from the series."

Detroit faced the St. Louis Cardinals "Gas House Gang," featuring Frankie Frisch, Joe Medwick, Pepper Martin, Leo Durocher, Dizzy Dean, and Paul Dean. In a result reminiscent of the 1909 Fall Classic, the Tigers lost the series by getting shutout in Game 7. Disappointed in all four of their team's World Series trips, Detroiters wondered if they would ever claim baseball's top prize. The Tigers won the AL flag again in 1935 to set up a series rematch against the Chicago Cubs, the team that had bested them in 1907 and 1908. This time the Tigers prevailed, capturing the championship four games to two. Long-suffering Detroit fans finally celebrated a World Series title. But sad news would soon temper the good feelings. Just a month after watching his team win its first World Series, longtime owner Frank Navin died from a heart attack while horseback riding.

By the mid-1930s, the number of active big leaguers who had shared the field with Crawford had dwindled to just a handful. One of the last of them, Babe Ruth, played only a few games in 1935 before retiring. Ty Cobb had hung up his spikes after the 1928 season. Even Sam's replacement, Harry Heilmann, ended his MLB career in 1932. He had been a magnificent hitter for Detroit, winning four batting titles en route to a .342 lifetime batting average.

The soaring averages and power numbers that big league hitters like Heilmann posted through the 1920s and into the 1930s continued the speculation about what Crawford could have done in this later era. Even during Sam's playing days, long before the home run barrage commenced, many players and writers believed he had been denied his fair share of big hits. Noting the frequency that deep-stationed outfielders like Fielder Jones tracked down his long drives, M.W. Bingay of *The Detroit News* wrote that Crawford was robbed of more hits than any other big leaguer. In January 1911, *The Detroit Times* commented that "seldom has a ball player gone through a season as he [Sam] did in 1910, hitting the ball terrifically and missing so many long drives because outfielders just managed to pull down his smashes." Several opposing pitchers admitted that Crawford hit the ball harder than anybody, but his drives often found their way into fielders' gloves. Teammate Donie Bush said that he saw Sam hit five deep fly balls in a single game that were caught near the wall for outs. *Sporting Life* summed up the trend by calling Sam a notoriously hard-luck batter.

Though acknowledging that luck can impact a player's numbers, Crawford himself refused to use it as an excuse for his poor hitting stretches. He believed that all he could do was hit the ball hard. Sometimes they went for hits, sometimes not. He said that he hit as many hard drives during his best statistical years as he did during his worst. Over the long-term, the effects of luck evened out. "I believe my poorest year was about as far below my general average as my best was above that average," Crawford said. "But luck teaches the ball player not to put too much dependence upon mere records and not to feel inflated by apparent success nor discouraged by apparent failure."

Whatever hard luck Crawford had to endure, he achieved far more successes as a hitter than all but a few who wore the uniform. His .309 lifetime batting average placed him in MLB's all-time top-30 hitters at the time of his retirement. Sam's diamond achievements, however, somehow lost their luster just a couple decades after his retirement. In 1936 the Baseball Writers' Association of America (BBWAA) voted for the inaugural class of the National Baseball Hall of Fame. Only Ty Cobb, Honus Wagner, Babe Ruth, Christy Mathewson, and Walter Johnson received the 75 percent of votes required for admission. And none of those legends was a unanimous selection. Other giants of the game, Napoleon Lajoie, Cy Young, and Tris Speaker, did not gain admission in that first vote. Given the incredibly high standards the 200-plus writers had initially set for Hall admission, it is not surprising that Crawford did not gain entry in 1936. What is surprising, astonishing even, is that only one voter named him on his ballot. And so the top power hitter of his day was deemed less worthy of enshrinement than Lou Criger (7 votes), a defensive-specialist catcher who topped 100 games just once in his career, while posting a .221 lifetime batting average.

The next year, the BBWAA voted in Lajoie, Speaker, and Young. Crawford, however, collected just five votes, 11 fewer than Criger and Jimmy Archer, a former Cubs catcher with all of 660 career hits. The following two years, Grover Cleveland Alexander, George Sisler, Wee Willie Keeler, and Eddie Collins gained admission to the Hall of Fame. Crawford's vote total peaked at 11 in 1938, nowhere near the 197 needed to punch a ticket to Cooperstown. He received six votes in 1939, two votes in 1942, and four votes in 1945. In 1946, the BBWAA held a nominating election to determine who would be named on the next official ballot. Crawford fell well short of the total needed for nomination. After that, he never appeared on a BBWAA ballot again.

That the writers never even came close to inducting Crawford was a shocking snub. But perhaps it should not have been that surprising. Though Walter Johnson, Joe Tinker, Jimmy Collins, and other players who had seen Sam play extolled his greatness, by the late 1930s the number of writers with first-hand knowledge of his exploits had dwindled. And there was no film footage of his big hits to remind them. Yes, veteran scribes like Hugh Fullerton and H.G. Salsinger still lauded Sam's batting virtues, but the bar for a top power hitter had been raised by Ruth hitting 60 home runs in a season and Jimmie Foxx and Hank Greenberg each reaching 58. Sam may have collected triples by the cartload, but that achievement faded in glamour during the Age of Ruth. Wahoo's top year of 16 homers paled in comparison to the leading sluggers of the 1920s and 1930s. And so the hardest hitter of the first two decades of the twentieth century was left on the outside looking in as the National Baseball Hall of Fame held its formal opening in 1939.

The Great Depression continued to hold the nation in its grip in the mid-1930s. Crawford hoped to weather the prolonged downturn by investing in a pecan grove, but eventually his savings eroded away. Needing a new source of income, he looked again to baseball. In December 1934, Sam applied to become an umpire in the Pacific Coast League. Former big leaguers Duster Mails, George Burns, and Wally Hood joined him in submitting applications to the league office at this time.

While waiting to hear the status of his application, Crawford made a backup plan. Apparently not soured by his experience two years earlier, he planned to join another touring team of old-timers. With many familiar faces, including Orndorff, Wambsganss, and Hooper, the troupe again planned to play local teams and instruct youngsters who came out to the ballpark. This time though, Sam did not hit the road with Orndorff's crew. Early in 1935 the PCL hired Crawford as an umpire for the upcoming season.

As a player, Sam had few major disagreements with the umpires. In a big league career of more than 2,500 games, he was ejected only five times. Veteran ump Billy Evans related a story that reflected Crawford's relationship with the men in blue. Evans once called Sam out on a close play at the plate, ending a game that Detroit lost by one run. As the angry crowd hurled insults at the umpire, Crawford dusted off his uniform and engaged him in conversation as they walked off the field. While riding a trolly home from the game, Evans overheard fans speculating about how Wahoo bawled him out after the game. The umpire later relayed what they actually said to each other:

> **Crawford:** "Well, Billy, I was out all right, but it was close and it was worth taking this chance."
>
> **Evans:** "That's right, Sam. The throw had to be good to get you, and if you'd scored that run you had a chance to win the game. It was a good chance to take with two out."
>
> [walking together] **Crawford:** "How's the wife, Bill?"
>
> **Evans:** "Fine, thank you, Sam. I've got her along with me this trip."
>
> **Crawford:** "Well, if you've got nothing on for tonight I'll bring the car around and we'll go for a drive."

Now wearing the blue himself, Sam tried to maintain cordial relations with the players. San Diego Padres catcher Bill Starr described Crawford as "the kindest person ever to wear an umpire's uniform." Observing that Sam did not like confrontations, Starr said he always felt remorse after criticizing one of his calls. Many managers and other players in the PCL felt the same way. Starr recalled a time when Portland's manager screamed at Sam to call a balk on the opposing pitcher. Both the angry skipper and the pitcher approached the plate to argue their case. Crawford's calm responses soon ended the dispute with both adversaries apologizing for causing trouble.

Sam sometimes liked to kid around with the players. Once after he called a strike on Frankie Morehouse, the batter turned around and told Crawford he missed the call. "Oh, yeah," Sam replied. "Well, if I'd had that bat in my hand, I wouldn't have missed it." Crawford's umpiring partner on the field, Jack Powell, warned him not to fraternize with the players. He said if you get too friendly with them, they will use that against you and put you on the spot. Sam eventually found out that Powell was right.

Crawford earned $100 a week as a PCL umpire, good wages during the depression. After a year in the minors, he turned his eye to the Big Show. In April 1936, he wrote a note of thanks to National League president Ford Frick for sending him a lifetime silver pass granting free admission to all NL games. Crawford continued by asking Frick to consider him as an NL umpire. In 1918, Sam had turned down a chance to continue his big league playing career due to family considerations. Now that his youngest child, Sam Jr., had just turned 18, Crawford hoped to return to the majors. This did not happen though, and he remained a PCL umpire.

Following Sam's second season as arbiter, PCL president W.C. Tuttle announced that he wanted a young, yet experienced and efficient umpiring staff. Deciding that Crawford did not fit these criteria, he dropped him. In August 1937, however, Tuttle rehired Sam to replace his old partner Jack Powell, who had been arrested at a game in Sacramento for public intoxication. While behind the plate that year, Crawford had the opportunity to watch a skinny teenager knocking out home runs for the San Diego Padres. The kid's name: Ted Williams. That was not the first time umpire Sam witnessed a rising star destined for major league greatness. A couple years earlier, a San Francisco outfielder named Joe DiMaggio tore up the PCL with a .398 batting average and 34 home runs.

After his mid-season return, Crawford apparently impressed his boss. Tuttle assigned him to one of the crews that would work the league semifinals that fall. In 1938 Sam returned to umpire another PCL season. At a game in Los Angeles on May 15, the Helms-Olympic Athletic Foundation awarded trophies to the most valuable Angels for each season since 1903. Crawford received the award for the 1919 Los Angeles team MVP.

After four years in blue, Sam had had enough. At the end of the 1938 season, he resigned as a PCL umpire. His time as an arbiter did not engender fond memories for Crawford, who never enjoyed being the target of fan criticism. Not that any player, manager, or umpire does, but many of them do not let acrimony bother them much. Some even channel it to drive their on-field performance. Sam, on the other hand, got worn down by it. Decades later he related his feelings about umpiring:

> Umpiring is a lonesome life.... You haven't got a friend in the place. Only your partner, that's all.... Everybody else is just waiting for you to make a mistake. There's a bench over here, and a bench over there, and thousands of people in the stands, and every eye in the whole damn place is watching like a hawk trying to get something on you.... It's a thankless and lonely way to live, so I quit it.

Earlier that year Sam had experienced a devastating loss. In February 1938, his beloved wife fell ill while visiting their daughter Virginia in Fullerton. Ada underwent a major operation at a local hospital but died a month later at the age of 57. She and Sam had been married 36 years. Following a funeral at the White-Emerson funeral chapel in Whittier, she was buried at Rose Hills Memorial Park in the same town. During her years in California, Ada had been active in social and philanthropic activities.

Sam Jr., almost 20 at the time of his mother's passing, still lived at home in Pico. Virginia remained in Fullerton, where her husband Arthur still taught and coached. Crawford had become a grandfather a year earlier, when the Johnsons' daughter Carole was born in September 1937. Three years later, Virginia gave birth to another daughter, Julie.

Sam's children remained close to home, but for most of his adult life he lived well over a thousand miles from his three siblings. Since her marriage to Arthur Monteen in 1901, Zadia had lived in Wahoo, Monowi, Fremont, Kearney, and Grand Island in Nebraska, as well as Denver, Colorado. After she and her husband divorced in the 1930s, Zadia moved to Lincoln, Nebraska, where she lived downtown on Q Street. This location was only a mile from where her daughter Lucile Jacoby and her family lived.

Sam's brother Step had moved to Deadwood, South Dakota, in the early 1900s to play baseball. He lived there for a few years with his wife Lailah, while following the family tradition of barbering. He later returned to Nebraska, where he resided in Omaha with his second wife Fern. By the early 1930s, he had given up cutting hair to work as a salesman. A few years later, he moved west to southern California, near his older brother. According to his 1942 draft registration card, 57-year-old Step was unemployed at the time and living on Menlo Avenue, about a mile west of downtown Los Angeles.

The youngest Crawford brother, Neal, moved from Wahoo to Omaha as a young man. After a term in the United States Army Air Service during World War I, he moved to Le Sueur, Minnesota, where he worked for the town's newspaper. He later resided in Peshtigo, Wisconsin, before settling in Minneapolis, where he was a newspaper circulation manager. On October 29, 1940, he died from encephalomalacia (softening of brain tissue) at the age of 51. Neal is buried in the Fort Snelling National Cemetery in Minneapolis.

After Sam's resignation as a PCL umpire, his membership in the Association of Professional Ball Players of America was his last remaining organizational tie to baseball. In 1936 members selected Crawford from a field of 76 candidates to serve as one of the APBPA's ten directors. Two years later he was re-elected to the board of directors. Other board members serving with Sam included Lou Gehrig, Mickey Cochrane, Joe Cronin, and Gabby Hartnett.

Receiving more than $130,000 in proceeds from the 1934 and 1935 major league All-Star Games allowed APBPA secretary Russ Hall to broaden the organization's work and help more needy ballplayers. The hard times of the 1930s increased the relevance of the association's mission. Its membership book at that time conveyed a strong message to the active players:

> This Association is the humanity part of baseball, and it all simmers down to one thing—do you want to help the old, injured, and sick ballplayers and umpires when they cannot help themselves? For you must remember, you are going to get old yourself and may possibly become sick with an incurable disease or you may become permanently injured through no fault of your own and it is mighty nice to have something to fall back on and find some relief.

In June 1939, 59-year-old Crawford again took the field. Traveling to Detroit, he played in an old-timers' game at his former ballpark—now called Briggs Stadium. His former Tiger teammates Davy Jones, Bobby Veach, and Marty Kavanagh joined him for this contest. The exhibition preceded a regular game between Detroit and Philadelphia. Organizers staged the event to honor Connie Mack. Following the games, the former ballplayers and longtime Athletics manager attended a banquet held in their honor.

Back in southern California, Crawford found employment driving a truck. The job paid him $18 a week. He soon found a better-paying job with Barker Bros., an LA-based furniture company, working as a shipping packer and freight elevator operator. His new employer paid him $1,200 a year. Though a fraction of his major league salary, it was decent pay for the late depression era. The average income in the United States in 1940 was $1,368.

Around this time, Crawford moved to an apartment in the Westlake neighborhood of Central Los Angeles. With Sam Jr. having moved into his own place on San Gabriel Boulevard in Pico, Sam Sr. lived by himself for the first time. His apartment was in the four-story Hotel Chelsea on South Bonnie Brae Street, a building originally constructed in the 1920s to lodge tourists visiting Westlake Park (today MacArthur Park) and other nearby attractions. The solid brick structure with decorative trim was a mile west of downtown and about two miles southwest of where Dodger Stadium would be built in Chavez Ravine two decades later.

No longer employed in baseball, Sam entered uncharted waters in the new decade. Events halfway around the world, meanwhile, would drag the nation into a global conflict that impacted the life of nearly every American.

Chapter 14

The Desert

Sam Crawford turned 60 in April 1940. No longer a coach or an umpire, he maintained one official connection to Organized Baseball. Earlier that year, he defeated former Red Sox outfielder Chester Chadbourne in a vote-by-mail election to become treasurer of the Association of Professional Ball Players of America. Soon after the election, organization members gathered at what was described as one of their most successful dinners. Held in Los Angeles, the event featured a rousing speech by San Francisco Seal owner Charley Graham. The outgoing APBPA president urged his listeners to practice patience and perseverance to avoid ill-feelings when recruiting new members. The singing talents of Cincinnati (soon to be Pittsburgh) outfielder Vince DiMaggio provided the highlight of the evening's entertainment.

Crawford won subsequent reelections to remain in office as treasurer for four years. His popularity among fellow APBPA members was evident in his landslide 874 to 282-vote win over Marty Krug in the 1943 contest. During Sam's tenure as treasurer, the organization disbursed more than a quarter-million dollars in aid to sick and indigent ballplayers each year. Proceeds from the major league All-Star Game provided the principal source of income for the APBPA during these years.

Babe Ruth attended the organization's annual banquet in February 1942. The retired slugger was in town to portray himself in *The Pride of the Yankees*, a film tribute to Lou Gehrig, who had died a year earlier. Speakers at the banquet included Crawford, Ruth, Graham (once again APBPA president), Bob Meusel and Bill Dickey. Like Ruth, Meusel and Dickey would portray themselves as Gehrig's teammates in the upcoming movie.

Crawford continued to work at Barker Bros., but his residence soon changed again. In 1941 he moved to a house on Hollyridge Drive in Hollywood, just a half-mile northwest of the home he and Ada shared on Canyon Drive two decades earlier. Sam again lived south of the famous "HOLLYWOODLAND" sign on Mount Lee, and not quite a mile northeast of the famous Hollywood and Vine intersection.

The house where Crawford now lived was owned by Mary Carter. Born Mary Blazer in Illinois in December 1884, the new lady in Sam's life was not a recent acquaintance. Mary and her husband George, a dry cleaner, had been longtime friends of Sam and Ada. Like Crawford, Mary had lost her spouse a few years earlier. Sam and Mary wed in 1942. The groom was 62, the bride 57.

At the time Crawford's bachelor days ended, the United States was once again fighting in a world war. The country that had drawn the nation into WWII was the same one that Crawford and many other American ballplayers had visited years earlier to promote baseball. Following Japan's attack on Pearl Harbor, many former players expressed their disdain for the people across the Pacific. Honus Lobert, a member of the 1913-14 World Tour, said of the Japanese, "Well, we gave 'em the game, and now it's almost a disgrace to think that they've played it." *The Sporting News* went even further in distancing America's game from the country's new wartime enemies:

> So, we repeat, Japan never was converted to baseball.
> They may have acquired a little skill at the game, but the
> soul of our National Game never touched them. No nation

which has had as intimate contact with baseball as the Japanese, could have committed the vicious, infamous deed of the early morning of December 7, 1941, if the spirit of the game ever had penetrated their yellow hides.

The United States' entry into World War II impacted almost every American family. The Crawfords were no exception. Sam left his position with Barker Bros. to work in a defense plant. His son would soon experience the war firsthand.

As a teenager, Sam Jr. had hoped to follow in his father's baseball footsteps. Similar to his dad, he played outfield and sometimes first base. Sam Jr. twice attended a tryout for Portland in the Pacific Coast League, but did not land a roster spot either time. In February 1940, at age 22, he arrived at the Los Angeles Angels training camp in Ontario, California, and asked for a tryout. Team officials granted this request from the son of one of their most famous players, but Sam Jr. did not make the Angels roster.

With baseball not in his future, Sam Jr. found employment with Kern Oil Company. Like his father, he did not remain in the petroleum industry for long. In April 1941, eight months before Pearl Harbor, Sam Jr. enlisted in the United States Marine Corps. During World War II, he saw action in the South Pacific. Rising to the rank of gunnery sergeant, he remained in the Marines until 1948, three years after the war ended. Sam Jr. married in 1952 and later moved to San Francisco.

In the early 1940s, Sam's daughter Virginia still lived in Fullerton with her husband Art and their two daughters. But all was not well within the Johnson household. Virginia's daughter Julie later described her mother as attentive and kind when sober, but abusive and angry when drunk. Unfortunately, Virginia's drinking increased at this time. Plagued by ulcers, Art did not share his wife's taste for gin. Distance between the spouses widened. Seeking a different lifestyle than that provided by her husband, Virginia filed for divorce.

Virginia then relocated to La Habra, a few miles north of Fullerton, where she moved in with a man whom she would later marry. Virginia and Art shared custody of the girls, who spent weekends with their father. Julie paints a bleak picture of her time in Virginia's new home, due to the frequent drinking of her mother and her new stepfather. In 1954 Virginia moved to Venezuela, where her husband had secured lucrative employment repairing equipment for an American oil company. The girls, teenagers by this time, lived full-time with Art in Fullerton.

Although a quarter century had passed since he last played in the majors, Crawford's name still occasionally popped up in the sports pages in the 1940s. The mentions usually came as part of a tribute to great outfield trios of Detroit's past. In 1945, for example, Washington sportswriter John B. Keller named the Cobb-Crawford-Veach unit as the best-ever hitting outfield. Noted sportswriter Hugh Fullerton similarly hailed the Cobb-Crawford-Jones triumvirate as one of a handful of "super-super outfields" in baseball history.

In 1943 another veteran sportswriter, Harry Grayson, published a series of newspaper articles profiling the great players in baseball history. A year later, this series was compiled into a book, *They Played the Game.* Crawford was among the featured diamond legends. Calling him one of the best-liked players in the game, Grayson credits Sam with playing a major role in helping Cobb score so many runs. "Crawford was a pull, line drive hitter of tremendous power," Grayson writes. "He leaned back slightly as his bat sailed into the ball. His swing was perfect."

The success of spread-stance hitters like Joe DiMaggio and Vern Stephens in the 1940s drew comparisons to Crawford, who similarly stood in the batter's box with his feet wide apart. Eddie Lawler, who had played against Sam during their semi-pro days, further elaborated on Wahoo's presence in the batter's box. "There was a half-smile on his face, and he was never tensed up," Lawler recalled. "He just stood there planted and waiting, chewing gum. He had the most beautiful swing you ever saw." Detroit manager Steve O'Neill, who saw plenty of Sam when catching for the Indians in the 1910s, also remembered his splendid swing. The Tiger skipper recalled that Wahoo swung with an uppercut, which, though departing from conventional batting wisdom, allowed him to drive the ball a great distance.

The defensive shift, which many believe was first used by Cleveland manager Lou Boudreau against Ted Williams in the 1940s, actually traces its origins back to the days of Wahoo Sam. *The Sporting News* reported that decades earlier, when Crawford came to bat, the New York Highlanders moved in their third baseman to the infield grass, shifted their shortstop to second, placed their second baseman closer to first on the outfield grass, and backed their first baseman Hal Chase well behind the bag on the foul line. Unorthodox in the Deadball Era, this type of shifted alignment is commonplace today.

Although a few former old-time ballplayers and veteran sportswriters still spoke of Crawford's skills, when it came to Hall of Fame admission their preaching failed to penetrate the deaf ears of the baseball scribe choir. As discussed in the previous chapter, Sam's chances of gaining a Cooperstown endorsement from the Baseball Writers' Association of America had dwindled to nothing by the mid-1940s.

What makes this rejection even more surprising is that it occurred while some believed that Crawford was part of the 3,000-hit club. Back in the mid-1920s, sports pages of certain newspapers listed Sam's career hit total at 3,051. A sporadic recognition of this achievement continued until 1942, when the Al Munro Elias Baseball Bureau reviewed the records. The Bureau reported that Crawford had recorded 87 hits while playing for Columbus and Grand Rapids in the Western League in 1899. Because the Western League later became the American League, some sportswriters added these hits to Sam's big league total. The Western League in 1899, however, was a minor league, and so Elias, the official statisticians for MLB, did not count the 87 hits, leaving Crawford three-dozen shy of 3,000.

Even with the subtraction, Sam's career hit total had been surpassed by only eight other major leaguers as of 1942. That he had more hits than the already-inducted Wee Willie Keeler and Rogers Hornsby did not impress the BBWAA. Neither did his career record for triples. Nor did his 1,500-plus RBI. Even being a perceived member of the 3,000 hit-club in the 1930s and early 1940s did not help his case. The all-knowing Cooperstown gatekeepers had issued their verdict—the hardest hitter of the Deadball Era was somehow not even close to worthy of Hall of Fame consideration.

Crawford did receive a modest consolation prize from his former home city. In 1944, William Pfau, a Detroit sports show promoter, conducted an annual poll for what he touted as the Tigers Hall of Fame. Motor City voters selected Crawford as one of the "original ten immortals," along with Cobb, Jennings, and Heilmann. Though not an official team honor, the selection showed that the fans who saw Sam play had not forgotten him.

In the years following World War II, Crawford sought a more secluded lifestyle. He still attended the conventions held by Southern California's growing community of former big leaguers, but city congestion grew more tiresome for him. In the first two decades after Sam had arrived in the city, Los Angeles had nearly tripled in population from a little over a half-million in 1920 to 1.5 million in 1940. The city would pass the two million mark in the early 1950s. The surrounding areas expanded rapidly as well. Los Angeles County, home to less than a million people in 1920, topped four million residents by 1950.

Crawford did not welcome this rapid urbanization springing up all around him. He and Mary moved to a frame bungalow on North Hudson Avenue in Hollywood, but he grew less enchanted with the city, as he later explained:

Too much smog. Too many cars, all fouling up the air. Can hardly breathe down there. Too many people, too. Have to stand in line everywhere you go. Can't even get a loaf of bread without standing in line. Pretty soon they'll be standing in line to get into the john! That's not for me.

To escape the crowded city, he bought a cabin on a half-acre of land about 40 miles northeast of Los Angeles. Located on the edge of the Mojave Desert, Sam's second home was near the small Antelope Valley town of Pearblossom (pop. 680). He found the desert location to his liking, with its healthy climate and friendly townspeople. Crawford's unpretentious cabin had a few modern conveniences, such as a television set and an outdoor shower, but no telephone connection.

Rarely accompanied by Mary, who did not like the desert, Sam spent up to six months a year by himself in his shack. He kept busy with several activities during his retirement years, such as whittling chains from balsa and teak to keep his hands in shape, and pruning fruit trees—his own and those on his neighbors' property. Crawford also liked to read, his favorite author being the 19th-century French novelist Honoré Balzac. Sam also admired the works of American writer and lecturer, Robert Ingersoll. Originally a lawyer in Peoria, Ingersoll gained fame in the late 1800s for his speeches on politics, Shakespeare, moral issues, and agnosticism.

Crawford even planned to author his own book. He sought to create an encyclopedic work containing the statistics, records, and characteristics of past big league players. He looked through old files at libraries and queried friends to find information for his project. Sam was correct about the level of public interest in such a publication, though perhaps not aware of the similar works that had been appearing in print. In the 1920s, sportswriter Ernest Lanigan published a statistical compendium of records called *The Baseball Cyclopedia.* In the 1930s, J.G. Taylor Spink, publisher of *The Sporting News,* started releasing editions of *Daguerreotypes of Great Stars of Baseball*, which also contained the records of many leading players. In 1951, sportswriter Hy Turkin, along with researcher S.C. Thompson, published an even more comprehensive baseball encyclopedia.

Sam's granddaughter Julie recalls riding with her dad to her grandfather's cabin in the desert. She holds fond memories of Sam, whom she remembers as funny and playful. During these visits, he would always take time to play catch with her. Art and Sam would sit in the shade of the shack and talk baseball. Young Julie loved hearing about the far-off places her grandfather had visited during his playing days. She said that when he talked, she could "almost hear the clatter of the railroad tracks in his voice."

Although Crawford freely recounted his playing days with his former son-in-law and granddaughter, he rarely talked baseball with his neighbors in the desert. The residents of Pearblossom he became acquainted with did not even know he was a former major league ballplayer. There were still fans, players, and writers across the country who remembered him, but the number of people who appreciated his impact on the game was shrinking. In 1950 New York sportswriter Tom Meany published a book titled *Baseball's Greatest Hitters*. The work profiled 20 top sluggers from the game's history, but Crawford did not make the cut. Even within the Association of Professional Ball Players of America, Sam declined in significance. In 1951 APBPA members selected 10 directors from a list of 69 nominees. Though a former treasurer and director within the organization, Crawford finished 42nd in the voting.

Wahoo Sam had faded from prominence by the early 1950s. Would he be remembered as anything more than Ty Cobb's teammate or the answer to a trivia question about triples?

Chapter 15

Cooperstown

Similar to Crawford, Ty Cobb relocated to California after his major league playing days had ended. In 1931 the Georgia Peach and his family moved into a mansion in Atherton, a town near San Francisco. Cobb's new abode was more than 300 miles away from Sam's residence in the Los Angeles area. Though living in the same state, the former Tiger teammates did not keep in touch.

Harry Heilmann remained in Detroit after hanging up his spikes. In 1933 he became a play-by-play radio broadcaster for the Tigers. With a captivating style that appealed to fans, Heilmann's skills in the broadcast booth were nearly as brilliant as those he had employed in the batter's box. In 1951, at the age of 56, he collapsed during spring training. Doctors diagnosed his ailment as lung cancer. Heilmann tried to keep this news from the public and even briefly resumed his broadcast duties. By late June, however, his illness had worsened and he was hospitalized in Detroit.

Following Heilmann's collapse that spring, Cobb led a campaign to enshrine his former teammate in the Hall of Fame. He even called for a special election to accelerate the process. That did not happen, but in late June a sportswriter informed Cobb that an advance poll showed that Heilmann would gain admission into the Hall with the next BBWAA vote. The Peach promptly wrote a letter sharing this news with Harry, which greatly pleased him.

The 1951 All-Star Game would be played at Briggs Stadium in Detroit on Tuesday, July 10. The festivities for this event included a banquet the night before the game and an on-field ceremony at the ASG honoring the all-time greatest Tigers. Both Crawford and Cobb traveled to the Motor City for this event. The long-estranged former teammates spoke again on friendly terms. They even planned to visit Heilmann together at the hospital on Monday, but Harry died earlier that day.

Before the All-Star Game, the 52,000 fans at Briggs Stadium observed a moment of silence for Heilmann. He, Crawford, and Cobb were named the all-time greatest outfielders in Tigers history as determined by a popular poll. Sam watched the game from Commissioner Happy Chandler's box. Along with his fellow honorees, Crawford received a gift of recognition at the game.

Six months later, in January 1952, baseball writers voted Heilmann into the Hall of Fame. Cobb then devoted his energies to sending another former teammate to Cooperstown. Even before their All-Star Game rapprochement, Cobb had long been extolling the baseball virtues of Wahoo Sam. In 1940, for example, he told Grantland Rice that Crawford might have hit 70 home runs a year had he played in the era of the "modern ball." Following their 1951 reunion, the Georgia Peach launched a full-scale campaign for Sam's enshrinement.

Though Cobb occasionally issued public statements calling for Crawford's admission into the Hall, most of his work occurred behind the scenes. He wrote hundreds of letters pleading Sam's case to influential sportswriters, baseball figures, and members of the Veterans Committee, the body that considered long-retired players for admission into the Hall of Fame. In his voluminous correspondence, Cobb cited his former teammate's .309 batting average in the Deadball Era, his power that would have produced 40-plus home runs a year in the modern game, and his impressive base-stealing totals. Though relations between them were chilly for much of their time together in Detroit, Cobb respected Sam's talent and accomplishments. He believed Crawford had earned his spot in the Hall.

Although Sam received copies of some of Cobb's letters, the public knew nothing about this campaign. That's how the Peach wanted it. When a San Francisco journalist told him he planned to write an article about his efforts on behalf of Crawford, Cobb threatened to never tell him anything in confidence again. The writer backed off, agreeing to keep the story quiet until after Cobb died. But the question remained, would Cobb's influence carry enough weight to convince the Cooperstown gatekeepers?

Crawford himself remained out of the public discourse on the Hall of Fame and other baseball issues in the early 1950s. Spending much of his time off the grid, the septuagenarian read stacks of books, tended the fruit trees surrounding his cabin, and chatted with Pearblossom neighbors who brought him pies. He still kept an eye on events in the baseball world though. One development that caught the attention of the former Nebraskan was the rise of Bob Cerv from Weston, a small town just a few miles from Wahoo. Following World War II service in the U.S. Navy and a successful athletic career at the University of Nebraska, Cerv joined the powerful New York Yankee juggernaut. Though a part-time player through his early years in the majors, the Cornhusker State slugger started four games in the 1955 World Series. After the following season, New York traded him to the Kansas City Athletics, where he emerged as an MVP candidate in 1958.

Crawford also followed the news about which players made it to Cooperstown. In 1953 the Hall of Fame created a new Committee on Veterans, which would hold biennial meetings to evaluate the candidacy of old-time players, managers, umpires, and executives no longer considered by the writers. Though earlier versions of this committee had existed, the creation of this new 11-member body headed by J.G. Taylor Spink breathed new life into Crawford's chances of enshrinement. Aside from Spink, other committee members included Tigers legend Charlie Gehringer and Branch Rickey, the former Dodgers GM who had brought Jackie Robinson into Major League Baseball. Sam was one of 51 nominated players for the class of 1953, but the Veterans Committee selected Chief Bender and Bobby Wallace that year.

Despite the worthiness of the selections (Bender was a top ace for Connie Mack's pennant-winning teams and Wallace was the best defensive shortstop of his day), some fans grumbled about who was passed over. Articles and letters to the editor calling for Crawford's induction appeared in sports publications. *Detroit News* sports editor H.G. Salsinger joined the campaign, pointing out that Sam's lifetime batting average was more than 50 points higher than recent inductee Rabbit Maranville.

Meeting every other year, the Veterans Committee next voted in February 1955. Existing rules at the time limited the body to selecting just two new Hall members at each election. With so many candidates, this restriction placed steep odds against any one individual player. That year the committee chose Ray Schalk and Frank "Home Run" Baker. Both were worthy candidates, though Baker recorded 1,100 fewer hits than Sam, and the defensive-oriented Schalk batted a modest .253 for his career. Crawford turned 75 in April of that year. Given the trickling pace at which players of his era entered the Hall, the chances that he would be around to see his own induction at Cooperstown seemed to be fading.

Though still shut out of the Hall of Fame, Crawford did receive some honors during this period. In 1951 the *Lincoln Journal* named him to the Nebraska Sports Hall of Fame. Wahoo Sam joined pitching legend Grover Cleveland Alexander as one of the first two native Nebraskan baseball players to receive this honor. Crawford also received the occasional fan letter. One of his favorites came from a ten-year-old boy who began his missive by writing, "I've been a fan of yours for years." Such attention helped remind Crawford that he had not been forgotten during a time when despondency threatened to creep in.

On February 3, 1957, the Veterans Committee met in New York to select two new members of the Hall of Fame. Once again, the 11 members weighed the merits of a long list of nominees. The baseball greats under consideration included: Billy Hamilton (career .344 BA), Jack Coombs (career 2.78 ERA), Amos Rusie (eight straight 20-win seasons), Tim Keefe (342 wins), Sam Thompson (.331 BA), Jake Beckley (1,575 RBI), Ross Youngs (.322 BA), and Harry Hooper (four World Series titles). Managerial legends Joe McCarthy and Miller Huggins added to the competition. With all these worthy candidates, *The Sporting News* speculated that the Veterans Committee meeting "might have to go into extra innings."

In addition to Spink, Rickey, and Gehringer, the 11-man body included committee secretary Paul Kerr, MLB secretary-treasurer Charles Segar, both major league presidents, the International League president, and three longtime sportswriters. These members had certainly heard from Ty Cobb in the months preceding the vote. The number of letters he sent is unknown, but the Peach had no qualms about expressing his opinions.

The Veterans Committee met at the Hotel Commodore on the afternoon of the first Sunday in February to cast their votes. On the first ballot all 11 members selected Sam Crawford for membership in the Hall of Fame. Former Yankee manager Joe McCarthy also gained a unanimous endorsement. After the vote, Paul Kerr informed the press of the committee's selections.

Hearing the news on the radio at his home in Atherton, Ty Cobb was elated at the success of his long campaign. He called his friend Jack McDonald, a sportswriter in San Francisco. "He made it. He made it," Cobb blurted in an excited voice, "Old Wahoo Sam. He just made the Hall of Fame."

Eager to convey his congratulations, the Georgia Peach called the Crawfords' home in Hollywood. He reached Mary, who in turn contacted her husband at his cabin near

Pearblossom—a process that involved calling one of the neighbors there who owned a telephone. When Sam got on the line, his wife told him he needed to talk to Cobb—she did not tell him why. Crawford then made the call to Atherton, reaching a delighted former teammate who told him he was a Hall of Famer. "It was a great climax to my career to get the news from Ty," Sam later said.

Congratulatory telegrams started arriving at the Crawfords' Hollywood home even before Wahoo had learned of his election. Reporters, unaware of Sam's desert refuge, struggled to track down the newest member of the Hall of Fame. When the press finally found him at his cabin, Crawford was busy with his chores—pruning fruit trees and pushing a wheelbarrow through the remains of an uncharacteristic snowfall that had covered the ground a week earlier. Journalists took note of Sam's rustic lifestyle, as well as the leftovers of his most recent meal, a half-eaten can of beans. One writer called his desert abode "as unpretentious as one can get."

Pearblossom residents wondered about the commotion at Crawford's cabin. Initially, they did not understand why reporters and photographers were at Sam's place. They did not know that he used to be a major league baseball player. When they learned this, and of his election to the Hall of Fame, excitement spread through the small desert community.

Mary told reporters that "Sam always was keenly interested when any of his old baseball associates were named to the Hall of Fame, but he never dreamed he would be chosen himself." Recent voting results had certainly given Crawford reason to be discouraged about his chances for enshrinement any time soon. When it finally happened, joy and gratitude filled his heart. He promptly hand wrote a letter of thanks to J.G. Taylor Spink:

> I could not use the cold letters and words of a typewriter to convey to you how grateful I am to you and to the other members of your committee for making this great climax to my life possible. I have written Ty Cobb along these lines. I had to write this personally to you with my own

hand and heart, for I wanted you to know what a wonderful thrill it is to have reached the Hall of Fame and am to be placed among all that diamond brilliance which is the ultra-ultra of all leagues.

And so the question arises: Would Crawford have made it into the Hall of Fame without the efforts and influence of Cobb? While a definitive answer cannot be known, it seems likely that Sam's career numbers would have eventually carried him to Cooperstown—but probably not in 1957. Given the previously discussed backlog of Deadball Era nominees, plus the lack of appreciation for Wahoo's diamond feats, Crawford possibly would not have been enshrined until the late 1960s, or maybe the 1970s when Harry Hooper, Jake Beckley, and Sam Thompson were inducted. Without Cobb, Sam might not have lived to see his own plaque. As it was, Crawford's enshrinement highlights the often-overlooked selfless work of Ty Cobb. Say what you want about the Georgia Peach, and many people have, but he devoted much time, energy, and financial resources during his golden years to helping others.

All but forgotten by the baseball world, Crawford now found himself a celebrity in demand. In April the Los Angeles Angels made him the guest of honor at the Opening Day ceremonies for the Pacific Coast League. In May, he was flown to San Francisco to receive an achievement scroll composed by California's governor Goodwin Knight. The ceremony took place at home plate of Seals Stadium between the games of a doubleheader. In June, Sam traveled to Kansas City to take part in an Athletics Hall of Fame event honoring Mickey Cochrane. Among the other baseball legends present in KC were Ty Cobb, Charlie Gehringer, Tris Speaker, and Jimmie Foxx.

Induction ceremonies at Cooperstown took place on Monday, July 22, before a crowd of about 2,000. July heat pushed temperatures into the 90s for the morning events. The cloudy sky mercifully provided shade to prevent the thermometer from reaching triple digits. Commissioner Ford Frick conducted the proceedings. In his comments about the

Kent Krause

honorees, baseball's top man cited Joe McCarthy's amazing success of winning eight pennants and seven World Series as Yankee manager, plus another pennant with the Cubs. For Crawford, Frick recited the slugger's many hitting feats during his 19-year career in the majors.

Following the commissioner's introduction, McCarthy arose to deliver his speech. Speaking for several minutes, he thanked his players, coaches, scouts, team officials, and his wife Babe. The manager even mentioned the umpires, whom he said had taught him lessons in humility. McCarthy summarized his gratitude by saying, "a man who makes the Hall of Fame because of success as a manager owes big debts of thanks to those without whose help he could not possibly have achieved the honor."

Next it was Sam's turn at the lectern. His remarks would be brief. "When I walked up to this mike, I had a speech all ready for delivery," he said. "but the words have escaped me. All I can say, over and over again, is thank you." Tears streamed down his face as he returned to his seat next to Mary, who similarly could not keep from crying.

If you would have traveled to Sam Crawford's desert cabin a few years earlier and asked him if he wanted to be in the Hall of Fame, he likely would have said something along the lines of, "It doesn't matter much to me. It's not a big deal." Those words would not have been the truth. The Hall of Fame did matter to Sam; it was a big deal.

Following the induction ceremony, which concluded after a brisk 45 minutes, the baseball luminaries, former ballplayers, and other attending guests headed to the Otesaga Hotel for a buffet luncheon. Crawford reminisced with his former Tiger teammates Cobb and Davy Jones. A reporter took a picture of the three outfielders sitting shoulder to shoulder at a table, happily conversing, all hatchets from the past buried.

After lunch, the St. Louis Cardinals squared off against the Chicago White Sox in an exhibition game at Cooperstown's Doubleday Field. The clouds unleashed a sharp rain before the

236

game, washing out the pregame ceremonies. When the deluge slowed to a drizzle, Ford Motor Company officials presented Crawford with a new Lincoln. Noting the age of Sam's current vehicle, a 1935 Ford, Tigers president Harvey Hansen had convinced the car manufacturer to make this donation. Sam very much appreciated the gift. Mary did too, telling reporters that she looked forward to driving the 1957 Lincoln when they returned to California. The White Sox prevailed 13-4 in the subsequent ballgame played before 8,500 rain-soaked fans.

For this occasion, Crawford donated gifts of his own. The Hall of Fame requests that each new inductee provide for its museum mementos of his time in the game. Weeks earlier Sam had sent to the Hall a 40-ounce bat that he once used to terrorize American League pitchers. He also donated the red, white, and blue uniform he wore during the World Tour of 1913-1914.

For his plaque, Crawford insisted that the engraving include his nickname, "Wahoo Sam." The Hall complied, ensuring that Crawford's hometown accompanied him into the pantheon. On induction day, he and McCarthy held their plaques for photographers. The inscription on Sam's tablet reads:

> Samuel Earl Crawford
> "Wahoo Sam"
> Cincinnati N.L. 1899-1902
> Detroit A.L. 1903-1917
> Had lifetime record of 2964 hits,
> batting average of .309. Played 2505
> games. Holds Major League record
> for most triples, 312. League leader
> one or more seasons in doubles, triples,
> runs batted in, runs scored, chances
> accepted, home runs (N.L. 1901 – A.L. 1908)
> and total bases (N.L. 1902 – A.L. 1913).

The festivities for Crawford did not end on that rainy Monday in Cooperstown. Five days later, he and McCarthy were the top guests of honor for the annual Old-Timers' Day and Salute to the Hall of Fame at Yankees Stadium. About 50 former

Tigers and Yankees attended the event. A crowd of 44,000 cheered the baseball legends as their names were announced. Hometown fans reserved the largest ovations for Yankee greats Joe DiMaggio and Phil Rizzuto. Crawford, Cobb, and Davy Jones, each in his 70s, did not play in the old-timers' game, but they did offer coaching advice to the participants. Al Schacht, the "Clown Prince of Baseball," and funnyman Phil Silvers served as umpires, livening up the contest with their comedic antics.

That evening, following a game between the current Yankees and Tigers, the old-timers and other guests gathered at the dining hall of Toots Shor's Restaurant in Manhattan. The newest Hall of Fame inductees gave speeches, with Crawford again delivering the briefest remarks. Current Yankee skipper Casey Stengel closed out the proceedings by ranting about the superiority of the American League over the National and arguing that if the Dodgers left Brooklyn (which they did after the season), then New York did not need another team. Five years later, Stengel became the manager of the city's new "other" team, the Mets.

Having never been to the east coast before, Mary appreciated the hospitality shown to her and her husband in Cooperstown and New York City. "I'm very proud and happy to have shared in all this glory," she said, "and have enjoyed every minute of the past hectic weeks." A salesman at Saks Fifth Avenue even provided an unexpected highlight for Mary by asking for her autograph.

After the festivities in New York concluded, the Crawfords boarded a train heading west. But they did not head straight home to California. Wahoo Sam was returning to Nebraska.

While in Cooperstown, Crawford had received a telegram from the Wahoo Lions Club. Part of the message from its 100-plus members read, "We want the world to know that your home town, the place of your birth, is very proud of its own Wahoo

Sam Crawford." In less than two weeks, the recipient would have the opportunity to thank the Lions in person.

In October 1917, following the end of his last season with Detroit, Sam had traveled to Nebraska to visit family members in Fremont and Omaha. He also dropped by Wahoo on this trip. Four decades would pass before he returned to his hometown.

The Crawfords' train arrived in Omaha in the late afternoon of Friday, August 2. A special delegation from Wahoo, Omaha dignitaries, and members of the press greeted them at the station. A televised ceremony followed, during which Crawford received a gold key from the Omaha officials. Hosts then ushered Sam and Mary into an automobile that would be accompanied on its journey by a police and Shriner escort. The caravan zipped through the city at 40 miles per hour. Mary observed, "That's the first time I've ever run red lights and got by with it." The Wahoo delegation and guests of honor dined at an Omaha restaurant, but Sam was too excited to eat much of his steak and baked potato.

Following dinner, the party traveled 30 miles west to Wahoo. Town mayor Lloyd Torrens, boyhood friend John Schmidt, and local baseball star Brownie Rohman rode with Sam in the lead convertible driven by Lee Bronson, the executive secretary of the Wahoo Chamber of Commerce. They arrived at the town ballpark at 8:30 pm. Fans stood and cheered as Crawford strode onto the field. Among those in attendance were Kansas City A's outfielder and local hero Bob Cerv, and Connie Mack III, the grandson of the legendary Athletics owner/manager who had died a year earlier. During the pregame ceremony, Mayor Torrens presented Sam with an honorary key to the city. Master of ceremonies Bill Keefer then gave him a gold plaque bearing the image of a left-handed batter.

Next came the big announcement. Dr. J.R. Swanson, speaking on behalf of the city, announced to all in attendance that the ballpark would now be called Wahoo Sam Crawford Field. Appropriately, the park was located on the same site as the ballfield where Sam had played as a teenager. The new brick and wood grandstand bore a sign proclaiming the ballpark's new name. Following a brief message of thanks, Crawford threw out the first pitch. He and Mary then sat in a bunting-draped box to watch five innings of the game between Fremont and Wahoo.

The next day, a local café hosted a testimonial luncheon for Crawford. More than a hundred people showed up, many of them former teammates or acquaintances from his youth. Toastmaster Clyde Worrall from the Wahoo Lions Club presented Sam with a gold desk calendar set. He also received a scrapbook of clippings from his early games that had been collected by Ada's sister, Belle Johnson. A representative from the governor's office proclaimed Sam an admiral in the Great Navy of Nebraska. Worrall then read letters and telegrams sent by Crawford's old friends and schoolmates who could not attend the weekend events in Wahoo. Reminiscences filled the room, and many a story from Sam's youthful baseball and barbering days were shared. Eddie Lawler, who played against Crawford back then commented, "He hasn't changed in the 60 years I've known him. The same Sam."

When called upon to address the gathering, Sam opened with his trademark understated wit: "After hearing all these laudatory remarks, I thought Mr. Worrall must be talking about somebody else." Crawford then recounted old memories, such as receiving his first uniform from Tom Killian, and new memories from his recent trip to Cooperstown. He said he planned to donate the plaque he had been given the night before to the Hall of Fame. Sam concluded the luncheon by taking questions from the audience.

Crawford next went to the Wahoo Chamber of Commerce office. There, he spent an hour autographing baseballs for the long line of children and adults awaiting him. One of the people in line was Lucile Jacoby, Sam's 46-year-old niece (Zadia's daughter). He did not recognize her until after he had signed the ball and handed it back. That brief oversight amused the crowd.

Crawford spent the rest of the afternoon on a chauffeured tour of his hometown. Wahoo residents put up festive decorations for their celebrated visitor. Stopping by the homes of childhood friends, Sam impressed the accompanying town officials and reporters with his ability to recall people and places he had not seen in decades. One newsman described him as courtly, with the fluency of an ex-professor. On Main Street, Crawford visited the site of the basement barber shop where he had worked as a teenager 60 years earlier. He noted that the stairs leading to the shop used to be much wider. He also visited the house where the late Tom Killian once lived.

Crawford then returned to the house on North Orange Street where he had grown up. The current occupants, Mrs. Marie Herrick and her daughter Lucille, hung a sign on the door that read, "Welcome Home, Wahoo Sam." Though commenting that his former homeplace looked much like he remembered it, Crawford noted that new rooms had been added, and the roof was no longer tin. While Sam was at the house, Mrs. F.W. Anderson, who had lived across the street since the 1890s, came over to say hello. Mrs. Anderson had been friends with Nellie Crawford and on occasion looked after young Sam and his brothers.

Wahoo had changed considerably since Crawford's last visit 40 years earlier. He noted that the trees had grown larger and more beautiful. Aside from Main Street, Linden Street, and his old neighborhood, much of the city was not familiar to him. He continued his tour throughout the afternoon. Despite the sticky 90-degree August heat, he did not remove his coat or tie for his public appearances. When asked if he might be more comfortable without his coat, Sam replied, "No, I believe the people prefer to meet me this way."

On Saturday evening, the Crawfords rode with Sam's niece Lucile and her husband, Lieutenant Colonel Henry Jacoby, to their home in Lincoln. Henry was the commanding officer of the Lincoln Air Force Base. After Sam and Mary spent the evening in Nebraska's capital city, on Sunday the Jacobys drove them to Omaha. There, they boarded a train for California.

The past six months had been a whirlwind for Crawford. And he loved every minute of it. In September he wrote to the

Hall of Fame historian, Ernie Lanigan, thanking him for sending the latest edition of *The Little Red Book of Baseball*—a book of baseball records. In his letter, Sam told Lanigan, "Mrs. Crawford and I are getting back to normal after our wonderful trip back east. We talk of Cooperstown a great deal and the opportunity it gave us to make so many new friends and to visit with our old friends once more."

Sportswriter Oscar Ruhl said that election to the Hall of Fame "made a new man out of Sam." It put him in the spotlight again and filled his schedule with baseball functions. Indeed, Crawford remained in demand after his return home. On October 28, he was an honored guest at a large civic luncheon celebrating the Dodgers' move to Los Angeles and the arrival of Major League Baseball in California.

The following summer, Tigers officials invited Crawford to attend their Hall of Fame Day and Old-Timers' game to honor the team's greats. Though most of the past Tiger heroes at the event had played after Sam's retirement, Cobb and Jones joined him in representing the 1907-1909 pennant winners. Refusing to wear a uniform, Crawford waved to the fans at Briggs Stadium wearing a coat and tie. "When they think of Sam Crawford in a Detroit uniform I want them to think of me the way I was way back then," he said, "and no other way."

Crawford received another honor in 1958, when he was inducted into the Michigan Sports Hall of Fame, along with Hughie Jennings and Hank Greenberg. In January 1959, Crawford attended a testimonial dinner honoring Casey Stengel as baseball's top manager. In addition to Cobb, Sam's former Angels teammate Arnold Statz was in attendance. So too were the current Dodgers, Sandy Koufax, Don Drysdale, and Carl Furillo, as well as broadcaster Vin Scully and boxer Joe Louis. Former Dodger turned actor Chuck Connors, star of the TV series *The Rifleman,* provided entertainment by reading the classic poem, "Casey at the Bat."

As his 80th birthday approached, Crawford was indeed a new man. Now immortalized in Cooperstown, his fame had reached its highest level since his playing days in Detroit more than four decades earlier. And soon another opportunity would appear, allowing his voice to reach multitudes of baseball fans for decades to come.

Chapter 16

The Interview

Neither of Crawford's children attended his induction ceremonies in Cooperstown. Sam's daughter Virginia still lived in Venezuela in the summer of 1957. She ran a gift shop at the Halliburton compound, where her husband and the other oil company employees lived. Jungle surrounded the encampment, which was located near the small town of Anaco. Sam Jr. lived in San Francisco at this time. Injuries from a head-on car crash years earlier had left him with a physical disability. Sam's 16-year-old granddaughter Julie had wanted to go to the ceremonies in Cooperstown, but her parents made her stay in California for summer school.

Sam's brother Step still lived in Los Angeles, where he taught classes at the Vail Art School. His sister Zadia had married a widower named Frank Hassell and moved to Delta, Colorado. She remained there following Frank's passing in 1951. Zadia died in Delta in July 1959 at the age of 81.

News of Crawford's election into the Hall of Fame greatly increased the flow of postal traffic arriving in his mailbox. He received scores of letters from across the United States, most of them from children, who sometimes included a stamped return envelope and sometimes did not. Either way, Sam answered every one of them with a handwritten reply. He obliged autograph requests by signing the small cards from the Hall of

Fame that showed a picture of his plaque. He generously sent them out to his legion of new fans. Eventually he had to ask Hall of Fame historian Lee Allen for more cards because the Little Leaguers had cleaned out his supply.

In the spring of 1961, Crawford decided it was time for a new hideout away from the city. Perhaps his Pearblossom cabin no longer felt so secluded and private. Whatever the reason, in May of that year he moved north to Cayucos, a small coastal community about halfway between Los Angeles and San Francisco. To make the 200-mile trip to and from the house he and Mary still shared in Hollywood, Sam did not drive the Lincoln given to him in Cooperstown. Finding that vehicle "a little too much car," he traded it in for a Ford.

A couple months after Crawford settled in Cayucos, Ty Cobb died in an Atlanta hospital from cancer, heart disease, and diabetes at the age of 74. Crawford was named an honorary pallbearer at his funeral in Cornelia, Georgia. And so the baseball world said goodbye to one of the most successful, most discussed, and most controversial ballplayers of all time. Cobb is also the player whose name was, and still is, most closely associated with Sam. As historian Charles Alexander said of Crawford, "It had been both his fortune and his fate to spend his best years playing in the shadow of the great Cobb."

In the years that followed Ty's passing, Sam offered several reflective thoughts about his former teammate. "Cobb was great, there's no doubt about that," Crawford said. He considered Ty one of the best to ever play the game. Sam rejected allegations that Cobb played dirty, arguing that he never intentionally tried to spike anybody. Wahoo also praised the Georgia Peach's quick thinking and exemplary baserunning skills. Regarding their off-field interactions, on the other hand, Sam said that Cobb was not friendly or good-natured.

Crawford and Cobb's relationship during their 13 years as Tiger teammates might best be characterized as "complicated." Tension divided the two men, marked by hard words, extended periods of silence, and occasional public criticisms. And yet, they still socialized at times, cooperated on double-steal attempts, and defended each other from outside criticisms. As the kids today might say, Sam and Ty were "frenemies." This status continued into the years following their playing days. They had little contact with each other through the 1920s, 1930s, and 1940s. In the 1950s, they reunited like long-lost friends. When Cobb learned of his former teammate's election to the Hall of Fame, he celebrated as joyously as perhaps Crawford himself. In June 1965, in his last public statement about Cobb, Sam told a reporter that Ty was "one of the nicest guys that ever lived."

Yes, those were Crawford's exact words about Cobb. Let them sink in for a while: *"one of the nicest guys that ever lived."* The quote provides a happy coda to one of the longest and most complicated relationships between big league teammates.

That Sam could make such a statement is even more noteworthy given the publication of Cobb's "autobiography" soon after his death. The passage of time and friendly relations in the 1950s had certainly taken the edge off their rivalry, but Cobb's *My Life in Baseball: The True Record* once again stoked the fires of ill-feeling. In recounting his early years with the Tigers, Ty blamed Crawford for heading the persecution campaign against him. According to the book, a jealous Sam encouraged his teammates to destroy Cobb's bats.

But the so-called autobiography was in fact penned by writer Al Stump, who riddled the book with embellishments, fabrications, and factual errors. Upon reading the manuscript a month before his death, a furious Cobb demanded that Stump be fired and the book be rewritten. Ty at this point was too weak to pursue the fight, however, and the publisher and Stump just waited him out, releasing the book two months after his death. It is thus possible that Cobb did not endorse what "he" allegedly said about Crawford in his book. But Sam did not know this when he read the biography soon after it arrived in bookstores in the fall of 1961.

In August 1962, Nebraskan Richie Ashburn hit his 2,099th single to pass Crawford for 18th place in the all-time singles list. The longtime Phillies outfielder, now playing for the Mets, would soon conclude a career that eventually landed him in Cooperstown. Ashburn is arguably the second greatest major league hitter who was born and raised in the Cornhusker State.

In 1964 Crawford moved from Cayucos a few miles south to another small coastal community, Baywood Park. Valuing his privacy and smog-free air, he spent much of the year at his small-town hideaway. Mary, meanwhile, still lived in the couple's Hollywood home year-round. As in Pearblossom, Sam did not have a telephone. He also no longer bought a newspaper because so much of it was filled with trouble, war, and misery. A self-described non-conformist, Crawford also rarely watched television anymore. His only must-watch programs were the World Series games in October.

Sam remained busy as an octogenarian. Without *Bonanza*, *Combat!* or *The Andy Griffith Show* filling his hours, he continued to devour stacks of books and go on walks. He was always on the move, a leftover trait, he said, from his years on the road as a big leaguer. Spending much of his time off the grid in his remote hideaways, he was not the easiest person to track down. Little did he know that somebody was in fact looking for him. This stranger traveled all the way across the country, spending weeks searching for Sam Crawford.

Lawrence Ritter was a finance professor at New York University. Earning a Ph.D. in economics from the University of Wisconsin, he expounded his knowledge of markets, financial institutions, and monetary theory in many articles and in a textbook he co-authored. He served as president of the American Finance Association and consulted for many organizations, including the Treasury Department and Federal Deposit Insurance Corporation.

Ritter also loved baseball. He held fond childhood memories of attending games with his father. His dad died around the same time that Ty Cobb passed in 1961. These sad events left him wanting to recapture baseball's past and the meaning it held for him as a child. With the number of early twentieth century players declining, he wanted to hear their stories first-hand while they could still tell them. At the age of 39, Ritter embarked on a grand mission to interview the players from the early days of baseball. Armed with his tape recorder, he spent five years on the road crisscrossing the United States and Canada.

With no central repository of addresses, finding the long-retired ballplayers was not easy. Ritter searched baseball record books to find their birthplaces. He then scoured the telephone directories held at the New York Public Library to learn if a retired player had returned to his hometown. Some of them had, and for those who had not, the phonebook often revealed the number of a relative who knew the player's current whereabouts. Slowly but surely, Ritter tracked down the diamond greats of the early 1900s.

Sam Crawford, however, proved elusive. Ritter first found the address for his house in Hollywood. He arrived there to find Mary, but no Sam. She said that her husband had been away for months. When Ritter asked where he could find him, Mary refused to say. She said that Sam wanted peace, quiet, and privacy and would be angry with her if she revealed his location. Determined to find his man, Ritter beseeched Mrs. Crawford for hours. Finally, she reluctantly agreed to give him a hint. She told him to drive north, and somewhere between 175 and 225 miles was the right area. Mary also let slip that her husband enjoyed tending his garden and watching the sun set into the Pacific Ocean.

With those vague directions, Ritter departed. He knew a general area near the ocean where Crawford might be. After traveling up the coast about halfway between Los Angeles and San Francisco, he started inquiring at post offices, real estate agencies, and grocery stores for the whereabouts of a man named Sam Crawford. This needle-in-a-haystack approach yielded just enough clues for Ritter to continue his search. Sam had occasionally left his Hall of Fame plaque card at places he had visited. He valued his privacy, but he also liked a little recognition.

Ritter eventually ended up in the small town of Baywood Park. After spending two days there, however, the trail went cold. Discouraged, the finance professor decided it was about time to give up. The next morning, he sat in his car in front of a laundromat, where he planned to wash his clothes. A tall gaunt man then passed by carrying a stack of books. He took them into a drugstore, where customers could trade used paperbacks. After this man emerged a while later, he went to the neighboring laundromat to wash some clothes he had been carrying along with his books. Ritter went in with his load and started up a machine. Sitting next to the man, he figured he might as well ask, "Do you know anybody around here named Sam Crawford?"

"Well, I should certainly hope so," the man said, "bein' as I'm him."

Ritter and Crawford hit it off, spending a lot of time together. The finance professor found Sam to be a perceptive observer of the human condition. They would remain friends for years, with Ritter later calling Wahoo one of his favorite people of all time.

The interview took place in March 1964, a month before Crawford's 84th birthday. Following his usual laissez-faire interviewing style, Ritter set up his tape recorder and let his subject reflect. What Sam provided for posterity proved well worth the time and effort it took to find him.

The reach of Crawford's memory extended back nearly eight decades to his childhood in Wahoo. He talked about playing with his friends and how they made their own balls and bats. He recalled seeing another famous Wahoo son, movie producer Darryl Zanuck, running about the streets as a towheaded boy. Sam recounted his experiences as a teenage barber and the lumber wagon baseball tour of eastern Nebraska.

He described his big break that took him to Chatham, Canada, for his start in professional baseball.

Crawford provided a wealth of information about the big league experience in the early 1900s. He described travelling by train and how the lack of respect afforded ballplayers made it difficult to find good hotels. He recounted how opposing infielders tried to trip and bump him as he ran the bases. He spoke of players treating spike wounds with wads of chewing tobacco and handkerchief wraps. He talked about hitting lopsided, discolored balls saturated with tobacco juice.

Sam spoke about many of the players and managers with whom he had interacted in the big leagues. He recalled the laughs and disappointments he shared with teammates. He described Tiger manager Bill Armour's aversion to cross-eyed boys, and how he and his teammates tried to recruit such kids as batboys to torment their skipper. Sam offered a host of comments about the top stars of the Deadball Era.

- Rube Waddell: "How good he'd have been if he'd taken baseball seriously is hard to imagine."
- William Hoy: "... he was a fine outfielder. A *great* one."
- Ed Delahanty: "... the best right-handed hitter I ever saw."
- Walter Johnson: "... the best I ever faced, without a doubt."
- Tris Speaker: "... the best centerfielder of them all."
- Honus Wagner: "... greatest all-around player who ever lived."

Ritter, of course, asked Crawford about Ty Cobb. Sam acknowledged the Georgia Peach's greatness, praising his hitting and baserunning skills, and his drive to be the best. Crawford believed Cobb's mind was the key to his success. "He didn't outhit the opposition and he didn't outrun them," Sam said. "He outthought them!"

Crawford also defended Cobb against the accusations of being a dirty player. But, speaking in the wake of Cobb's "autobiography," Sam criticized his teammate's antagonistic attitude for escalating the normal rookie hazing directed at him into a bitter conflict with the other Tigers. Crawford said that Ty was still fighting the Civil War and viewed his teammates as "damn Yankees." Similar to Davy Jones, who was also interviewed by Ritter, Sam said that Cobb's sour disposition made it difficult to get along with him.

Like many old-time ballplayers, Crawford shared plenty of opinions about how the current game compared to the game back in the day. Years earlier, he had told Fred Lieb that the pitching he faced was much tougher than that of the current era. Wahoo expressed similar views to Ritter. Explaining that baseball in his day required strategy and tactics, Sam maintained that players back then were smarter than current players. He felt that the lively ball and shorter fences had erased the need for strategy in modern baseball, since current players just try to hit home runs. Crawford also noted that the frequent replacement of balls during a game made it easier for modern hitters.

Sam's interview with Ritter was not the first time he had expressed his opinions about how the game had changed, and not for the better, since his era. A few years earlier, Crawford criticized modern outfielders for playing too deep. He said they did this out of insecurity, because they were too fearful of a ball being hit over their heads. Sam also did not like the longer time required to play a major league game. Even worse was playing under the lights. "Baseball wasn't meant to be played at night," Crawford told *The Sporting News* in 1957. "You've gotta sweat to play good ball, and the hotter the weather, the better."

Long before Sam expressed these views, old-time ballplayers had been griping about how the game had declined since their day. Each generation of retired players typically expounds upon the superiority of their own era. This still goes on today. In criticizing the modern game of the 1950s and 1960s, Crawford continued a time-honored baseball tradition.

Throughout his interview with Ritter, Sam recalled specific details about events and people from more than a half-century earlier. But how accurate was the 83-year-old's memory with these distant facts? The following are some of the specific claims Crawford made, and an assessment of their accuracy:

- *Rube Waddell won about 30 games for Grand Rapids/Columbus in 1899.* Very close, Rube won 29.

- *The Tigers and A's won all but two AL pennants from 1905 to 1914.* Right on the nose.

- *Tommy Leach led the NL with six home runs in 1906. Sam led the AL with seven home runs in 1908. Frank Baker's top home run year was 12.* Correct on all counts.

- *Wee Willie Keeler and Ed Delahanty had lifetime batting averages close to .350.* We'll give it to him; according to the official stats at the time both players hit .345.

- *William Hoy was 5'5" and stole more than 600 bases.* Close on both counts: Hoy is listed at 5'4" and stole 594 bases.

- *In Walter Johnson's first game, Sam hit a home run to help Detroit win 3-2.* Exactly right.

- *In 1911 Sam hit .378, Cobb hit .420, and Joe Jackson hit .408.* Correct on all three.

- *Noodles Hahn pitched 41 complete games in 1901.* Right on target.

All told, Crawford displayed an impressive accuracy in the details he shared with Ritter. His feats of memory are even more amazing considering that many of the events he described occurred nearly 60 years earlier.

Ritter published *The Glory of Their Times: The Story of the Early Days of Baseball Told by the Men Who Played It* in September 1966. The original edition featured first-person accounts of 22 ballplayers, including Crawford, Davy Jones, Harry Hooper, and Smoky Joe Wood. The book garnered positive reviews upon its release, and in the years and decades that followed it has emerged as a classic of baseball literature. Ritter published an expanded version in 1984 with first-person recollections from four more ballplayers. Many baseball aficionados today consider Ritter's book one of the great works on the history of the game.

Throughout his chapter, Sam provides an engaging, informative, and sometimes witty view of baseball in the 1890s and early 1900s. His voice rings with the authority of one of the towering figures of the early game. This stature is even more evident when listening to the audio recording of the interview.

Crawford jestingly asked Ritter why he would want to spend his time writing a book about baseball in the old days. Legions of scholars, students, and fans of the game and its history are thankful the finance professor did undertake this project. *The Glory of Their Times* preserved hundreds of first-person stories of early baseball that would have otherwise been lost. Crawford's words have been quoted in countless publications and projects, including the 1994 Ken Burns documentary *Baseball*. Thanks to Ritter, Wahoo Sam and his contemporaries can speak directly to each new generation about what the game was like in the Deadball Era.

Chapter 17

"We'll Miss Him"

When Lawrence Ritter found him in Baywood Park in 1964, Sam Crawford had no more living siblings. His brother Stephen had died a year earlier in Los Angeles. Step was 77 years old at the time of his passing in March 1963. Aside from his wife Mary, Sam's closest family members included his daughter Virginia, who had returned to the states and again resided in La Habra in Orange County, and Sam Jr., who lived in the small northern California town of Ukiah. Crawford's granddaughter Julie also lived in California, and he remained in contact with his niece Lucile Jacoby in Nebraska.

In November 1964, Sam's former teammate Oscar Stanage died at the age of 81. His passing left only three surviving players from Detroit's 1907-1909 pennant-winning teams: Crawford, Donie Bush, and Davy Jones. The latter continued to attend baseball functions. In September 1965, the 85-year-old Jones was honored at Tiger Stadium as part of the festivities celebrating the team's 10,000th American League game. Impressing the current players with his mobility, Jones strode onto the field at a brisk pace to receive a portable television set.

Crawford continued to follow baseball developments in the mid-1960s. And he occasionally reflected on the old days in his periodic correspondence with Lee Allen. The Hall of Fame historian looked forward to receiving Sam's letters handwritten in bold script with green ink. The two men discussed past players and events dating back to Crawford's early career in Cincinnati. Wahoo admitted to Allen in one of his letters, "I get kind of garrulous when I think of the old days."

Regarding the modern players, Sam identified Mickey Mantle and Willie Mays as the cream of the crop. He praised Mantle as baseball's best-ever switch hitter, with the potential to become the game's greatest slugger. Crawford said Mays was one of the few current players whose talent matched that of the top players of his day. When prompted to pick his all-star team from his era, Sam selected: Hal Chase (1B), Napoleon Lajoie (2B), Bill Bradley (3B), Honus Wagner (SS), Tris Speaker (OF), Ty Cobb (OF), Joe Jackson (OF), Ray Schalk (C), Eddie Plank (LHP), and Walter Johnson (RHP). When asked why Ruth was not on his team, Crawford said the Babe struck out too often.

In March 1965, Sam found a new hideaway even more distant from his Hollywood home. His new retreat was a small rustic cabin near the northern California town of Oroville. It was located 130 miles northeast of San Francisco, and more than 400 miles from Los Angeles. Crawford was not kidding when he said he wanted to get away from the smog of LA.

Not long after Sam moved to Oroville, two reporters visited him, independent of each other, seeking an interview. The first was Carolyn Richards from the local newspaper and the second was Vera Ludi of Wahoo, who was visiting her brother, a photographer who resided in the nearby town of Paradise. The resulting articles they wrote about Sam covered similar ground.

Both women noted Crawford's excellent health. Ludi said he guided her up the rocky steps to his cabin with a strong "baseball arm." She also found him to be "courteous, alert, well read, and rugged." Richards described Sam as spry, straight, and handsome, with a happy smile on his face. For both interviews, the 85-year-old jokingly gave his age as 69. Ludi said he looked much younger than that.

Crawford reflected on his playing days for Richards, recalling the "dead" ball, treating spike wounds with tobacco juice, and his lumber wagon tour. Sam also discussed former teammates, such as William Hoy. Crawford told Richards that he had written to the commissioner calling for Hoy's enshrinement in the Hall of Fame.

With both interviewers, Sam spoke about how baseball in his era differed from the modern game. The conversation segued into the earnings of current baseball players. Four decades earlier, when his playing days with the Angels were coming to an end, Crawford disapprovingly noted the growing salaries for untried minor leaguers. In 1965 he decried the practice of teams handing out signing bonuses, stating that they were done just for publicity. Sam did not complain, however, about the escalating big league salaries, which had climbed into six-figures for the game's top players. "As to the money the stars are making today, more credit to them," Crawford had earlier told Fred Lieb. "It's a different game now … and the dollar has much less purchasing value than when I was making $3,500."

Wahoo did not hide his disdain for Major League Baseball's pension plan. The system at the time allowed for no payments for players who had retired before 1947. Big leaguers retiring after that time qualified if they had five years of MLB service. Crawford found this system favoring the younger players unfair. He felt that he and other older retirees were entitled to the pension because of their contributions to building the game into a profitable national institution. "Not many of us old-timers are left and I don't think it would wreck the two big leagues to hand out some kind of a small pension," Sam wrote to a sportswriter. "So give some of these young mediocre players a blast that they should give a thought to the old-timers who put them in the driver's seat."

Crawford's views are certainly understandable. Had he played in the 1950s and 1960s, he would have commanded a much heftier salary, potentially supplemented by lucrative product endorsements and radio and television appearances. And a pension would have awaited him in retirement. Instead, though one of the top professional athletes of his day, he lived modestly in his golden years. As Ludi wrote, "Sam's cabin is small, and his income is smaller."

The other complaint Crawford mentioned to his interviewers related to his career hit total. He told both women that his bronze plaque in the Hall of Fame lists the wrong number: 2,964. He argued that his 87 Western League hits should be counted, bringing his career mark to more than 3,000. Sam maintained that the National Commission had awarded him the extra hits back in the day. He wrote to the Hall of Fame and others stating his case. Detroit sportswriter H.G. Salsinger supported his claim, but baseball officials did not. The Western League was not considered a major league back in 1899, and this classification never changed. Thus, the official Elias ruling of 1942 omitting the extra hits still stands.

Despite the aforementioned two complaints, Crawford appears mostly upbeat and positive in the two articles. Ludi said that he remained active whittling wood chains, growing flowers, and collecting rock specimens for his cabin. She reported that the Ford he had received as a trade-in for the gifted Lincoln looked new and well-maintained. Sam expressed his approval of American Legion Baseball and Little League, indicating that he planned to talk to the local youth teams later that spring. As he stated in a letter to Lee Allen a year earlier, "[I] am doing what I can to help the old 'National Pastime.'"

Current members of the Hall of Fame often attend the annual summer ceremonies for the new inductees. Making the cross-country trek, however, did not appeal to Crawford. When asked by Allen one year if he would be coming to Cooperstown, Sam replied in his letter, "[I] don't know about coming east again." Crawford never did return to the Hall of Fame after his own enshrinement. He remained on the go in his Ford in the first half of the 1960s, but within the state of California.

In March 1967, the city of Bradenton, Florida, hosted a Hall of Fame Day, inviting all 33 living members to attend. Citing illness, Crawford declined. It would have been a surprise if the

86-year-old traveled across the continent for the festivities. Even if Sam himself had not been sick, his bank account may not have been in the greatest of health for such a trip. And his general enthusiasm for reflecting on the game may have been starting to wane. Later that year, when David Zimmett offered to send him a book about the World Tour of 1913-14, Crawford declined, stating "I don't like [to] retrospect that far back."

Sam still enjoyed relatively good health as the calendar flipped to 1968. In early January, he sent a letter with an accompanying picture to his niece Lucile. Written in his typical strong script, Crawford identified the people in an enlarged photograph from five decades earlier. Taken at the 1917 Crawford family gathering in Fremont, the picture showed his mother Nellie, step-grandfather Milton Runyon, brother Neal, sister Zadia, and Lucile, along with Sam, Ada, and Virginia. There were also a young man and a boy in the photo whom Sam could not identify. They were likely Lucile's brothers, Carl and Delbert. Crawford signed this letter to his niece, "Mary & Wahoo."

That spring Sam remained at his Hudson Avenue duplex in Hollywood with his wife. In April his granddaughter Julie Ann Johnson came over for a visit. Julie by this time was emerging as a top stuntwoman in television and film. Doubling for Stephanie Powers in the TV series *The Girl from U.N.C.L.E.* and for Doris Day in the movie *Caprice* were among her career highlights thus far. Julie took Wahoo to a nearby park, where they played catch just like they had when she was a child. One of Julie's friends took a few pictures of them together. At 88 Crawford still liked to throw the ball around.

Sam's first major league employer, the Cincinnati Reds, floundered around .500 in the spring of 1968, though their roster featured some promising young players, like Pete Rose, Tony Perez, and Johnny Bench. This was not to be their year, but in 1970 Sparky Anderson would arrive to take the helm. The fiery skipper transformed his team into a Big Red Machine that went to the World Series in four of his first seven seasons in Cincy.

Sam's principal big league employer, the Detroit Tigers, had not appeared in the Fall Classic since 1945, when they won their second title by defeating the Chicago Cubs in seven games. After Detroit's narrow miss in 1967, Tiger fans hoped to end their pennant drought in '68. Led by the slugging of Willie Horton, Norm Cash, Bill Freehan, and Al Kaline, and the pitching of Denny McClain and Mickey Lolich, the team burst out of the gate winning nine of its first ten. By late May, the Tigers had nosed ahead of Baltimore for the top spot in the AL standings.

Hollywood basked in summer weather on Sunday, May 26, 1968. Skies were clear and the thermometer topped out at 94 degrees. A mild breeze complemented the California sunshine. That afternoon the Tigers faced the Oakland Athletics in front of 14,500 fans at Oakland-Alameda County Coliseum. The home crowd cheered as the A's pushed across the winning run in the 10th inning to cut into Detroit's lead in the standings. About 350 miles to the south, a Tiger legend was taking his final at-bat.

That Sunday started like a typical day at the Crawford household in Hollywood. Sam seemed fine that morning. There was no sign that anything was wrong prior to the moment he collapsed to the floor. Mary called an ambulance, which rushed him to nearby Hollywood Community Hospital. Virginia and Julie arrived to find him hooked up to an oxygen machine with IVs in his arms. He had suffered a stroke and was in a coma.

Crawford remained unconscious for nearly three weeks. Over that time his condition worsened with pneumonia. On Saturday, June 15, Virginia's 61st birthday, the hospital called to tell her that the end was near. She and Julie arrived at Sam's bedside, each taking hold of one of his hands. There they sat unspeaking—the only sounds being the gurgling noise of the suctioning machine that came with each breath. After two hours the gurgling abruptly stopped. Sam was gone.

Funeral services were held at Hollywood Presbyterian Church on Wednesday, June 19. Sam was buried in Inglewood Park Cemetery, about eight miles south of Hollywood. The large cemetery provides the final resting place for many entertainment and sports figures, including a few ballplayers from Sam's era—Bobby Wallace, Beals Becker, and Fred McMullin.

Years earlier, Crawford had told Lawrence Ritter that he wanted to be remembered as a straight sort of a guy. Upon his death, he wanted people to say, "Well, good old Sam, he wasn't such a bad guy after all. Everything considered, he was pretty fair and square. We'll miss him."

Many people did miss Sam. He left behind a wife, a daughter, a son, and two granddaughters. Davy Jones, Donie Bush, and Arnold Statz were among the former teammates who survived him. Old friends, acquaintances, and fans who had seen him play in the majors, minors, and as a town team star in Nebraska also remembered the baseball legend. The entire town of Wahoo mourned the passing of one of its most famous men. The city's Chamber of Commerce sent to the funeral a floral wreath consisting of red carnations, white roses, white mums, white orchids, bells of Ireland, and satin ribbon tufts. Wahoo mayor Jack Swanson changed the name of Sam Crawford Field to Sam Crawford Memorial Field.

Obituaries appeared in newspapers across the nation. Fred Lieb wrote a lengthy tribute that covered an entire page of *The Sporting News*. The baseball historian recounted Crawford's many diamond accomplishments from his semipro days through the Pacific Coast League, lauding him "one of the game's great hitters." A week later, Lee Allen penned his tribute to Wahoo. He reflected on his years of correspondence with Sam and praised his individualism. Allen called Crawford "a free thinker and a free man ... who exuded love in a world that seemed to produce an increase in petty and irrational hatred."

Prior to his passing, Crawford was the second oldest living member of the Hall of Fame. Only Elmer Flick at age 92 was older. Later that summer, on July 22, the Hall of Fame inducted its newest members, Goose Goslin, Kiki Cuyler, and Joe Medwick. A moment of silence was held before the ceremony to remember Crawford. Five days after this event, former Pirate pitcher Babe Adams died at the age of 86. With three complete-game victories in the 1909 World Series, Adams was one of Sam's most formidable Fall Classic adversaries.

The 1968 baseball season produced two more notable Crawford-related developments. These "tributes" seemed like they may have been penned by a screenwriter in the town where Sam drew his last breath. But they actually happened. On June 15, the same day Crawford died, USC won the college World Series. This triumph occurred at Rosenblatt Stadium in Omaha, Nebraska—just 35 miles from where Sam had played his first baseball games in Wahoo. The Trojans' title, their fourth in 11 years, cemented USC's status as the country's most dominant college baseball team. More championships would soon follow for this program that arose from the foundation that Sam had built from almost nothing four decades earlier.

Later in 1968, another former Crawford team reached the top of the baseball mountain. Riding Denny McClain's 31 wins and Willie Horton's 36 home runs, the Tigers captured the AL pennant with a 103-59 record. Similar to Sam's team from 60 years earlier, Detroit fell behind three games to one in the World Series. But this time the Tigers rallied, winning three straight games against St. Louis to capture the championship.

The following season, as part of Major League Baseball's 100th anniversary promotions, Detroit fans voted on the all-time "Greatest Tiger Team." The outfield they selected consisted of current star Al Kaline, as well as Ty Cobb and Sam Crawford. As he did for much of his career, Wahoo would spend posterity alongside the Georgia Peach.

Chapter 18

The Legacy of Wahoo Sam

For years Crawford lobbied Major League Baseball and the Hall of Fame to change his official statistics. As discussed, he believed his career hit total exceeded 3,000. In the decades after his passing, Sam's official numbers were indeed revised—though not in the way he wanted. Crawford's Hall of Fame plaque lists his career hit total at 2,964 and career triples at 312. Though his plaque remains unchanged, Sam today is officially credited with three fewer hits (2,961) and three fewer triples (309) than originally recorded.

Modern stat revisions have tweaked the career totals of many Deadball Era ballplayers. Baseball recordkeeping was not as precise in the early 1900s as it later became. In recent decades, researchers scoured old newspaper game accounts and box scores to verify the official statistics of yesteryear. Their efforts uncovered occasional mistakes—for example, a game's stats being counted twice in the season totals, a sacrifice fly being counted as an at-bat, or an error being counted as a hit. The revisions have impacted some iconic numbers, most notably reducing Ty Cobb's career hit total from 4,191 to 4,189 and lowering his MLB-best lifetime batting average from .367 to .366. Do you think it's possible for someone to actually spin in his grave?

Though noticeable because of the alteration to baseball's all-time triples record, the stat corrections for Crawford had a negligible impact on his legacy. A review of Wahoo's career achievements reveals nothing less than one of the greatest players ever to wear a major league uniform:

- He has a higher batting average (.309) than George Brett.
- He drove in more runs (1,525) than Mickey Mantle.
- He scored more runs (1,391) than Joe DiMaggio.
- He stole more bases (366) than Willie Mays.
- He recorded more hits (2,961) than Rogers Hornsby.

While Crawford's 97 career home runs are not impressive by today's standards, it was a formidable mark for the era in which he played. When he concluded his big league career in 1917, Sam's home run total placed him in the top ten at that point. Since the 1920s, sportswriters, managers, fans, and fellow players have speculated on the impressive power totals Crawford would have accumulated had he played in a later era. Given his longevity in the game, a career total of more than 500 homers seems likely. But we will never know. Despite his power-bereft era, Wahoo does hold a home run record that still stands. In 1901 he hit 12 inside-the-park home runs, setting a single-season mark that remains unsurpassed.

Speaking of records, let's talk triples. Crawford hit 309 of them. Cobb is second on the list with 295 career three-baggers. Honus Wagner is third with 252. Only eight players in major league history have hit more than 200 career triples, and all of them finished their careers before 1930. Baseball has a number of "unbreakable" records: Cobb's .366 career batting average, Cy Young's 511 wins, and Cal Ripken Jr.'s 2,632 consecutive games played. Having not been approached for nearly a century, Crawford's triples record is as unbreakable as any other mark on this list.

When baseball aficionados speculate on Sam's potential home run totals had he played in a later era, the underlying thought is that he missed out on something. But many fans, past and present, consider the triple the most suspenseful and thrilling hit in a baseball game. Writer Roy Blount Jr. famously called the triple "the most exciting 12 seconds in sports." If that is the case, then Sam Crawford is the most exciting player in baseball history. Had he accumulated hundreds of home runs in a later era, he certainly would not have set the all-time triples record. Many of his long hits would have cleared the fence, limiting him to only a handful of triples each year. So the hypothetical choice comes down to hitting 500-plus home runs or holding the big league record with 309 triples. In baseball, a hit falls into one of only four categories: single, double, triple, or home run. Sam is one of only four players to hold an all-time record in one of those categories. The others: Pete Rose (singles), Tris Speaker (doubles), and Barry Bonds (home runs).

In retirement, Crawford once told a reporter that it would have felt good to hit a lively ball and watch it travel. But he repeatedly expressed his preference for the strategy and tactics of his era over the home run-laden modern game. If given the choice, it seems likely he would not have traded in his status as the all-time triples king to hit more home runs.

Crawford struck out 580 times in his major league career. That averages out to 36 strikeouts over a 154-game season, an impressively low total for a hard swinger. By comparison, Babe Ruth struck out an average of 82 times a season. For another comparison, place Crawford's season strikeout average of 36 next to today's hitters. With a strikeout rate of more than 20%, the average modern player with 600 plate appearances strikes out 120 times over a season—more than three times the rate that Sam whiffed.

On the other hand, Crawford did not draw a great number of walks for a feared slugger. His single-season high was 69 bases on balls. Over his career, he averaged 46 walks in a full season. Ruth averaged 127 walks per season throughout his career. Cobb drew about 60 walks per year. Modern players have a walk rate of around 9%, translating into 54 walks over a full season of 600 plate appearances. Crawford struck out far less frequently than twenty-first century hitters, and he walked somewhat less often. Wahoo liked to swing the bat, and when he did, he usually made contact.

In the late twentieth century, researchers started using more advanced metrics to measure ballplayer performance. Bill James, the grandmaster of baseball statistical analysis, called this new emphasis on objective measurements, *Sabermetrics*. Lengthy books have been written about the advanced methodologies assessing player and team performances. For Crawford, we will focus on a few of the most widely-used metrics.

Modern baseball analysts use OPS (on base percentage + slugging average) instead of batting average as a better measure of a hitter's true value. Crawford's career OPS stands at .814, an impressive figure but well below many players of lesser talent whose slugging numbers benefited from playing in power-laden eras. A better statistical indicator of Sam's on-field impact as a ballplayer is WAR (wins above replacement), which measures a player's overall value above that of a generic replacement (e.g. a high-level minor leaguer) from his era. Crawford's career WAR is 75.3, placing him among the top 80 players in MLB history. He ranks higher than such Hall of Famers as Johnny Bench, Reggie Jackson, Harry Heilman, Paul Waner, and Ed Delahanty.

Not surprisingly, the bulk of Crawford's WAR came from his offensive production. Modern metrics are less kind in evaluating his defensive skills. Contemporary accounts of his outfield abilities varied. During the first two-thirds of his career, observers generally described him as a somewhat above average fielder with a decent arm. From 1900 through 1910, he usually finished around the middle of the pack in putouts and assists per year as an outfielder. As the 1910s progressed, sportswriters increasingly noted Crawford's diminishing abilities in the field. After 1911 his putouts and assists per season declined. His fielding percentage actually increased during this period, though the fewer errors were likely a result of reaching fewer fly balls to attempt a catch.

His late career defensive shortcomings aside, Wahoo Sam was one of the dominant players of his day. Modern stat-savvy researchers have confirmed his towering presence on the diamond. In 2001 Sabermetric godfather Bill James ranked Crawford as the 10th greatest right fielder in baseball history. In so doing, he placed Wahoo ahead of fellow Tiger RF legends, Al Kaline (11th) and Harry Heilmann (16th). James, moreover, pioneered a methodology that combined all of the factors affecting a player's contributions (hitting, fielding, baserunning, level of competition, etc.) into a single number known as Win Shares—a metric similar in concept to WAR. According to James, Sam's 266 Win Shares in the 1900-1909 years was the third highest in the majors for a position player, behind only Honus Wagner (421) and Napoleon Lajoie (296). The following decade (1910-1919), Crawford had the eighth highest Win Share total among hitters, even though he played in what amounted to just seven full seasons during that span.

James used his Win Shares system to determine the greatest outfields of all-time. After crunching the numbers, he found the top set of fly-chasers in baseball history to be the 1915 Tigers, with LF Bobby Veach (30 shares), CF Ty Cobb (49 shares), and RF Sam Crawford (28 shares) combining for 107 total Win Shares. Crawford is also a member of James' second all-time greatest outfield, the 1908 Tigers, with Cobb and Matty McIntyre. That outfield's combined 101 Win Shares is actually tied for second with the 1941 Yankees outfield of Joe DiMaggio, Charlie Keller, and Tommy Henrich. The fourth all-time best outfield is the 1907 Tigers with Crawford, Cobb, and Davy Jones.

In his ranking of the 100 greatest players of all time (through 2000), Bill James rated Crawford 89th. That placed him one slot behind Frankie Frisch, and one slot ahead of Al Kaline. Sam made other Top-100 lists compiled at the end of the twentieth century, including those issued by the Society for American Baseball Research (90th) and *The Sporting News* (84th). Crawford's most impressive ranking is found in

Baseball-Reference's Gray Ink Test of rating players. This metric, which counts seasonal top ten appearances in important statistical categories (doubles, triples, HRs, RBI, etc.), ranks Sam as the 9th best hitter in baseball history, just ahead of Rogers Hornsby, Ted Williams, and Frank Robinson.

Crawford's career numbers place him among the leaders in several baseball hitting categories. He is a member of the Baseball Hall of Fame, the Nebraska Sports Hall of Fame, the Michigan Sports Hall of Fame, and the Cincinnati Reds Hall of Fame. Detroit fans in 1969 voted him a member of the all-time greatest Tigers team. Though he dropped out of school after seventh grade, the Nebraska High School Sports Hall of Fame inducted Crawford for his football accomplishments.

Wahoo Sam is certainly deserving of all these accolades. And yet, numbers, plaques, and ranking lists do not reveal the true picture of Sam. The number *309*, doubly tied to Wahoo (career triples and batting average), does not fully convey his towering stature on baseball's landscape. To truly understand Crawford's overall value to his teams, we must look beyond the statistics and lists.

Throughout his career, Crawford continually worked to succeed on the ballfield. Playing baseball was his profession, and he took it seriously. He dependably showed up for work, playing in 98% of his team's games from 1906 to 1915. He pursued a consistent conditioning regimen at a time when many of his colleagues neglected such off-field preparations. Sam followed a regular schedule with plenty of sleep and few diversions. Hughie Jennings said that Crawford took better care of himself than any other player he had seen. He moderated his diet, rarely indulging in red meat. Sam usually went to bed before 10:00 pm and awoke at 7:00 every morning. Wahoo was first to arrive at the clubhouse in the morning and first to report back after the noon-hour break.

Jennings also noted Crawford's even temper and disposition. "No player ever gave [his] manager or owner less trouble than Sam," the Detroit skipper said. Most teammates on the Reds and Tigers admired Crawford, who provided a positive clubhouse presence. He emerged as a team leader in Detroit, and his quiet aggressiveness on the field inspired the other players. "Sam's example and his occasional word of encouragement go farther than almost any other factor to inspire the Tigers in a tight game," Jennings said.

In an era noted for dirty tactics, Crawford played a clean game. Despite his many triples and stolen bases, he avoided using his spikes on opposing players. Research for this book uncovered only one incidence of that type involving Sam, a 1913 spiking of White Sox infielder Rollie Zeider. The article does not say one way or the other, but it almost certainly was accidental.

Sam also drew praise for aspects of his defensive game. *Baseball Magazine* noted that he was always on the move, alertly backing up infield plays in case a bad throw was missed by one of the infielders. Crawford furthermore limited the opportunities of opposing baserunners. Recalling the difficulty of trying to take an extra base on Sam, Honus Wagner said "Crawford was the best of them all in handling ground balls in the outfield."

Sam provided scant fodder for those looking to criticize him. Age eventually diminished his speed, range, and fielding skills, but the same fate befalls all who wear the uniform. Should he have displayed more willingness to shift from the outfield to first base in 1915 and 1916? Probably. But he had done so earlier in his career and did not like the experience.

In one of his few offensive shortcomings, Crawford sometimes neglected to run out ground balls to the infield. Observers noted that he could have logged a few more hits had he ran out grounders more diligently. Donie Bush described this flaw a bit more euphemistically. "He [Sam] never wasted a step any more than he ever wasted a cent," the Tiger shortstop said. "He was strictly for economy."

In contrast with many of his colleagues, Crawford did not seek to engage in verbal or physical altercations. Yes, he moaned in frustration when an outfielder would catch one of his deep fly balls at the wall, but he did not often argue with umpires or quarrel with other players. Only five ejections in more than 2,500 big league games shows an amazing level of restraint for that era. Kid Elberfeld, in contrast, got tossed 23 times while playing in half as many games as Wahoo. Crawford moreover did not run afoul of the law like many of his fellow ballplayers. His worst "offense" came in 1908, when a police court named him on a blanket warrant with the other Tigers for playing baseball on Sunday in violation of a Detroit ordinance. The players duly made their appearance in court, but nothing came of the matter. The few traditionalists in the Motor City who still opposed Sunday ballgames were a shrinking minority, and the restriction was freely ignored after 1908 until the laws were officially expunged a few years later.

Ironically, Crawford's reputation as a quiet, law-abiding baseball citizen worked against his legacy as a great ballplayer. He was not considered a colorful player in an era that produced many memorable characters. His sobriquet provided the lone exception. As *The Sporting News* explained, "the nickname of 'Wahoo Sam' gave him a touch of the unusual which his style of playing failed to provide him." Regarding this on-field style, H.G. Salsinger described Crawford as "thorough, but never brilliant; reliable, but never daring … conventional and strictly orthodox." As such, scribes labeled Sam a fine ballplayer, but lacking the color or spectacular style to become a box office attraction.

The presence of Ty Cobb in the same outfield reinforced this perception of a bland Crawford, further casting him into the shadows of sports history. Cobb during his playing days was the most dynamic force in baseball. He transformed the game with his bold, aggressive tactics. He won batting titles, stole bases, and rattled pitchers like no one before him. He brawled with teammates, opposing players, loudmouthed fans, and pretty much anybody who besmirched his honor. Cobb collected headlines like base hits, becoming the most visible sports celebrity of the Deadball Era. When it came to drawing attention, what baseball player did not pale in comparison to the Georgia Peach?

Although the hardest hitting slugger in the game during his playing days, Crawford eventually became known as just a talented member of Cobb's supporting cast. This perception solidified after Crawford faded from the sports pages in the 1920s, while Ty continued to play. By the 1930s, Sam's status as an elite ballplayer had been obscured. Baseball writers barely gave him a passing glance when voting for the Hall of Fame. In yet another irony, it took the man who had cast the shadow to pull Crawford back into the light of baseball recognition in the 1950s.

A century has passed since Crawford concluded his career as a ballplayer. His Hall of Fame induction occurred more than 60 years ago. And so today we may ask, what is Wahoo Sam's larger significance to the game of baseball?

When Crawford debuted for Cincinnati in 1899, professional baseball occupied a prominent place in American life. Boys across the nation played the game on urban lots and in rural fields. Thousands of fans rooted for their city's teams to vanquish their rivals. Newspapers covered the professional leagues, and men discussed pennant races at various gathering places. But baseball at the turn of the century still lacked acceptance among many segments of American society. Elites largely dismissed the game. Many middle-class Protestants considered ballplayers to be loafers at best and crude, hard-drinking, immigrant ruffians at worst. Respectable women balked at attending games. Few parents viewed the major leagues as a viable career option for their sons.

These negative perceptions dissipated over the first two decades of the twentieth century. By the early 1920s, baseball had increased its emotional appeal across American society.

Press coverage and fan enthusiasm soared to new heights. The top ballplayers became celebrities and heroes who commanded hefty salaries. Women attended games in greater numbers. Presidents, senators, and business leaders watched from box seats. While still maintaining its appeal to the masses, the game won over the middle and upper classes. It forged patriotic links as a national symbol, and a shaper of proper values among young people. Baseball had not only become respectable, it had entered a golden age as America's game.

The rise of a core group of reputable diamond stars played a key role in baseball's ascendancy of the early 1900s. Walter Johnson from rural Idaho eschewed both tobacco and alcohol. Though an unhittable fireballer, the Big Train reflected modesty and small-town values. The "Christian Gentleman" Christy Mathewson embodied the urban sophistication of a college man. His presence on the mound allowed respectable young ladies to ask their beaus to take them to the ballpark.

And then there was Sam Crawford. He hailed from a small town in the Midwest. He showed up every day at the ballpark, where he pursued his craft with an admirable work ethic. He treated children with kindness. He did not drink or smoke—not during the season anyway. He was not a brawler, nor did he draw negative publicity. Many fans looked to him as an example for the nation's boys to follow. His teammates liked and respected him. He was a family man who wisely saved his money. During World War I, he was the first Detroiter to purchase Liberty bonds—buying $5,000 worth. H.G. Salsinger called him one of the finest men in all of baseball. *The Omaha Bee* rated him as one of the city's "most estimable citizens." *Baseball Magazine* called him "one of the greatest players and one of the greatest credits to the game that baseball has ever produced."

For a decade-and-a-half, Crawford stood as one of the top players in the game. He was a sports hero in Detroit, and people across the nation knew the name Wahoo Sam. As baseball magnates sought to increase their game's respectability and appeal to the wealthy and middle classes, they looked to men like Crawford to support their cause. Owners still wanted players like Cobb to create excitement, thrills, and the unexpected at the ballpark. But they *needed* players like Sam to show the public that the game was played by decent individuals—men who could serve as role models for America's children.

Crawford's significance extended even beyond promoting a respectability that helped elevate baseball to greater cultural acceptance. He embodied a broader American dream as it related to the national pastime. He showed what was possible. He lived the idealized baseball life.

Sam grew up in a small Nebraska town. Though not destitute, he came from a family of limited means. As a boy in Wahoo, he developed a love for baseball. He ate, breathed, and slept the game. Like millions of youngsters across the nation, he dreamed of emulating his big league heroes. But that was just a dream. Sam would enter the workforce, toiling as a barber. While he showed promise in the tonsorial arts, his heart remained elsewhere.

On the diamond Sam emerged as the most talented of his youthful peers. In his teen years a local businessman gave him the chance to play on the town's semi-pro team. Sam excelled. He joined a traveling team that toured rural Nebraska in a horse-drawn wagon. His talent impressed another player who had played in the minors. That player told his manager, who gave Sam a shot. He dominated in a low-level minor league for two months, before moving to a high-level minor league. Two months after that, the Cincinnati Reds signed him. He had made it to Major League Baseball in his first season as a pro, when he was just 19 years old.

The small-town kid impressed in the big city ballparks, soon becoming one of the greatest sluggers in the game. After two teams fought for his services, he landed in Detroit. There, he emerged as his club's leader, helping them reach the top of the American League. He awed fans and terrorized pitchers with his deep blasts. He drove in runs and set records. He became known as the "King of Sluggers."

When the passage of years pushed him from the field, Wahoo Sam remained in baseball. He coached at USC, building the foundation for the most dominate collegiate team of the twentieth century. He worked as an umpire. He designed an innovative new bat that became a favorite of the great Babe Ruth. Despite seeing his fortune wiped out by the Great Depression, he served as an officer in the APBPA to help other former ballplayers in need. He crusaded for a pension to assist the aging players of his generation who helped build the modern game. He signed autographs for the countless children who wrote to him. At age 77, the kid from Wahoo, Nebraska, gained enshrinement into the National Baseball Hall of Fame.

Sam Crawford lived out his boyhood dream. He embodied the American success story on the diamond. Though certain individual and team accomplishments eluded him, he reached levels of success that few have exceeded.

"I had a fine career," Sam said in his later years, "I enjoyed every minute of it."

National Baseball Hall of Fame and Museum

Acknowledgments

Thank you to my mentor Benjamin G. Rader for recommending me to the Saunders County Historical Society to give a talk on Sam Crawford. His suggestion resulted in Mary Bergan and Erin Hauser at the SCHS asking me to speak about Wahoo Sam in the spring of 2020. Though the pandemic postponed that event, their lecture invitation started me on the research journey that led to the writing of this book. I am further grateful to Mary and Erin for directing me to the documents, artifacts, and images of Sam Crawford at the Society's museum locations in Wahoo.

Much gratitude to Jodi Fuson for her Wahoo Sam-level editorial skills in improving this book's wording and content. My thanks to Julie Ann Johnson for sharing with me her insights, memories, and photos of her grandfather Sam. Thank you to Rhonda Andresen of the Saunders County Register of Deeds for finding Crawford family property records for me. And many thanks to John Horne at the National Baseball Hall of Fame and Museum for helping me acquire several excellent photographs of Sam.

I also express my appreciation to the Society for American Baseball Research for providing a wealth of information on baseball history, including access to voluminous primary source materials. This book would not have been possible without the newspaper and magazine collections made available by SABR, the Library of Congress, and the LA84 Foundation. Similarly useful were the microfilm newspaper holdings at the Nebraska Historical Society.

Finally, thank you to my wife Jill for her continuing support, encouragement, and multifaceted assistance with my writing projects.

Sources

Chapter 1

• Mitch Lutzke, "October 14, 1909: Tigers top Pirates in 'most exciting' Game Six," SABR.org, 2016, https://sabr.org/gamesproj/game/october-14-1909-tigers-top-pirates-most-exciting-game-six
• *Sporting Life*, October 30, 1909, page 10.
• *The Detroit Times*, December 4, 1912, page 1.
• Trey Strecker, "George Gibson," SABR.org, 2004, https://sabr.org/bioproj/person/7715c135
• F.C. Lane, "Where the Dope Went Wrong," *Baseball Magazine* (Dec. 1914), p. 13.

Chapter 2

• "General History: The History & Function of Minor League Baseball," MiLB.com, 2020, http://www.milb.com/milb/history/general_history.jsp
• "Major League Players by Birthplace During the 1909 Season," Baseball Almanac, 2020, https://www.baseball-almanac.com/players/birthplace.php?y=1909
• Charles Perky, ed., *Past and Present of Saunders County, Vol. 1* (Chicago: The S.J. Clarke Publishing Company, 1915), pages 77-79, 82-83, 88, 257.
• Saunders County Book Committee, *Saunders County History* (Wahoo: Saunders County Historical Society, 1983), page 119.
• 1850 United States Federal Census; Milton, Chittenden, Vermont; Roll 923, p. 203A.
• *The Burlington Courier* (Burlington, VT), October 17, 1850, page 3
• *Sauk Rapids* (MN) *Frontiersman,* Sept. 10, 1857, p. 5; Nov. 3, 1859, p. 2
• *St. Cloud Democrat* (St. Cloud, MN), February 20, 1862, page 1; January 7, 1864, page 4; December 15, 1864, page 3; June 22, 1865, page 2; November 9, 1865, page 2.
• Ralph Orson Sturtevant, *Pictorial History of the 13th Regiment Vermont Volunteers* (n.p., 1910), pages 305, 307, 447.
• "Patients in the Marine Hospital," *The Daily Freeman* (Montpelier, VT), January 12, 1863, page 1.
• *The Caledonian* (St. Johnsbury, VT), January 30, 1863, page 1
• *The Gordon Journal* (Gordon, NE), April 17, 1930.
• 1870 U.S. Federal Census; Fremont, Dodge, Nebraska; roll M593_828, page 325A.
• 1870 U.S. Federal Census; Skull Creek, Butler, Nebraska; roll M593_828, page 57A.
• *The Iowa Capital Reporter* (Iowa City, IA), February 8, 1854, page 3
• 1860 United States Federal Census; Washington, Washington, Iowa; Family History Library film: 803344, page 75.
• Iowa Adjutant General's Office, *Roster and Record of Iowa Soldiers in the War of the Rebellion, Vol. III, 17th-31st Regiments—Infantry* (Des Moines: Emory H. English, State Printer; E.D. Chassell, State Binder, 1910), 120-121, 136.
• 1870 U.S. Federal Census; Trenton, Dade, Georgia; roll M593_146, page 471B.

• 1890 United States Federal Census Veterans Schedules; Belton, Bell, Texas; microfilm M123, Enumeration District 10.

• 1880 United States Federal Census; Precinct 6, Bell, Texas; Roll 1290, page 416A.

• 1900 United States Federal Census; Temple Ward 2, Bell, Texas; Family History Library microfilm 1241610, page 5.

• 1870 U.S. Federal Census; Des Moines, Boone, Iowa; roll M593_378, page 17A.

• Butler County, NE, Marriage Records, S.O. Crawford and Ellen A. Blanchard, July 22, 1872.

• Charles Perky, ed., *Past and Present of Saunders County, Vol. 1* (Chicago: The S.J. Clarke Publishing Company, 1915), pages 51, 82, 88-89, 117, 257.

• *The Wahoo Democrat*, April 22, 1904, page 1.

• Delayed Birth Registration, Zadia M. Crawford, Saunders County, Nebraska, October 20, 1941, Saunders County Historical Society.

• A.T. Andreas, *History of the State of Nebraska* (Chicago: The Western Historical Company, 1882), "Saunders County," Part 8, https://www.kancoll.org/books/andreas_ne/saunders/saunders-p8.html#clearcreek

• *The Columbus Journal,* January 21, 1880, page 4.

• 1880 United States Federal Census; Union Precinct, Saunders, Nebraska; Roll 755, Enumeration District 179, page 332B.

• Delayed Birth Registration, Earl Lee Crawford, Saunders County, Nebraska, October 20, 1941, Saunders County Historical Society.

• 1885 Nebraska State Census; Yutan Village, Union Township, Saunders County; Roll 755, Enumeration District 706, page 5.

• *The Independent* (Wahoo, NE), April 9, 1885, page 2.

• Property Transfer Deed, Henry Anderson to S.O. Crawford, September 2, 1880, Saunders County Register of Deeds.

• "Wahoo Sam Crawford was a Slugger, Medina Recalls," undated clipping in Wahoo Women's Club Binder, Saunders County Historical Society.

• Lawrence Ritter, *The Glory of Their Times* (New York: William Morrow and Company, 1984), page 66.

• *Omaha Daily Bee,* March 9, 1888, page 4; September 22, 1890, page 1.

• Charles H. Morrill, "Drought and Depression in 1890s Nebraska," History Nebraska (from *The Morrills and Reminiscences*, 1918), https://history.nebraska.gov/publications/drought-and-depression-1890s-nebraska

• Jim McKee, "Wahoo's Early Banks, Buildings," *Lincoln Journal Start,* December 21, 2019, https://journalstar.com/news/state-and-regional/nebraska/jim-mckee-wahoos-early-banks-buildings/article_5ccdadf7-c4a3-59ad-b6d8-2b12fa5401a8.html

• "Local "Old Timers' Remember Wahoo Sam Crawford," June 5, 1975 clipping in Wahoo Women's Club Binder, Saunders County Historical Society.

• *Omaha Daily Bee,* May 6, 1897, page 7.

• "Wahoo Sam Crawford is Dead," June 20, 1968 clipping in Wahoo Women's Club Binder, Saunders County Historical Society.

• "Times have changed quite a lot since Wahoo Sam Crawford lived in these parts," undated clipping in Wahoo Women's Club Binder, Saunders County Historical Society.

• *The New Era* (Wahoo, NE), April 27, 1893, page 5.

• "Mr. S.E. Crawford Known as Wahoo Sam," undated handwritten note in Wahoo Women's Club Binder, Saunders County Historical Society.

• David L. Robb with Julie Ann Johnson, *The Stuntwoman* (Coppell, TX: CreateSpace, 2013), page 63.

• "Death of 'Steve' Crawford," *The Wahoo Democrat,* April 22, 1904, page 1.

• "Wahoo's 'Hall of Fame' Wahoo Sam Crawford," undated fact sheet in Sam Crawford folder, Saunders County Historical Society.

• "Daguerreotypes Taken of Former Stars of the Diamond: Samuel E. (Wahoo Sam) Crawford," *The Sporting News,* August 31, 1933, page 2.

• "Hometown Tribute Overwhelms Sam," 1957 clipping in Wahoo Women's Club Binder, Saunders County Historical Society.

• Sam Crawford, "Playing the Outfield," *The American Boy* (1909 article in Sam Crawford folder, Saunders County Historical Society), pp. 307-308.

• Paul Means, "Town, Sam Change—But Both Prosper," *Lincoln Sunday Journal and Start*, August 4, 1957, page 2B.

• "Recollections of 'Wahoo' Sam," April 1957 clipping in Wahoo Women's Club Binder, Saunders County Historical Society.

Chapter 3

• "Hometown Tribute Overwhelms Sam," 1957 clipping in Wahoo Women's Club Binder, Saunders County Historical Society.

• Charles Perky, ed., *Past and Present of Saunders County, Vol. 1* (Chicago: The S.J. Clarke Publishing Company, 1915), page 82.

• F.C. Lane, "The King of Sluggers," *Baseball Magazine* (February 1916), pp. 59-61.

• *The New Era* (Wahoo, NE), June 29, 1893, page 5.

• Saunders County, Nebraska, Marriage Records, Tracy K. Crawford and Myrtle B. Miller, October 17, 1895.

• *The New Era* (Wahoo, NE), June 15, 1893, page 8; February 7, 1895, page 5.

• "Death of Tracy K. Crawford," undated newspaper clipping in Sam Crawford folder, Saunders County Historical Society.

• Lawrence Ritter, *The Glory of Their Times* (New York: William Morrow and Company, 1984), pages 66-68.

• "Recollections of 'Wahoo' Sam," April 1957 clipping in Wahoo Women's Club Binder, Saunders County Historical Society.

• Frederic G. Lieb, "'Wahoo' Sam Crawford: The Famous Slugging Outfielder of the Detroit Tigers," *Outdoor Sports,* 1911 article in Sam Crawford folder, Saunders County Historical Society.

• Paul Means, "Town, Sam Change—But Both Prosper," *Lincoln Sunday Journal and Start*, August 4, 1957, page 2B.

• Robert Phipps, "Wahoo Honors Hall of Fame Son—Crawford Recalls No-Smoke Deal," 1957 *Omaha World-Herald* clipping in Wahoo Women's Club Binder, Saunders County Historical Society.

• "Diamond Meteors of the Past—Slugger Sam Crawford," *Reading Eagle,* March 10, 1940, clipping in Sam Crawford folder, Saunders County Historical Society.

• "Baseball Fete Keynote of Pair Wed 58 Years," September 28, 1935, clipping in Wahoo Women's Club Binder, Saunders County Historical Society.

• "Local "Old Timers' Remember Wahoo Sam Crawford," June 5, 1975 clipping in Wahoo Women's Club Binder, Saunders County Historical Society.

• "Wahoo Sam Crawford is Dead," June 20, 1968 clipping in Wahoo Women's Club Binder, Saunders County Historical Society.

• *The Wahoo Democrat,* May 29, 1896, page 5; August 20, 1896, page 5.

• *Omaha Daily Bee,* July 5, 1896, page 5.

• *Wasp* (Wahoo, NE), July 9, 1896, page 8; July 16, 1896, page 5.

• *Omaha Daily Bee,* July 16, 1896, page 2.

• "Averages of the Killian Bros. Base Ball Team, Season 1896," *The Wahoo Democrat,* December 10, 1896, page 10.

• "Our Foot Ball Team," *The Wahoo Democrat,* October 1, 1896, page 5.

• "Wahoo's Foot Ball Team," *Omaha Daily Bee,* September 23, 1896, page 7.

• Jerry Mathers, *Nebraska High School Sports*, 2nd ed. (Lyons, NE: unidentified publisher, 1980), pages 7, 107.

• *Sporting Life*, September 19, 1908, page 11.

• "Base Ball Team at Wahoo," *Omaha Daily Bee,* April 17, 1897, page 2.

• "Council Bluffs Wins," *Wasp* (Wahoo, NE), May 6, 1897, page 6.

• "Snake's Colts Gets 0," *Wasp* (Wahoo, NE), May 13, 1897, page 5; "Three Straight Victories," *The Nebraskan,* May 15, 1897, pages 1, 4.

• *The Wahoo Democrat,* June 3, 1897, page 5; June 17, 1897, page 5; June 24, 1897, page 5; July 8, 1897, page 1.

• "Wahoo Clerks Organize," *Omaha Daily Bee,* July 15, 1897, page 7.

• *Omaha Daily Bee,* May 19, 1896, page 2; June 1, 1896, page 2; July 21, 1897, page 7; July 22, 1897, page 7; July 25, 1897, page. 3.

• "Mr. S.E. Crawford Known as Wahoo Sam," undated handwritten note in Wahoo Women's Club Binder, Saunders County Historical Society.

• *The Wahoo Democrat,* August 12, 1897, page 5.

• *Omaha Daily Bee,* August 2, 1897, page 7; August 3, 1897, page 7; August 11, 1897, page 2; August 31, 1897, page 2; September 10, 1897, page 7; September 11, 1897, page 2; September 12, 1897, page 6.
• "West Point Wins the Championship," *Cuming County Advertiser,* Sept. 14, 1897, page 4.
• *Omaha Sunday Bee,* October 9, 1897, page 6.
• Benjamin G. Rader, *Baseball: A History of America's Game,* 4th ed. (Urbana: University of Illinois Press, 2018), page 101.
• *The St. Paul Globe,* January 25, 1903, page 6.
• *Omaha Sunday Bee,* April 4, 1906, page 6.
• Guy W. Green, *The Nebraska Indians and Fun and Frolic with an Indian Ball Team,* (Jefferson, NC: McFarland & Company, 2010), page xi.
• *"Nebraska Indians Baseball Team," History Nebraska,* https://history.nebraska.gov/publications/nebraska-indians-baseball-team
• Jeffrey Powers-Beck, *The American Indian Integration of Baseball,* (Lincoln, NE: University of Nebraska Press, 2004), pages 53, 62.
• *Omaha Daily Bee,* June 23, 1897, page 7; June 26, 1897, page 2.
• *The Weekly Arbor State* (Wymore, NE), June 24, 1898, page 8; July 8, 1898, page 7.
• *The Weekly Wymorean,* July 9, 1898, p. 1; July 23, 1898, p. 1; Aug 13, 1898, page 1.
• *Omaha Daily Bee,* July 28, 1898, page 4; August 9, 1898, page 4.
• *Omaha Sunday Bee,* August 28, 1898, page 9.

Chapter 4

• "Recollections of 'Wahoo' Sam," April 1957 clipping in Wahoo Women's Club Binder, Saunders County Historical Society.
• Lawrence Ritter, *The Glory of Their Times* (New York: William Morrow and Company, 1984), pages 49, 67-69.
• F.C. Lane, "The King of Sluggers," *Baseball Magazine* (Feb. 1916), pages 60-62.
• "Canada's League," *Sporting Life,* April 29, 1899, page 5.
• Frank Moore Colby and Talcott Williams, eds., *The New International Encyclopedia,* 2nd ed., Vol. 5 (New York: Dodd, Mead and Company, 1923), page 94.
• "Daguerreotypes Taken of Former Stars of the Diamond: Samuel E. (Wahoo Sam) Crawford," *The Sporting News,* August 31, 1933, page 2.
• *Sporting Life,* May 20, 1899, page 7; May 27, 1899, page 8; June 10, 1899, page 9; June 17, 1899, page 5; June 24, 1899, page 8; July 8, 1899, pages 8, 10; July 15, 1899, pages 8, 9; July 22, 1899, page 8; August 5, 1899, pages 7, 8, 11; August 12, 1899, pages 7, 8, 11; August 19, 1899, pages 4, 8, 9, 11; September 2, 1899, page 5; September 16, 1899, pages 3, 4, 11; September 23, 1899, pages 3, 11; September 30, 1899, pages 3, 4; October 7, 1899, pages 5, 7, 10; November 29, 1902, page 6.
• Alan H. Levy, *Rube Waddell: The Zany, Brilliant Life of a Strikeout Artist* (Jefferson, NC: McFarland & Company, 2000), page 41.

• *Sporting Life*, October 21, 1899, page 6.

• Charles Alexander, *John McGraw* (Lincoln: University of Nebraska Press, 1988), pages 66-67.

• Paul Wendt, "Jimmy Barrett," SABR.org, 2006, https://sabr.org/bioproj/person/jimmy-barrett/

• Lawrence Ritter, *The Glory of Their Times* sound recording, (St. Paul, MN: HighBridge Audio, 1998), Sam Crawford interview.

• *Sporting Life*, October 28, 1899, pages 4, 9.

• Walt Dobbins, "Nebraska Sports Fame Hall Fetes Sam E. Crawford," undated clipping in Wahoo Women's Club Binder, Saunders County Historical Society.

• *North Plate Semi-Weekly Tribune,* November 28, 1899, page 7.

• *Omaha Sunday Bee*, October 1, 1899, page 11.

• Fred Lieb, "Crawford Dead at 88; Three-Base Hit King," *The Sporting News*, June 29, 1968, page 15.

• *Sporting Life*, November 4, 1899, page 9.

Chapter 5

• Harold Seymour, *Baseball: The Early Years* (New York: Oxford University Press, 1960), pages 17, 304-305, 307-315, 321.

• "Cincinnati, Ohio," *Ohio History Central*, 2015, https://ohiohistorycentral.org/w/Cincinnati,_Ohio

• Lawrence Ritter, *The Glory of Their Times* (New York: William Morrow and Company, 1984), pages 53-54, 69.

• Gilson Willets, *Workers of the Nation: An Encyclopedia of the Occupations of the American People and a Record of Business, Professional and Industrial Achievement at the Beginning of the Twentieth Century* (New York: P.F. Collier and Son, 1903), page 1047.

• *Sporting Life*, March 10, 1900, p. 6; March 24, 1900, p. 2; March 31, 1900, p. 6; April 14, 1900, p. 2; April 28, 1900, p. 2; May 5, 1900, p. 2-3; May 12, 1900, p. 4; May 19, 1900, p. 3; May 26, 1900, p. 3; June 2, 1900, pp. 4, 9; June 9, 1900, pp. 3, 5; June 23, 1900, p. 3.

• *The Scranton Tribune*, May 19, 1900, page 3.

• 1900 United States Federal Census; Cincinnati Ward 18, Hamilton, Ohio; Family History Library microfilm 1241277, page 4.

• Lee Allen, "Cooperstown Corner: An Unusual Man Was Sam Crawford," *The Sporting News,* July 6, 1968, page 6.

• letter from Sam Crawford to Lee Allen, November 11, 1963, National Baseball Hall of Fame Library.

• Benjamin G. Rader, *Baseball: A History of America's Game*, 4th ed. (Urbana: University of Illinois Press, 2018), pages 66-68, 87-89.

• John Saccoman, "John T. Brush," SABR.org, 2004,
https://sabr.org/bioproj/person/john-t-brush/
• *Sporting Life*, July 21, 1900, pages 1-2; July 28, 1900, page 5; August 18, 1900, page 4; September 8, 1900, pages 3-4; August 4, 1900, page 4; August 11, 1900, page 5; August 25, 1900, page 4; Sept. 15, 1900, pages 4-5; Sept. 29, 1900, page 7; October 13, 1900, page 5; October 27, 1900, page 6; November 10, 1900, page 6; November 24, 1900, page 7; December 15, 1900, page 8; February 2, 1901, pages 2, 6; March 23, 1901, pages 4-5; April 27, 1901, pages 2-3; May 4, 1901, pages 2, 4; May 11, 1901, pages 3-4; June 1, 1901, pages 2, 5; June 8, 1901, page 3; June 29, 1901, page 3.
• *Omaha Daily Bee,* July 20, 1901, page 9.
• *The St. Louis Republic,* August 4, 1901, page 2; August 10, 1901, page 5.
• *Washington Evening Star,* August 24, 1901, page 8.
• "Wahoo Sam Crawford is Dead," June 20, 1968 clipping in Wahoo Women's Club Binder, Saunders County Historical Society.
• *Omaha Daily Bee,* October 31, 1901, page 5; November 3, 1901, page 5.
• Saunders County, Nebraska, Marriage Records, Samuel E. Crawford and Ada M. Lattin, October 30, 1901.
• *The Wahoo Democrat,* October 31, 1893, page 5.
• "Mrs. Sam Crawford Dies; Had Attended Wahoo Schools," March 10, 1938, clipping in Sam Crawford folder, Saunders County Historical Society.
• *Wasp* (Wahoo, NE)*,* May 9, 1895, page 5.
• *The New Era* (Wahoo, NE), May 25, 1893, page 5; September 7, 1893, page 5; March 22, 1894, page 5.
• *The Independent* (Wahoo, NE)*,* October 2, 1879, page 2.
• Saunders County, Nebraska, Marriage Records, Arthur Monteen and Zadia Crawford, September 12, 1901.
• *Sporting Life*, April 19, 1902, page 4.
• Jeff Suess, "Reds' Legendary Palace of the Fans Symbol of Baseball's Growth," Cincinnati.com, April 5, 2017,
https://www.cincinnati.com/story/news/2017/04/05/reds-legendary-palace-fans-symbol-baseballs-growth/100063096/
• *Sporting Life*, April 26, 1902, pages 2-3.
• Ralph Berger, "Dummy Hoy," SABR.org, https://sabr.org/bioproj/person/dummy-hoy/
• *Sporting Life*, May 17, 1902, page 11; May 24, 1902, page 10; June 7, 1902, pages 3, 10; June 14, 1902, page 7; June 21, 1902, page 8; June 28, 1902, pages 8-9.
• *Washington Evening Star,* June 5, 1902, page 9.
• *The St. Louis Republic,* July 21, 1902, page 4.
• *Sporting Life*, July 12, 1902, page 3.
• Jimmy Keenan, "Joe Kelley," SABR.org, 2011, https://sabr.org/bioproj/person/joe-kelley/

• Charles Alexander, *John McGraw* (Lincoln: University of Nebraska Press, 1988), pages 89-93.

• *Sporting Life*, July 26, 1902, page 5; Aug. 2, 1902, page 9; Aug. 23, 1902, page 9.

Chapter 6

• *Sporting Life*, August 16, 1902, pages 2-3, 5; August 23, 1902, page 5; August 30, 1902, pages 2, 8-9.

• *The St. Louis Republic,* August 20, 1902, page 7.

• *The St. Paul Globe,* August 25, 1902, page 5.

• Rob Edelman and Michael Betzold, "Mike Donlin," SABR.org, 2004, https://sabr.org/bioproj/person/mike-donlin/

• *Omaha Daily Bee,* August 28, 1902, page 2.

• *Topeka State Journal,* August 29, 1902, page 2.

• Mitch Lutzke, "How Sam Crawford Became a Tiger after Signing with Two Different Teams," The Tigers History Project, August 1, 2019, https://tigershistory.com/features/how-sam-crawford-became-a-tiger-after-signing-with-two-different-teams/

• *Sporting Life*, September 6, 1902, pages 5, 8.

• *Omaha Daily Bee*, August 31, 1902, page 8.

• John Saccoman, "Garry Herrmann," SABR.org, 2004, https://sabr.org/bioproj/person/garry-herrmann/

• Frederic G. Lieb, *The Detroit Tigers* (Kent, OH: The Kent State University Press, 2008; originally New York: G.P. Putnam's Sons, 1946), page 94.

• *The Sporting News*, November 7, 1903, page 5.

• *Sporting Life*, September 20, 1902, page 9; September 27, 1902, pages 3, 9; October 11, 1902, pages 1, 3, 5; October 18, 1902, page 7.

• *Sporting Life*, Oct. 4, 1902, pp. 7, 9; Oct. 25, 1902, pp. 2, 5; Nov. 1, 1902, p. 7.

• *Omaha Daily Bee*, October 19, 1902, page 10; October 20, 1902, page 6.

• Harold Seymour, *Baseball: The Early Years* (New York: Oxford University Press, 1960), pages 307, 322-323.

• Morris A. Eckhouse, "Detroit Tigers: The Cornerstone of Detroit Baseball is Stability" in Peter C. Bjarkman, ed., *Encyclopedia of Major League Baseball: American League* (New York: Carroll & Graf Publishers, 1993), page 141.

• *Sporting Life*, November 8, 1902, page 7; November 15, 1902, pages 3, 7; November 29, 1902, page 8; December 6, 1902, page 3; December 27, 1902, page 2; January 4, 1903, page 4; January 17, 1903, pages 2, 4.

• Benjamin G. Rader, *Baseball: A History of America's Game*, 4th ed. (Urbana: University of Illinois Press, 2018), pages 87-90, 110.

• *Sporting Life*, January 24, 1903, pages 3, 5.

• William Akin, "Win Mercer," SABR.org, https://sabr.org/bioproj/person/win-mercer/

• F.C. Lane, "The King of Sluggers," *Baseball Magazine* (February 1916), pp. 63-64.

Chapter 7

• J. Edward Grillo, "Stays With Reds," *The Sporting News*, Nov 29, 1902, page 1.
• *Washington Evening Star*, January 24, 1903, page 9.
• *Sporting Life*, February 21, 1903, p. 5; March 7, 1903, p. 4; March 21, 1903, pp. 7-8.
• "Industrial Detroit (1860-1900)," Detroit Historical Society, 2020, https://detroithistorical.org/learn/timeline-detroit/industrial-detroit-1860-1900
• Peter Weber, "The Rise and Fall of Detroit: A Timeline," *The Week*, July 19, 2013, https://theweek.com/articles/461968/rise-fall-detroit-timeline
• Terry Simpkins, "Kid Elberfeld," SABR.org, 2006, https://sabr.org/bioproj/person/kid-elberfeld/
• Daniel R. Levitt, "Ed Barrow," SABR.org, 2008, https://sabr.org/bioproj/person/ed-barrow/
• Charles Leerhsen, *Ty Cobb: A Terrible Beauty* (New York: Simon and Schuster, 2015), pages 53-55, 71-78, 83-85, 94-99, 101, 112-117, 125-126, 132-133, 139.
• Scott Ferkovich, "Bennett Park (Detroit)," SABR.org, 2012, https://sabr.org/bioproj/park/bennett-park-detroit/
• Ron Selter, "Bennett Park Historical Analysis," Baseball Almanac, 1999-2020, https://www.baseball-almanac.com/stadium/st_bp.shtml
• *Sporting Life*, April 11, 1903, p. 6; April 18, 1903, p. 8; May 2, 1903, p. 8; May 9, 1903, p. 8; May 23, 1903, pp. 8-9; May 30, 1903, p. 9; June 13, 1903, p. 8.
• Dan D'Addona, *In Cobb's Shadow* (Jefferson, NC: McFarland & Company, 2015), pages 10, 13, 20.
• Benjamin G. Rader, *Baseball: A History of America's Game*, 4th ed. (Urbana: University of Illinois Press, 2018), pages 101, 111.
• Lawrence Ritter, *The Glory of Their Times* (New York: William Morrow and Company, 1984), pages 51-52, 60, 62, 65.
• John Saccoman, "Ed Delahanty," SABR.org, 2006, https://sabr.org/bioproj/person/ed-delahanty/
• *Sporting Life*, July 25, 1903, p. 11; August 1, 1903, p. 10; August 8, 1903, p. 10.
• *Omaha Daily Bee*, July 11, 1903, page 9.
• "Just Like Big Sam," *Omaha Daily Bee*, August 19, 1903, page 5.
• *Sporting Life*, Jan. 23, 1904, pp. 4-5; Jan. 30, 1904, p. 6; Feb. 13, 1904, p. 10.
• Morris A. Eckhouse, "Detroit Tigers: The Cornerstone of Detroit Baseball is Stability" in Peter C. Bjarkman, ed., *Encyclopedia of Major League Baseball: American League* (New York: Carroll & Graf Publishers, 1993), page 142.
• *The St. Louis Republic*, February 25, 1904, page 6.
• *Sporting Life*, February 27, 1904, page 4; March 19, 1904, page 1; April 2, 1904, page 4; April 16, 1904, page 5; April 23, 1904, page 8.
• "Death of 'Steve' Crawford," *The Wahoo Democrat,* April 22, 1904, page 1.

• "Crippled Tigers," *The Sporting News*, April 30, 1904, page 2.

• *Sporting Life*, May 7, 1904, page 6; May 14, 1904, page 8; May 21, 1904, page 8.

• David Southwick and Bill Nowlin, "Cy Young," SABR.org, 2006, https://sabr.org/bioproj/person/cy-young/

• *Sporting Life*, May 28, 1904, pages 8-9; June 4, 1904, pages 8-9; June 11, 1904, page 8; June 25, 1904, page 8; July 9, 1904, page 1; July 30, 1904, pages 8-9.

• *Omaha Daily Bee*, December 22, 1905, page 6.

• *Sporting Life*, March 24, 1906, page 7; March 13, 1909, page 15.

• Frank Navin, "A Good Word for Sam Crawford," *Baseball Magazine* (February 1916), page 31.

• *Sporting Life*, September 24, 1904, page 11; August 6, 1904, page 11; October 22, 1904, pages 7-8; December 5, 1904, page 5; April 21, 1906, page 6.

• Charles Alexander, *Ty Cobb* (New York: Oxford University Press, 1984), pages 30, 41-42, 45, 47.

• Al Stump, *Cobb: A Biography* (Chapel Hill, NC: Algonquin, 1994), page 58-60.

• *Sporting Life*, March 4, 1905, p. 3; March 11, 1905, p. 6; March 25, 1905, p. 8; Apr. 1, 1905, p. 12; Apr. 29, 1905, p. 7; May 13, 1905, p. 10; May 20, 1905, p. 8; June 10, 1905, p. 7; June 24, 1905, pp. 6-7; Aug. 19, 1905, p. 7; Sept. 2, 1905, p. 6; March 10, 1906, p. 12.

• B.T. Wright, "Tigers are Lucky," *The Sporting News*, March 24, 1906, page 3.

• Paul Wendt, "Jimmy Barrett," SABR.org, 2006, https://sabr.org/bioproj/person/jimmy-barrett/

• Mike Grahek, "Davy Jones," SABR.org, 2006, https://sabr.org/bioproj/person/davy-jones/

• *Sporting Life*, April 7, 1906, p. 7; April 21, 1906, p. 6; April 28, 1906, pp. 6-7.

• J.G. Taylor Spink, "The Ty Cobb that I Knew," *The Sporting News,* December 13, 1961, page 4.

• *Sporting Life*, May 12, 1906, page 6; June 2, 1906, page 5; June 9, 1906, page 7; July 7, 1906, page 6; July 21, 1906, page 7; August 11, 1906, page 3; September 1, 1906, page 6; September 15, 1906, page 6.

Chapter 8

• *Omaha Daily Bee*, October 12, 1906, page 8.

• *Sporting Life*, October 13, 1906, page 14.

• Charles Alexander, *Ty Cobb* (New York: Oxford University Press, 1984), pages 30, 44-45, 53, 58-59, 68-69, 75, 80-81.

• Charles Leerhsen, *Ty Cobb: A Terrible Beauty* (New York: Simon and Schuster, 2015), pages 146, 151-157, 174-177, 185-187, 200, 213, 216-221.

• *Sporting Life*, March 9, 1907, page 17; March 30, 1907, page 2; April 20, 1907, pages 10-11; May 4, 1907, page 11; May 11, 1907, page 10; June 1, 1907, page 10; June 8, 1907, page 11; June 22, 1907, pages 6, 13; August 10, 1907, page 10.

• Lawrence Ritter, *The Glory of Their Times* (New York: William Morrow and Company, 1984), pages 56-57.

• Ty Cobb with Al Stump, *My Life in Baseball* (Lincoln: University of Nebraska Press, 1993), page 65.

• *Sporting Life*, September 7, 1907, page 7; September 21, 1907, page 12; October 5, 1907, pages 7, 10-11; October 12, 1907, page 12; November 9, 1907, page 7.

• Richard Smiley, "Matty McIntyre," SABR.org, 2006, https://sabr.org/bioproj/person/matty-mcintyre/

• Jerry Clark, *Nebraska Diamonds* (Omaha: Making History, 1991), page 25.

• *Omaha Daily Bee*, October 10, 1907, page 4; October 19, 1907, pages 5-6, 8; October 26, 1907, pages 9-10.

• Affidavit, M.M. Runyon to the Public, May 8, 1919, Saunders County Register of Deeds.

• 1910 United States Federal Census; Detroit Ward 1, Wayne, Michigan; Roll T624_679, page 4B.

• Jodie Adams Kirshner, *Broke: Hardship and Resilience in a City of Broken Promises* (New York: St. Martins Publishing Group, 2019), ebook.

• *The Detroit Times*, February 20, 1908, page 2; February 29, 1908, page 2; March 17, 1908, page 4; *The Detroit Times*, March 21, 1908, page 2.

• *Sporting Life*, May 2, 1908, page 11; May 9, 1908, page 7; June 13, 1908, page 11; June 20, 1908, pages 5, 10; July 4, 1908, pages 6, 10.

• *The Detroit Times*, June 25, 1908, page 2.

• Lawrence Ritter, *The Glory of Their Times* (New York: William Morrow and Company, 1984), pages 41, 56, 59.

• F.C. Lane, "The Spit-ball King," *Baseball Magazine* (March 1913), page 52.

• M.W. Bingay, "Game's Heaviest Batter," *The Sporting News*, January 16, 1908, p. 3.

• *Sporting Life*, July 18, 1908, page 5; August 1, 1908, page 11.

• Paul H. Bruske, "Crawford-Cobb Debate Again Rages in Fandom," *The Detroit Times*, September 5, 1908, page 6.

• Fred Lieb, "Crawford Dead at 88; Three-Base Hit King," *The Sporting News*, June 29, 1968, page 15.

• Dan Holmes, *Ty Cobb: A Biography* (Westport, CT: Greenwood Press, 2004), pages 41-42, 48.

• *The Detroit Times*, Aug. 31, 1908, p. 1; Sept. 1, 1908, p. 1; Sept. 11, 1908, p. 6.

• *Sporting Life*, September 5, 1908, p. 11; October 3, 1908, pages 10-11; October 10, 1908, page 11; October 24, 1908, pages 5-7; October 31, 1908, page 8.

• David Jones and Marc Okkonen, "Frank Navin," SABR.org, 2014, https://sabr.org/bioproj/person/frank-navin/

• *Omaha Daily Bee*, October 25, 1908, Sports section, page 1.

• *Omaha Daily Bee*, November 24, 1908, page 9; November 28, 1908, page 16.

• *Sporting Life*, January 2, 1909, page 7; January 30, 1909, page 5.

• *The Detroit Times*, February 18, 1909, page 7; March 2, 1909, page 2; March 13, 1909, page 7; March 23, 1909, page 2; March 30, 1909, page 2.
• *Sporting Life*, March 20, 1909, page 17; April 17, 1909, page 3; April 24, 1909, page 10; May 22, 1909, page 11.
• *The Detroit Times*, May 22, 1909, page 6; June 5, 1909, page 7; June 23, 1909, page 7; July 3, 1909, page 7.
• Dan Holmes, "Germany Schaefer," SABR.org, 2006, https://sabr.org/bioproj/person/germany-schaefer/
• *Sporting Life*, July 24, 1909, page 11; August 14, 1909, page 11; August 28, 1909, pages 3, 10; Sept. 25, 1909, page 10; Oct. 2, 1909, page 10; January 1, 1910, page 9.
• Hugh Fullerton, "Pittsburgh, Paced by Pitching of Young Babe Adams, Nipped Tigers, Favorites, in Historic Series of 1909," *The Sporting News*, Jan. 30, 1940, p. 9.
• *Omaha Daily Bee*, October 11, 1909, page 8.
• *The Calumet* (MI) *News*, October 20, 1909, page 7.
• *Sporting Life*, October 23, 1909, pages 4-6, 8.
• *The Sporting News*, October 21, 1909, page 3; October 30, 1909, pages 2, 8.
• Fred Lieb, "When Babe Adams Trimmed Tigers' Claws and Won a World's Pennant," *The Washington Times*, January 26, 1920, page 12.
• *The Calumet* (MI) *News*, October 29, 1909, page 7.
• *Omaha Daily Bee*, October 25, 1908, Sports section, page 1; November 24, 1908, page 9; November 28, 1908, page 16.
• *Sporting Life*, January 2, 1909, page 7; January 30, 1909, page 5.
• *The Detroit Times*, February 18, 1909, page 7; March 2, 1909, page 2; March 13, 1909, page 7; March 23, 1909, page 2; March 30, 1909, page 2.
• *Sporting Life*, March 20, 1909, page 17; April 17, 1909, page 3; April 24, 1909, page 10; May 22, 1909, page 11.
• *The Detroit Times*, May 22, 1909, page 6; June 5, 1909, page 7; June 23, 1909, page 7; July 3, 1909, page 7.
• *Sporting Life*, July 24, 1909, page 11; August 14, 1909, page 11; August 28, 1909, pages 3, 10; Sept. 25, 1909, page 10; Oct. 2, 1909, page 10; January 1, 1910, page 9.
• *Omaha Daily Bee*, October 11, 1909, page 8.
• *The Calumet* (MI) *News*, October 20, 1909, page 7; October 29, 1909, page 7.
• *Sporting Life*, October 23, 1909, pages 4-6, 8.
• *The Sporting News*, October 21, 1909, page 3; October 30, 1909, pages 2, 8.

Chapter 9

• *The Detroit Times*, January 26, 1910, p. 8; April 12, 1910, p. 4; March 15, 1911, p. 9
• *Sporting Life*, February 12, 1910, page 6; April 2, 1910, page 7; April 16, 1910, pages 5, 7; June 11, 1910, pages 6, 11; July 2, 1910, page 11.
• Henry P. Edwards, "Stars of Two Centuries Flashed at League Park," *The Sporting News*, April 2, 1947, page 15.

• *The Detroit Times*, March 20, 1910, p. 7; June 4, 1910, page 10; June 25, 1910, p. 6; July 2, 1910, p. 6; July 14, 1910, p. 6; September 26, 1910, p. 8; Nov. 16, 1910, p. 8.

• *The Calumet* (MI) *News*, July 15, 1910, page 7.

• *Sporting Life*, July 9, 1910, p. 5; July 23, 1910, p. 10; Aug. 13, 1910, p. 11; Oct. 1, 1910, p. 3; Oct. 8, 1910, p. 18; Oct. 15, 1910, p. 8; Dec. 31, 1910, p. 8.

• Charles Alexander, *Ty Cobb* (New York: OUP, 1984), pp. 98-99, 105, 113.

• *Sporting Life*, February 25, 1911, page 8.

• *The Detroit Times*, January 16, 1911, p. 6; March 4, 1911, p. 7; March 14, 1911, p. 6; March 25, 1911, p. 12; Apr. 15, 1911, pp. 2-3; Apr. 22, 1911, p. 11; May 6, 1911, p. 1.

• Alex Semchuck, "Addie Joss," SABR.org, 2006, https://sabr.org/bioproj/person/addie-joss/

• *The Detroit Times*, April 2, 1911, p. 6; April 22, 1911, p. 10; Sept. 18, 1911, p. 6.

• *Omaha Daily Bee*, June 7, 1911, page 4.

• *Sporting Life*, May 27, 1911, page 5; June 10, 1911, pages 10-11; June 29, 1911, page 11; July 22, 1911, page 11; August 19, 1911, page 11; Sept. 9, 1911, page 5.

• Charles Leerhsen, *Ty Cobb: A Terrible Beauty* (New York: Simon and Schuster, 2015), pages 8, 248, 255, 258-267, 269, 280-282, 295.

• *The Detroit Times*, December 16, 1911, page 12; December 22, 1911, page 10.

• *Sporting Life*, November 18, 1911, page 5.

• Scott Ferkovich, "Tiger Stadium (Detroit)," SABR.org, 2016, https://sabr.org/bioproj/park/tiger-stadium-detroit/

• Richard Bak, "The Day Frank Navin's Ballpark Came to Life," Vintage Detroit, April 20, 2012, https://www.vintagedetroit.com/blog/2012/04/20/the-day-frank-navins-ballpark-came-to-life/

• *Sporting Life*, April 13, 1912, p. 13; May 11, 1912, p. 13; May 18, 1912, pp. 12-13.

• Benjamin Rader, "Matters Involving Honor: Religion, Race, and Rank in the Violent Life of Tyrus Raymond Cobb," in Donald G. Kyle and Robert B. Fairbanks, eds., *Baseball in America and America in Baseball* (College Station: Texas A&M University Press, 2008), pages 189, 211.

• Ty Cobb with Al Stump, *My Life in Baseball* (Lincoln: University of Nebraska Press, 1993), page 133.

• *The Detroit Times*, May 11, 1912, p. 6; July 6, 1912, p. 13; July 20, 1912, p. 13.

• Fred Lieb, "Crawford Dead at 88; Three-Base Hit King," *The Sporting News*, June 29, 1968, page 15.

• *Sporting Life*, Sept. 28, 1912, p. 11; Dec. 14, 1912, pp. 1-2, 7; Dec. 21, 1912, p. 11.

• *The Sporting News*, December 19, 1912, page 6.

• *Omaha Daily Bee*, December 7, 1912, page 13.

• *The Detroit Times*, Dec. 4, 1912, p. 4; Dec. 14, 1912, p. 14; Dec. 31, 1912, p. 8.

• *Sporting Life*, Jan. 4, 1913, p. 6; Jan. 25, 1913, p. 11; Feb. 22, 1913, pp. 12, 17.

• *The Detroit Times*, January 24, 1913, page 1; January 31, 1913, page 1; March 13, 1913, page 1; March 15, 1913, page 1; March 20, 1913, pages 1, 7.

• *Sporting Life*, March 1, 1913, page 11; March 29, 1913, pages 6, 7, 11.

• Harold Seymour, *Baseball: The Golden Age* (New York: Oxford University Press, 1971), pages 172-176, 194.

• *Omaha Daily Bee*, April 6, 1913, sports section, page 4.

• *Sporting Life*, May 3, 1913, page 11; May 10, 1913, pages 2-3; May 24, 1913, page 17; June 7, 1913, page 15; June 21, 1913, page 12; August 2, 1913, page 12.

• *The Detroit Times*, March 17, 1914, p. 6; June 25, 1913, p. 6; July 15, 1913, p. 6.

• *Sporting Life*, June 7, 1913, p. 3; July 26, 1913, p. 12; August 9, 1913, p. 12; August 23, 1913, p. 7; October 25, 1913, pp. 1, 5; Nov. 1, 1913, p. 7; Nov. 15, 1913, p. 5.

• F.C. Lane, "The King of Sluggers," *Baseball Magazine* (February 1916), pp. 67-68.

• *Sporting Life*, November 29, 1913, pages 5, 9.

• Tom Clavin, "The Inside Story of Baseball's Grand World Tour of 1914," Smithsonianmag.com, March 21, 2014, https://www.smithsonianmag.com/history/inside-story-baseballs-grand-world-tour-1914-180950228/

• Frank McGlynn, "Striking Scenes from the Tour Around the World," *Baseball Magazine* (August 1914), pages 63, 66.

• *Sporting Life*, Jan. 10, 1914, p. 11; Feb. 21, 1914, p. 7; Feb. 28, 1914, p. 6; March 7, 1914, p. 14; March 14, 1914, pp. 9-11, 17; April 4, 1914, p. 6; Oct. 31, 1914, p. 8

• *The Detroit Times*, March 6, 1914, p. 13; March 27, 1914, p. 12; April 30, 1914, p. 9.

• *The Omaha Sunday Bee*, March 15, 1914, sports section, page 2.

• Frank Navin, "A Good Word for Sam Crawford," *Baseball Magazine* (February 1916), page 31.

• *Omaha Daily Bee*, July 3, 1917, page 10.

• *Loup City* (Nebraska) *Northwestern*, May 28, 1914, page 7.

• *Sporting Life*, May 16, 1914, page 9; July 25, 1914, page 8; Nov. 8, 1913, page 8.

• *The Detroit Times*, December 18, 1914, page 14.

• "Sam Crawford Excells Cobb" *The Calumet* (MI) *News*, Feb. 7, 1914, page 7

• Dan O'Brien, "Rube Waddell," SABR.org, 2018, https://sabr.org/bioproj/person/rube-waddell/

• *The Omaha Sunday Bee*, January 24, 1915, sports section, pages 1, 4; February 28, 1915, sports section, page 1.

• *The Detroit Times*, June 25, 1914, page 7; March 5, 1915, page 6; March 15, 1915, page 6; December 17, 1915, page 12; March 4, 1916, page 6.

• *Sporting Life*, January 23, 1915, page 15; July 10, 1915, page 15; August 28, 1915, page 13; September 4, 1915, pages 12-13; September 25, 1915, pages 7, 15; October 2, 1915, page 10; October 9, 1915, page 7.

Chapter 10

• F.C. Lane, "The King of Sluggers," *Baseball Magazine* (Feb. 1916), pp. 64-66, 68.

• "A Good Word for Sam Crawford," *Baseball Magazine* (Feb. 1916), p. 32.

• Charles Alexander, *Ty Cobb* (New York: Oxford University Press, 1984), pages 125-128, 135, 137.

• *The Detroit Times*, March 4, 1916, page 9.

• *Omaha Daily Bee*, April 23, 1918, page 8.

• *Sporting Life*, February 5, 1916, page 11; February 12, 1916, page 12; March 18, 1916, pages 6, 11; March 25, 1916, page 7; April 8, 1916, page 6; April 29, 1916, page 6; May 27, 1916, pages 5, 11; June 3, 1916, page 2; June 10, 1916, page 9.

• Dan D'Addona, *In Cobb's Shadow* (Jefferson, NC: McFarland & Company, 2015), pages 108-109.

• *The Detroit Times*, March 21, 1915, page 8; June 9, 1916, page 8.

• "Editorials," *Baseball Magazine* (July 1916), pages 31-32.

• John J. Ward, "Sam Crawford's Successor," *Baseball Magazine* (Oct. 1916), p. 76.

• H.G. Salsinger, "Tigers Cheer Up as Pitching Improves," *The Sporting News*, June 8, 1916, page 3.

• *Sporting Life*, June 17, 1916, page 15; July 29, 1916, page 8; August 19, 1916, page 8; October 28, 1916, page 8; December 23, 1916, page 10.

• *The Detroit Times*, July 19, 1916, page 3; July 29, 1916, page 6; August 1, 1916, page 6; September 22, 1916, page 10.

• William A. Phelon, "The Greatest Race in Baseball History," *Baseball Magazine* (November 1916), page 62.

• *Omaha Daily Bee*, December 10, 1916, sports section, page 2.

• Harold Seymour, *Baseball: The Golden Age* (New York: Oxford University Press, 1971), pages 237-242.

• *Omaha Sunday Bee*, January 21, 1917, sports section, page 3.

• *The Detroit Times*, March 10, 1917, page 9; March 20, 1917, page 6; March 24, 1917, page 10; April 2, 1917, page 4.

• Charles Leerhsen, *Ty Cobb: A Terrible Beauty* (New York: Simon and Schuster, 2015), pages 278-279.

• *Omaha Daily Bee*, April 8, 1917, sports section, page 3.

• Sam Crawford, "My Three Thousandth Hit," *The Baseball Magazine* (August 1917), pages 420, 457-458.

• H.G. Salsinger, "Testimonial Game for Sam Crawford," *The Sporting News*, August 23, 1917, page 2.

• *The Detroit Times*, August 25, 1917, page 1; August 27, 1917, page 4.

• *Omaha Daily Bee*, July 3, 1917, page 10; September 23, 1917, sports section, page 2; October 28, 1917, page 12.

• *Fremont Tribune*, October 24, 1917, page 8.

• H.G. Salsinger, "Here's That Story of Tiger Discord," *The Sporting News*, November 22, 1917, page 6.

• *The New York Tribune*, January 9, 1918, page 17.

• F.C. Lane, "Famous Rivals of the Diamond," *Baseball Magazine* (July 1913), p. 31.

• Al Stump, *Cobb: A Biography* (Chapel Hill, NC: Algonquin, 1994), pages 190-191.
• Edward Lyell Fox, "Baseball as the Players See It," *The Outing Magazine* (May 1911), pages 145-146.
• Lawrence Ritter, *The Glory of Their Times* (New York: William Morrow and Company, 1984), pages 59-61.
• *The Sporting News*, January 31, 1918, page 7; February 7, 1918, page 2.
• *The Oklahoma City Times*, January 5, 1918, page 5.
• *The Bulletin* (Norwich, CT), January 17, 1918, page 3.
• *The Seattle Star*, January 7, 1918, page 8.
• *The Standard* (Ogden, UT), January 30, 1918, page 8.
• *Evening Public Ledger (Philadelphia)*, February 2, 1918, sports section, page 14.
• *The Daily Gate City and Constitution-Democrat* (Keokuk, IA), Feb. 14, 1918, p. 6.
• *Evening Star (Washington, DC)*, March 5, 1918, page 17.
• *The Sporting News*, March 7, 1918, page 4.
• Matt Gallagher, "Coast has Advantage Through Early Start," *The Sporting News*, April 4, 1918, page 2.
• *The Fargo Forum and Daily Republican* (Fargo, ND), March 13, 1918, page 15.
• *The Daily Gate City and Constitution-Democrat* (Keokuk, IA), Mar. 27, 1918, p. 6.
• Samuel E. Crawford draft registration card, September 12, 1918.

Chapter 11

• Matt Gallagher, "Coast has Advantage Through Early Start," *The Sporting News*, April 4, 1918, page 2.
• Charlie Weatherby, "Red Killefer," SABR.org, https://sabr.org/bioproj/person/red-killefer/
• *The Standard* (Ogden, UT), April 3, 1918, page 10; April 4, 1918, page 10; April 10, 1918, page 11; April 17, 1918, page 12; May 14, 1918, page 8.
• H.C. Hamilton, "Crawford Flashing Through Coast League," *The Chickasha* (OK) *Daily Express*, April 29, 1918, page 6.
• *Grand Forks* (ND) *Herald*, April 27, 1918, page 6.
• *Evening Public Ledger* (Philadelphia), April 27, 1918, page 16.
• *The Fargo* (ND) *Forum and Daily Republican*, June 27, 1918, page 10.
• *The Southern Herald* (Liberty, MS), June 28, 1918, page 3.
• Linda D. Wilson, "War Bond Drives," Oklahoma Historical Society, https://www.okhistory.org/publications/enc/entry.php?entry=WA020
• *Omaha Daily Bee*, May 19, 1918, sports section, page 1.
• Benjamin G. Rader, *Baseball: A History of America's Game*, 4th ed. (Urbana: University of Illinois Press, 2018), pages 113, 115-116.
• Harold Seymour, *Baseball: The Golden Age* (New York: Oxford University Press, 1971), pages 248-252.

• *The Standard* (Ogden, UT), July 15, 1918, page 8; July 18, 1918, page 8; July 19, 1918, page 4.

• *Bisbee* (AZ) *Daily Review*, July 13, 1918, page 3.

• *The Washington Herald*, July 24, 1918, page 8.

• Samuel E. Crawford draft registration card, September 12, 1918.

• "The History of Montebello," City of Montebello, 2016, https://www.cityofmontebello.com/about-montebello/montebello-history.html

• *El Paso Herald*, March 24, 1919, page 10.

• *Tulsa Daily World*, February 16, 1919, page 8.

• *The Seattle Star*, April 5, 1919, page 10.

• *The Standard* (Ogden, UT), April 21, 1919, page 2; April 22, 1919, page 2.

• *Vicksburg Evening Post*, April 29, 1919, page 2.

• *The Wahoo Democrat*, May 1, 1919, page 8.

• Warranty Deed, Zada Monteen, et. al. to Chas J. Fair, May 16, 1919, Saunders County Register of Deeds.

• 1920 U.S. Federal Census; Stocking, Saunders, Nebraska; Roll T625_1001, page 3B.

• *The Seattle Star*, June 10, 1919, page 10; July 7, 1919, page 12; July 12, 1919, page 16; July 30, 1919, page 12; October 11, 1919, page 14.

• *Great Falls* (MT) *Daily Tribune*, July 24, 1919, page 11.

• *The Standard* (Ogden, UT), August 30, 1919, page 17; October 6, 1919, page 3.

• *The Sporting News,* November 27, 1919, page 6.

• *The News Scimitar* (Memphis, TN), December 15, 1919, page 12.

• Richard Beverage, *The Los Angeles Angels of the Pacific Coast League: A History, 1903-1957* (Jefferson, NC: McFarland & Company, 2011), pages 15, 19-20.

• *The Seattle Star*, April 27, 1920, p. 12; April 28, 1920, p. 12; Nov. 12, 1919, p. 12.

• *Perth Amboy* (NJ) *Evening News*, May 17, 1918, page 2.

• Robert W. Maxwell, "Hark! Hark! Here's a tale wherein our Gavvy Outslugs Ruth," *Evening Public Ledger* (Philadelphia), February 6, 1920, page 18.

• *The West Virginian* (Fairmont, WV), February 12, 1920, page 10.

• *The Bismarck* (ND) *Tribune*, April 14, 1920, page 6.

• *The West Virginian* (Fairmont, WV), May 19, 1920, page 10.

• *The Washington Herald*, June 7, 1920, page 11.

• *The Sporting News,* July 8, 1920, page 6.

• *Evening Public Ledger* (Philadelphia), July 30, 1920, page 12.

• *Chicago Eagle*, August 21, 1920, page 2.

• *The Bridgeport* (CT) *Times and Evening Farmer*, August 24, 1920, page 4.

• *The Sporting News,* October 21, 1920, page 8.

• *The Seattle Star*, October 18, 1921, page 15.

• Josh Jackson, "Truth Emerges about Tigers in Pennant Race," MiLB.com, January 6, 2020, https://www.milb.com/news/grand-jury-exposes-babe-borton-s-cheating-for-1919-vernon-tigers-in-pc-312312742

• Daniel R. Levitt, "Bill Essick," SABR.org, https://sabr.org/bioproj/person/bill-essick/

• *Omaha Sunday Bee*, October 17, 1920, page 8.

• *The Bridgeport* (CT) *Times and Evening Farmer*, October 23, 1920, page 4.

• *The Bismarck* (ND) *Tribune*, July 7, 1921, page 9.

• Rube Samuelsen, "News Brings Tears of Joy to Tiger Star," *The Sporting News*, February 13, 1957, page 8.

• *The Seattle Star*, March 28, 1921, page 10.

• *Omaha Sunday Bee*, June 19, 1921, page 2C.

• *The Sporting News,* August 4, 1921, page 8; August 18, 1921, page 6; September 8, 1921, page 2; October 13, 1921, pages 7-8.

• *Albuquerque Morning Journal*, October 26, 1921, page 5.

• Greg Erion, "Tom Hughes," SABR.org, 2014, https://sabr.org/bioproj/person/tom-hughes-2/

• *Evening Public Ledger* (Philadelphia), January 16, 1922, page 20.

• Robert W. Maxwell, "Morris Rath, Former Reds Infielder, Quits Baseball for Music," *Evening Public Ledger* (Philadelphia), December 13, 1921, page 18.

• *South Bend* (IN) *Times*, December 29, 1921, page 9.

• *Omaha Sunday Bee*, February 19, 1922, sports section, page 2.

• *The Sporting News,* January 12, 1922, page 2; March 9, 1922, page 7.

• Matt Gallagher, "Bushers Get Notice of Los Angeles Fans," *The Sporting News,* March 16, 1922, page 3.

Chapter 12
• *The Great Falls* (MT) *Tribune*, December 13, 1922, page 8.

• *Capital Journal* (Salem, OR), October 23, 1922, page 8.

• *Richmond Times-Dispatch*, December 10, 1922, sports section, page 1.

• *The New York Herald*, October 25, 1922, page 10.

• Harold Seymour, *Baseball: The People's Game* (New York: Oxford University Press, 1990), pages 100-101, 169-170, 175-177.

• *The Detroit Times*, March 19, 1910, p. 6; Aug. 27, 1910, p. 9; March 14, 1911, p. 6.

• *Sporting Life*, March 5, 1910, page 14.

• "Photographs," *The Baseball Magazine*, (February 1916), page 9.

• "Trade Notes," *The Baseball Magazine*, (April 1916), page 112.

• George Moriarty, "Bats Pride of Ball Players; Crawford Noted Connoisseur," *The Evening Star* (Washington, DC), January 25, 1928, page 29.

• F.C. Lane, "How a Ball Player Grips His Bat," *Baseball Magazine*, (September 1917), page 480.

• "The Cleveland Pitchers Admit Cobb's Greatness," *The Calumet* (MI) *News*, April 19, 1910, page 7.

• F.C. Lane, "The Tremendous Speed of a Star Batters Swing," *Baseball Magazine*, (July 1917), page 350.

• F.C. Lane, "When Pitcher Meets Batter in a Duel of Wits," *Baseball Magazine*, (August 1915), page 61.

• Hugh A. Jennings, "Rounding Third, Chapter XI" *The Evening Star* (Washington, DC), December 11, 1925, page 44.

• *The Evening Star* (Washington, DC), July 8, 1923, page 24.

• *The Indianapolis Times*, July 17, 1923, page 9.

• *New Britain* (CT) *Daily Herald*, July 19, 1923, page 3.

• *Perth Amboy* (NJ) *Evening News*, August 16, 1923, page 13.

• *The Sunday Star* (Washington, DC), August 12, 1923, sports section, page 1.

• *The Evening Star* (Washington, DC), August 22, 1923, page 25.

• *The Bismarck* (ND) *Tribune*, December 30, 1925, page 6.

• Richard Smiley, "Matty McIntyre," SABR.org, 2006, https://sabr.org/bioproj/person/matty-mcintyre/

• *Detroit Free Press*, February 5, 1920, page 14.

• Paul Wendt, "Jimmy Barrett," SABR.org, 2006, https://sabr.org/bioproj/person/jimmy-barrett/

• Dan Holmes, "Germany Schaefer," SABR.org, 2006, https://sabr.org/bioproj/person/germany-schaefer/

• *Sporting Life*, June 19, 1915, page 9.

• Jess Altenberg, "Letting Fans in on What One Player Thinks of Another," *The Sporting News,* February 24, 1924, page 7.

• C. Paul Rogers III, "Hughie Jennings," SABR.org, 2006, https://sabr.org/bioproj/person/hughie-jennings/

• *The Detroit Times*, September 14, 1910, page 4.

• *The Calumet News*, August 25, 1910, page 7.

• "A Good Word for Sam Crawford," *The Baseball Magazine* (February 1916), p. 32.

• *The Sunday Star* (Washington, DC), October 29, 1922, page 4.

• Benjamin G. Rader, *Baseball: A History of America's Game*, 4th ed. (Urbana: University of Illinois Press, 2018), pages 124-128.

• Billy Evans, "Graceful Batters of Present Day," *New Britain* (CT) *Herald,* January 12, 1925, page 9.

• Hugh A. Jennings, "Rounding Third, Chapter XL" *The Evening Star* (Washington, DC), January 15, 1926, page 39.

• *The Bismarck Tribune*, January 25, 1928, page 6.

• William McC. Walker, "Places of Colorful Old Diamond Athletes May Never be Filled," *The Sunday Star* (Washington, DC), April 8, 1928, page 3.

• Grantland Rice, "The Spotlight," *The Evening Star* (Washington, DC), July 19, 1929, page 19.

• Harold Seymour, *Baseball: The Golden Age* (New York: Oxford University Press, 1971), page 356.
• "About APBPA: Our History," Association of Professional Ball Players of America, https://apbpa.org/about-apbpa/
• Sam Greene, "Detroit Admits to a Pair of Holdouts," *The Sporting News,* February 14, 1924, page 1.
• "Trojan Memories: Where Have You Gone "Wahoo" Crawford?" USC News, February 1, 1999, https://news.usc.edu/9339/Trojan-Memories-Where-Have-You-Gone-Wahoo-Crawford/
• Sam Greene, "How Can Ty Cobb Harness Energy?" *The Sporting News,* December 16, 1926, page 6.
• *New Britain* (CT) *Daily Herald*, December 6, 1927, page 12.
• *The Sporting News*, October 16, 1957, page 6.
• *The Evening Star* (Washington, DC), February 25, 1927, page 38.
• *The Indianapolis Times*, March 1, 1927, page 8.
• *The Bismarck Tribune*, March 27, 1927, page 6.
• David Eskenazi, "Wayback Machine: Lou, Mel – the Almada Brothers," SportsPressNW.com, 8.28.2012, http://sportspressnw.com/2137082/2012/wayback-machine-lou-mel-the-almada-brothers
• Stephen V. Rice, "Red Badgro," SABR.org, 2019, https://sabr.org/bioproj/person/red-badgro/
• *The Daily Nebraskan*, October 10, 1928, page 4
• Passenger List, *Siberia Maru*, August 18, 1928
• *The Evening Star* (Washington, DC), October 29, 1925, page 28.
• *Napa* (CA) *Journal*, June 6, 1929, page 5.
• Rube Samuelsen, "News Brings Tears of Joy to Tiger Star," *The Sporting News*, February 13, 1957, page 8.
• Rod Edelman, "Buster Keaton, Baseball Player" SABR.org, 2010, https://sabr.org/journal/article/buster-keaton-baseball-player/
• Michael Phillips, "Review: 'College,'" *Chicago Tribune*, April 10, 2015, https://www.chicagotribune.com/entertainment/movies/ct-college-keaton-review-20150410-column.html
• Aurora, "Buster Keaton in COLLEGE (1927)" *Once Upon a Screen ... a classic film and TV blog*, June 1, 2016, https://aurorasginjoint.com/2016/06/01/buster-keaton-in-college-1927/
• David L. Robb with Julie Ann Johnson, *The Stuntwoman* (Coppell, TX: CreateSpace, 2013), pages 32, 63.
• Charles Leerhsen, *Ty Cobb: A Terrible Beauty* (New York: Simon and Schuster, 2015), pages 356, 371.
• Evan Comen, Thomas C. Frohlich, Samuel Stebbins, and Michael B Sauter, "How Much a Home Cost the Year You Were Born," 24/7 Wall St., January 13, 2020,

https://247wallst.com/special-report/2016/03/28/what-a-home-cost-the-year-you-were-born-draft/2/.

• 1930 United States Federal Census; Fullerton, Orange, California; Page 8B; Enumeration District: 0027; FHL microfilm 2339916.

• 1930 United States Federal Census; Whittier, Los Angeles, California; Page 10B; Enumeration District: 1557; FHL microfilm 2339910.

Chapter 13

• *The Bismarck Tribune*, October 3, 1930, page 5.

• Edwin M. Bradley, *The First Hollywood Musicals: A Critical Filmography of 171 Features, 1927 through 1932* (Jefferson: McFarland & Company, 2004), page 217.

• *The Indianapolis Times*, February 6, 1930, page 8.

• *The Pomona Progress Bulletin*, May 5, 1931, page 10.

• *The Evening Star* (Washington, DC), October 15, 1932, page B-6.

• "Old-Timers Schedule 55 Games for Long Tour," *The Sporting News,* March 16, 1933, page 6.

• "Old-Time Stars Begin Missionary Junket, Playing Exhibitions and Instructing Boys," *The Sporting News,* April 27, 1933, page 3.

• *The Sporting News,* May 11, 1933, page 3; May 25, 1933, page 5.

• Harold Seymour, *Baseball: The People's Game* (New York: Oxford University Press, 1990), pages 69-72.

• *The Evening Star* (Washington, DC), December 3, 1934, page A-15.

• "Daguerreotypes Taken of Former Stars of the Diamond: Samuel E. (Wahoo Sam) Crawford," *The Sporting News*, August 31, 1933, page 2.

• Scott Ferkovich, "Remembering the Day Frank Navin Died," Vintage Detroit, January 4, 2016, https://www.vintagedetroit.com/blog/2016/01/04/remembering-the-day-frank-navin-died/

• H.G. Salsinger, "Donie Bush Tells of Old Battlers of Game," *The Sporting News,* January 18, 1934, page 7.

• Hugh A. Jennings, "Rounding Third, Chapter XL" *The Evening Star* (Washington, DC), January 15, 1926, page 39.

• M.W. Bingay, "Game's Heaviest Hitter," *The Sporting News,* January 16, 1908, p. 3.

• Harry Neily, "Can't Start South Too Soon to Please Sam'l," *The Detroit Times,* January 16, 1911, page 6.

• *The Detroit Times*, February 20, 1911, page 12.

• *The Calumet News*, March 31, 1911, page 7.

• *Sporting Life*, April 26, 1913, page 7.

• Sam Crawford, "What I Think About Baseball," *Baseball Magazine* (Feb. 1916), pp. 42-43.

• Tris Speaker, "When a Champion Batter Slumps Below .300," *Baseball Magazine* (June 1920), page 318.

• *The Sporting News,* Mar. 12, 1931, p. 7; March 11, 1943, p. 5; Nov. 2, 1933, page 4

• Cy Kritzer, "Late Jimmy Collins, the 'King of Third Sackers,' Became Hot Corner Star by Ability to Handle Bunt," *The Sporting News*, March 11, 1943, page 5.

• Maclean Kennedy, "Period from 1900 to 1917 saw Remarkable Outfielders, Including Keeler, Called Game's 'Most Scientific' Hitter," *The Sporting News,* December 8, 1932, page 5.

• *The Evening Star* (Washington, DC), July 10, 1934, p. A-10; Sept. 8, 1934, p. A-12.

• Francis E. Stan, "Sport Scope," *The Evening Star* (Washington, DC), September 16, 1934, page B-11.

• Hugh Fullerton, "Fullerton Glorifies Gehringer as Detroit All-Time Star," *The Sporting News,* December 26, 1935, page 3.

• Dan D'Addona, *In Cobb's Shadow* (Jefferson, NC: McFarland & Company, 2015), pages 121-122.

• Andrew Martin, "Reviewing the Unusual 1936 Baseball Hall of Fame Ballot," seamheads.com, Dec. 6, 2015, https://seamheads.com/blog/2015/12/06/reviewing-the-unusual-1936-baseball-hall-of-fame-ballot/

• H.G. Salsinger, "Crawford Hit for Distance in Dead Ball Era," *The Sporting News*, February 13, 1957, pages 12, 18.

• *The Indianapolis Times*, December 29, 1934, page 8.

• *The Sporting News,* May 9, 1935, page 4; February 7, 1935, page 8.

• "Sam Crawford," Retrosheet.org, https://www.retrosheet.org/boxesetc/C/Pcraws101.htm

• Bill McGowan, "Umpiring Under Difficulties," *The Sporting News,* November 4, 1926, page 3.

• Edgar G. Brands, "Between Innings," *The Sporting News,* July 30, 1936, page 4.

• Bill Starr, *Clearing the Bases: Baseball Then & Now*, (New York: Michael Kesend Publishing, 1989), page 127-128.

• Lawrence Ritter, *The Glory of Their Times* (New York: William Morrow and Company, 1984), pages 55-56.

• Eddie Brietz, "Howard Sees Own Kayak II as Threat to Seabiscuit," *The Evening Star* (Washington, DC), February 8, 1939, page A-17.

• letter from Samuel E. Crawford to Ford. C. Frick, April 22, 1936, National Baseball Hall of Fame Library.

• Bill Nowlin, *The Kid: Ted Williams in San Diego* (Cambridge, MA: Rounder books, 2005), pages 152-153.

• Crawford, Samuel Earl, *The Sporting News* player contract card

• Bob Ray, "Angels' Wings Clipped on Final Day of Race," *The Sporting News,* September 23, 1937, page 2.

• Bob Ray, "Angels Pay Out $5,000 for Bush in Hill Fix-Up," *The Sporting News,* May 19, 1938, page 14.

• *The Sporting News,* November 17, 1938, page 1.

- *The Sporting News,* March 17, 1938, page 10.
- *The Wahoo Democrat,* March 10, 1938, page 1.
- "Mrs. Sam Crawford Dies; Had Attended Wahoo Schools," March 10, 1938, clipping in Sam Crawford folder, Saunders County Historical Society.
- *Los Angeles Times,* March 5, 1938, page 8.
- David L. Robb with Julie Ann Johnson, *The Stuntwoman* (Coppell, TX: CreateSpace, 2013), page 29.
- 1940 United States Federal Census; Fullerton, Orange, California; Page 64A; Enumeration District: 30-26; Roll m-t0627-00272.
- 1940 United States Federal Census; Lincoln, Lancaster, Nebraska; Page 10B; Enumeration District: 55-47A; Roll m-t0627-002254.
- 1942 Lincoln city directory, page 619.
- 1910 United States Federal Census; Deadwood Ward 3, Lawrence, South Dakota; page 1A; Enumeration District: 0043; FHL microfilm 1375496.
- 1930 United States Federal Census; Omaha, Douglas, Nebraska; Page 21B; Enumeration District: 100; FHL microfilm 2341012.
- Stephen Orlando Crawford, U.S. Draft Registration Card, 1942.
- 1910 United States Federal Census; Omaha Ward 4, Douglas, Nebraska; Page 12A; Enumeration District: 0025; FHL microfilm 1374856.
- 1920 United States Federal Census; Le Sueur, Le Sueur, Minnesota; Page 19A; Enumeration District: 73; Roll T625_843.
- 1930 United States Federal Census; Peshtigo, Marinette, Wisconsin; Page 18B; Enumeration District: 0022; FHL microfilm 2342317.
- *Star Tribune* (Minneapolis), October 30, 1940, page 27.
- Neal A. Crawford, Certificate of Death, Minnesota State Department of Health, November 4, 1940.
- Crawford, Neal A., U.S. National Cemetery Internment Control Form, Nov. 4, 1940.
- *The Sporting News,* November 19, 1936, page 9; February 17, 1938, page 10.
- "About APBPA: Our History," Association of Professional Ball Players of America, https://apbpa.org/about-apbpa/
- *Oakland Tribune,* July 12, 1934, page 12.
- *The San Bernardino Sun,* July 10, 1935, page 15.
- *The Sporting News,* June 15, 1939, page 10.
- Samuel Earl Crawford, U.S. WWII draft registration card, 1942.
- 1940 United States Federal Census; Los Angeles, Los Angeles, California; Page 6A; Enumeration District: 60-994A; Roll m-t0627-00420.
- Linton Weeks, "The 1940 Census: 72-Year-Old Secrets Reveals," NPR.org, https://www.npr.org/2012/04/02/149575704/the-1940-census-72-year-old-secrets-revealed
- Diane Petro, "Brother, Can You Spare a Dime?" *Prologue Magazine* (Spring 2012), https://www.archives.gov/publications/prologue/2012/spring/1940.html

• Samuel Earl Crawford Jr., U.S. WWII draft registration card, 1940.
• Penelope McMillan, "'Cheerless and Ugly': Life Inside L.A.'s Slums: A Window on Despair," *Los Angeles Times*, August 2, 1989, https://www.latimes.com/archives/la-xpm-1989-08-02-mn-540-story.html

Chapter 14
• *The Sporting News*, February 1, 1940, page 2.
• B. Ray, "400 Attend Players' Association Coast Dinner," *The Sporting News*, February 15, 1940, page 12.
• *The Sporting News*, February 25, 1943, page 10.
• Al Wolf, "$276,497 Paid Out in Benefits by Players' Aid Organization," *The Sporting News*, February 12, 1942, page 12.
• Al Wolf, "Pacific Coast Bits," *The Sporting News*, February 19, 1942, page 18.
• Samuel Earl Crawford, U.S. WWII draft registration card, 1942.
• Delayed Birth Registration, Earl Lee Crawford, Saunders County, Nebraska, October 20, 1941, Saunders County Historical Museum.
• "Proud Wife of Wahoo Sam Shuns Limelight," August 7, 1957 clipping in Wahoo Women's Club Binder, Saunders County Historical Society.
• 1930 United States Federal Census; Los Angeles, Los Angeles, California; Page 9A; Enumeration District: 0071; FHL microfilm 2339869.
• *The Sporting News*, December 18, 1941, page 4.
• Frederic G. Lieb, *The Detroit Tigers* (Kent, OH: The Kent State University Press, 2008; originally New York: G.P. Putnam's Sons, 1946), page 53.
• *San Pedro News Pilot*, March 1, 1940, page 6.
• *Santa Cruz Sentinel*, March 1, 1940, page 4.
• Samuel Earl Crawford Jr., U.S. WWII draft registration card, 1940.
• *The Los Angeles Times*, October 26, 1996, page 20.
• Samuel Crawford, U.S. Dept. of Veterans Affairs BIRLS Death File, Oct. 18, 1996.
• David L. Robb with Julie Ann Johnson, *The Stuntwoman* (Coppell, TX: CreateSpace, 2013), page 30, 32-34, 47-48, 63-64.
• John B. Keller, "Win, Lose or Draw," *The Sunday Star* (Washington, DC), August 19, 1945, page A-14.
• Hugh Fullerton, "Finest Outfields -- as Figured out by Fullerton," *The Sporting News*, January 3, 1946, page 7.
• "Frederick G. Lieb, "Majors Were All-Star Leagues in 1912 -- With No July Classic," *The Sporting News*, July 13, 1949, page 10.
• Harry Grayson, "They Played the Game ... No. 25: Sam Crawford, Tripling King, Hardest Hitting Barber Ever to Come from Wahoo, Nebraska," *The Daily Monitor Leader* (Mount Clemens, MI), May 27, 1946, page 20.
• Grantland Rice, "Deceptive Delivery, Control Won Him 512 Games in 22 Years, Cy Young Claims," *The Sporting News*, January 3, 1946, page 7.

• Tom Meany, "Interest Spreads Over Straddle-Style Stephens," *The Sporting News*, July 29, 1943, page 3.

• Stan Baumgartner, "Batting Lesson by O'Neill – 'Don't Uppercut, Hit Level,'" *The Sporting News*, February 14, 1951, page 17.

• H.G. Salsinger, "Cobb was First to Score from Second on Sacrifice," *The Sporting News*, June 7, 1950, page 16.

• Robert Phipps, "Beautiful Crawford Swing Lives in Lawler's Memory," undated clipping in Wahoo Women's Club Binder, Saunders County Historical Society.

• Arthur Flynn, "94 Nominated, None Gains Hall of Fame," *The Sporting News*, February 1, 1945, page 5.

• *The Evening Star* (Washington, DC), March 7, 1924, page 30.

• *The Sporting News*, July 23, 1942, p. 16; Jan. 22, 1947, p. 19; April 16, 1947, p. 44.

• "Historical General Population City & County of Los Angeles, 1850 to 2010, Los Angeles Almanac, 1998-2020, http://www.laalmanac.com/population/po02.php

• Lawrence Ritter, *The Glory of Their Times* (New York: William Morrow and Company, 1984), pages 48, 62-63.

• "Immortality Nebraska Native, McCarthy Named," February 4, 1957 clipping in Wahoo Women's Club Binder, Saunders County Historical Society.

• "Sam Crawford Still in Prime Physical Shape," June 10, 1965 clipping in Wahoo Women's Club Binder, Saunders County Historical Society.

• "Robert Green Ingersoll Biography," Free Inquiry, https://secularhumanism.org/ingersoll-museum/robert-green-ingersoll-biography/

• H.G. Salsinger, "Crawford Hit for Distance in Dead Ball Era," *The Sporting News*, February 13, 1957, page 18.

• *The Evening Star* (Washington, DC), May 15, 1950, page A-13.

• *The Sporting News*, January 24, 1951, page 4; February 14, 1951, page 17.

• Rube Samuelsen, "News Brings Tears of Joy to Tiger Star," *The Sporting News*, February 13, 1957, pages 5, 8.

• Steve Gietschier, "Henry Chadwick Award: J.G. Taylor Spink," SABR.org, 2011, https://sabr.org/journal/article/henry-chadwick-award-j-g-taylor-spink/

Chapter 15

• Charles Leerhsen, *Ty Cobb: A Terrible Beauty* (New York: Simon and Schuster, 2015), pages 374-375.

• Dan D'Addona, "Harry Heilmann," SABR.org, https://sabr.org/bioproj/person/harry-heilmann/

• *The Evening Star* (Washington, DC), July 10, 1951, page C-1.

• Sam Greene, "'I'll Be Back' Valedictory by Chandler," *The Sporting News,* July 18, 1951, page 6.

• Oscar K. Ruhl, "All-Star Glints," *The Sporting News,* July 18, 1951, page 23.

• Grantland Rice, "The Sportlight," *The Sporting News,* January 26, 1940, page A-19.

• *The Sporting News,* February 4, 1953, page 2.

• "Now It Can be Told: Cobb Wahoo Sam Booster," July 30, 1961 clipping in Wahoo Women's Club Binder, Saunders County Historical Society.

• J.G. Taylor Spink, "The Ty Cobb that I Knew," *The Sporting News,* December 13, 1961, page 4.

• Warren Corbett, "Bob Cerv," SABR.org, 2017, https://sabr.org/bioproj/person/bob-cerv/

• Dan Daniel, "Hall of Fame Group Sorts Candidates," *The Sporting News,* August 26, 1953, pages 1-2.

• *The Sporting News,* September 23, 1953, page 7.

• "Selection of Sam Crawford to Hall of Fame Overdue," *The Sporting News,* June 2, 1954, page 18.

• "Honor 'Great Climax' for Sam," February 5, 1957 clipping in Wahoo Women's Club Binder, Saunders County Historical Society.

• Walt Dobbins, "Nebraska Sports Fame Hall Fetes Sam E. Crawford," undated clipping in Wahoo Women's Club Binder, Saunders County Historical Society.

• "'Fan of Yours for Years,' Boy, 10, Wrote Crawford," *The Sporting News*, February 13, 1957, page 8.

• Oscar Ruhl, "From the Ruhl Book," *The Sporting News,* May 7, 1958, page 19.

• *The Sporting News,* January 16, 1957, page 25.

• Warren Brown, "Hall of Fame Vets' Committee Faces Difficult Choices, Feb. 3," *The Sporting News,* January 30, 1957, page 12.

• Joe King, "Spink Group Opens Pantheon Portals for McCarthy, 69, and Crawford, 76," *The Sporting News,* February 13, 1957, page 5.

• Rube Samuelsen, "News Brings Tears of Joy to Tiger Star," *The Sporting News*, February 13, 1957, pages 5, 8.

• *The Sporting News,* February 13, 1957, page 6.

• Lawrence Ritter, *The Glory of Their Times* (New York: William Morrow and Company, 1984), page 63.

• *The Sporting News,* February 20, 1957, page 13.

• "Recollections of 'Wahoo' Sam," April 1957 clipping in Wahoo Women's Club Binder, Saunders County Historical Society.

• Paul Means, "Town, Sam Change—But Both Prosper," *Lincoln Sunday Journal and Start,* August 4, 1957, page 2B.

• Jack McDonald, "Ex-Stars Join Gov. Knight in Tribute to Wahoo Sam," *The Sporting News,* May 29, 1957, page 20.

• *The Sporting News,* June 19, 1957, page 15.

• "Proud Wife of Wahoo Sam Shuns Limelight," August 7, 1957 clipping in Wahoo Women's Club Binder, Saunders County Historical Society.

• Dan Daniel, "Shrine Doors Open for McCarthy, Crawford," *The Sporting News,* July 31, 1957, page 13.

• "Baseball's Hall of Fame Honors Two Greats—McCarthy, Crawford," July 22, 1957 clipping in Wahoo Women's Club Binder, Saunders County Historical Society.
• Charles Alexander, *Ty Cobb* (New York: Oxford University Press, 1984), page 225.
• Davy Jones, Sam Crawford, and Ty Cobb Photograph, 1957, National Baseball Hall of Fame Online Collection, https://collection.baseballhall.org/PASTIME/davy-jones-sam-crawford-and-ty-cobb-photograph-1957-0
• Edgar Munzel, "White Sox Clout Cardinals, 13-4, at Cooperstown," *The Sporting News,* July 31, 1957, pages 13-14, 18.
• *The Sporting News,* May 14, 1958, page 6.
• "Hometown Tribute Overwhelms Sam," August 8, 1957 clipping in Wahoo Women's Club Binder, Saunders County Historical Society.
• Carolyn Richards, "Baseball Yesterday Recalled by 'Wahoo,'" March 22, 1965 clipping in Wahoo Women's Club Binder, Saunders County Historical Society.
• Dan Daniel, "Ex-Stars Before 44,184 at Yanks' Reunion," *The Sporting News,* August 7, 1957, page 13.
• "Stengel Says A.L. Has Four Teams Stronger than N.L.," *The Sporting News,* August 7, 1957, page 13.
• H.G. Salsinger, "Crawford Hit for Distance in Dead Ball Era," *The Sporting News,* February 13, 1957, page 18.
• "Crawford, McCarthy Enter Hall of Fame," *Omaha World-Herald*, July 23, 1957, page 17.
• *The Sporting News,* August 14, 1957, page 20.
• Robert Phipps, "Crawford Recalls No-Smoke Deal," undated clipping in Wahoo Women's Club Binder, Saunders County Historical Society.
• letter from Sam Crawford to Ernest Lanigan, September 27, 1957, National Baseball Hall of Fame Library.
• *The Sporting News,* October 30, 1957, page 16.
• Hal Middlesworth, "Tiger Stars of Yesteryear Turn Back Clock," *The Sporting News,* July 9, 1958, page 19.
• Frank Finch, "Casey Receives 'Bible' Award at Big L.A. Dinner," *The Sporting News,* January 21, 1959, page 19.

Chapter 16
• David L. Robb with Julie Ann Johnson, *The Stuntwoman* (Coppell, TX: CreateSpace, 2013), pages 65, 121, 132.
• author interview with Julie Ann Johnson, October 10, 2020.
• letter from Samuel E. Crawford to Derrel Ludi, May 11, 1957, Wahoo Women's Club Binder, Saunders County Historical Society.
• "Hometown Tribute Overwhelms Sam," August 8, 1957 clipping in Wahoo Women's Club Binder, Saunders County Historical Society.

• "Recollections of 'Wahoo' Sam," April 1957 clipping in Wahoo Women's Club Binder, Saunders County Historical Society.
• letter from Sam Crawford to Lee Allen, July 14, 1964, National Baseball Hall of Fame Library.
• *The Sporting News,* May 31, 1961, page 23.
• "Sam Crawford Still in Prime Physical Shape," June 10, 1965 clipping in Wahoo Women's Club Binder, Saunders County Historical Society.
• "Cobb Buried in Clay Hills," July 28, 1961 clipping in Wahoo Women's Club Binder, Saunders County Historical Society.
• Charles Alexander, Ty Cobb (New York: Oxford University Press, 1984), page 135.
• Charles Leerhsen, *Ty Cobb: A Terrible Beauty* (New York: Simon and Schuster, 2015), pages 385-389.
• *The Sporting News,* September 1, 1962, page 23.
• Lawrence Ritter, *The Glory of Their Times* (New York: William Morrow and Company, 1984), pages ix, xi-xiii, xvii-xviii, 41, 47-69 (Chapter 4).
• "Lawrence S. Ritter," SABR,org, https://sabr.org/authors/lawrence-s-ritter/
• Lawrence Ritter, *The Glory of Their Times* sound recording, (St. Paul, MN: HighBridge Audio, 1998), Sam Crawford interview.
• Frederic G. Lieb, *The Detroit Tigers* (Kent, OH: The Kent State University Press, 2008; originally New York: G.P. Putnam's Sons, 1946), page 53.
• Jack McDonald, "Ex-Stars Join Gov. Knight in Tribute to Wahoo Sam," *The Sporting News,* May 29, 1957, page 20.
• Rube Samuelsen, "News Brings Tears of Joy to Tiger Star," *The Sporting News*, February 13, 1957, pages 8.

Chapter 17

• *The Sporting News,* November 21, 1964, page 32.
• Watson Spoelstra, "Spry Davy Jones, 85, Helps Tigers Mark 10,000th Tilt," *The Sporting News,* October 9, 1965, page 47.
• Lee Allen, "Cooperstown Corner: An Unusual Man Was Sam Crawford," *The Sporting News,* July 6, 1968, page 6.
• letter from Sam Crawford to Lee Allen, November 11, 1963, National Baseball Hall of Fame Library.
• "Pictorial Highlights of Wahoo Sam's Homecoming, *Wahoo Newspaper*, August 7, 1957 clipping in Wahoo Women's Club Binder, Saunders County Historical Society.
• Lawrence Ritter, *The Glory of Their Times* (New York: William Morrow and Company, 1984), 47-48, 59, 69.
• Hugh Bradley, "Crawford Confirms It: Mantle is the Greatest," March 1957 clipping in Wahoo Women's Club Binder, Saunders County Historical Society.
• Sam Crawford's All-Star Team to Nick Acocella, National Baseball Hall of Fame Library.

• H.G. Salsinger, "Crawford Hit for Distance in Dead Ball Era," *The Sporting News*, February 13, 1957, page 18.
• "Sam Crawford Still in Prime Physical Shape," June 10, 1965 clipping in Wahoo Women's Club Binder, Saunders County Historical Society.
• Carolyn Richards, "Baseball Yesterday Recalled by 'Wahoo,'" March 22, 1965 clipping in Wahoo Women's Club Binder, Saunders County Historical Society.
• Michael Haupert, "MLB's Annual Salary Leaders Since 1874," SABR.org, 2012, https://sabr.org/research/article/mlbs-annual-salary-leaders-since-1874/
• "Taking Pen in Hand: Sports Fans Write," undated clipping in Wahoo Women's Club Binder, Saunders County Historical Society.
• "Great Scarcity of Baseball Material," *The Chicago Eagle,* March 18, 1922, page 2.
• letter from Sam Crawford to Lee Allen, July 14, 1964, National Baseball Hall of Fame Library.
• Kent Chetlain, "11 Hall of Fame Stars to Attend Bradenton Fete," *The Sporting News*, April 1, 1967, page 39.
• letter from Sam Crawford to David Zimmett, September 13, 1967, National Baseball Hall of Fame Library.
• letter from Sam Crawford to Lucile, Henry, and Jerry Jacoby, January 8, 1968, in Wahoo Women's Club Binder, Saunders County Historical Society.
• David L. Robb with Julie Ann Johnson, *The Stuntwoman* (Coppell, TX: CreateSpace, 2013), pages 177, 183, 193-194.
• "'Wahoo Sam' Crawford Dies at 88," *San Bernardino Sun*, June 18, 1968, page 13.
• letter from B. Capelot, Hollywood Florists, to Wahoo Green House, July 5, 1968, Sam Crawford folder, Saunders County Historical Society.
• "Wahoo Sam Crawford is Dead," June 20, 1968 clipping in Wahoo Women's Club Binder, Saunders County Historical Society.
• Fred Lieb, "Crawford Dead at 88; Three-Base Hit King," *The Sporting News*, June 29, 1968, page 15.
• Lee Allen, "Cooperstown Corner: Famed Old-Timers Get Together," *The Sporting News,* August 10, 1968, page 6.
• *The Sporting News,* September 27, 1969, page 17.

Chapter 18
• Herm Krabbenhoft, "How Many Hits Did Ty Cobb Make in his Major League Career? What is his Lifetime Batting Average?" SABR.org, 2019, https://sabr.org/journal/article/how-many-hits-did-ty-cobb-make-in-his-major-league-career-what-is-his-lifetime-batting-average/
• Roy Blount Jr., "The Most Exciting 12 Seconds in Sports," *Sports Illustrated,* September 29, 2003, pages 74-75.
• Lawrence Ritter, *The Glory of Their Times* (New York: William Morrow and Company, 1984), page 52.

• Bill James, *The New Bill James Historical Baseball Abstract* (New York: The Free Press, 2001), pages 367, 673-674, 795-796, 930-931.

• Sam Crawford, "What I Think About Baseball," *Baseball Magazine*, Feb 1916, p 40.

• Hugh A. Jennings, "Rounding Third: Chapter XXXIX," *The Evening Star* (Washington, DC), January 14, 1926, page 45.

• Paul Hale Bruske, "Big Wahoo Sam Gets Ready for Another Great Season," *The Detroit Times*, March, 1911, page 6.

• Joseph Vila, "New York's Complaint," *Sporting Life*, July 26, page 6.

• *The Sporting News*, January 7, 1959, page 15.

• Hugh Bradley, "Crawford Confirms It: Mantle is the Greatest," March 1957 clipping in Wahoo Women's Club Binder, Saunders County Historical Society.

• John J. Corcoran, "Inside Baseball," *Baseball Magazine*, July 1916, page 82.

• Hans Wagner, "Hans Wagner's Story," *The Evening Star*, January 12, 1924, page 17.

• H.G. Salsinger, "Donie Bush Tells of Old Battlers of Game," *The Sporting News*, January 18, 1934, page 7.

• *The Detroit Times*, September 1, 1908, page 1.

• Richard Bak, "How Sunday Baseball Came to Detroit," Vintage Detroit, February 26, 2012, https://www.vintagedetroit.com/blog/2012/02/26/how-sunday-baseball-came-to-detroit/

• Paul McDonald, "Colorful Nicknames Help "Make" Many Heroes," *The Sporting News*, November 13, 1924, page 7.

• H.G. Salsinger, "Ty Cobb: Remaker of Base Ball," *The Evening Star* (Washington, DC), December 22, 1924, page 30.

• Russell J. Cowans, "Thru the Sport Mirror," *The Detroit Tribune*, Oct. 14, 1933, p. 7.

• Benjamin G. Rader, *Baseball: A History of America's Game*, 4th ed. (Urbana: University of Illinois Press, 2018), pages 101, 104-105.

• Steven A. Riess, *Touching Base: Professional Baseball and American Culture in the Progressive Era*, revised ed. (Urbana: University of Illinois Press, 1999), pp. 168-169.

• Harold Seymour, *Baseball: The Golden Age* (New York: Oxford University Press, 1971), pages 3-6, 357-358.

• F.C. Lane, "The King of Sluggers," *Baseball Magazine* (February 1916), page 68.

• "Our Letter Box," *Baseball Magazine* (April 1916), page 85.

• H.G. Salsinger, "Crawford Big Bond Buyer," *The Sporting News*, June 3, 1943, p 16.

• *Omaha Daily Bee*, June 5, 1914, page 8.

• Fred Lieb, "Crawford Dead at 88; Three-Base Hit King," *The Sporting News*, June 29, 1968, page 15.

I am especially appreciative of the online resources, Retrosheet, Baseball Almanac, and Baseball-Reference.com. The box scores, player stats, game-by-game schedules, play-by-play listings, and other baseball facts provided by these websites were vital to my research.

Index

About the Author

Kent Krause writes content for online high school history courses and social studies textbooks. He holds bachelor's and master's degrees from Iowa State University and a doctorate from the University of Nebraska-Lincoln. In addition to his six books, he has published articles in *Great Plains Quarterly* and *The International Journal of the History of Sport*. A member of the Society for American Baseball Research, Kent lives in Nebraska just 30 miles south of where Sam Crawford played his first baseball games in Wahoo.

Visit Kent online at: **kentkrause.com**